SHAKING THE GATES OF HELL

SHAKING
the
GATES
of
HELL

*A Search for Family and Truth
in the Wake of the Civil Rights Revolution*

John Archibald

ALFRED A. KNOPF   NEW YORK   2021

THIS IS A BORZOI BOOK
PUBLISHED BY ALFRED A. KNOPF

Library of Congress Cataloging-in-Publication Data
Names: Archibald, John, 1963– author.
Title: Shaking the gates of hell : a search for family and truth in the wake
of the civil rights revolution / John Archibald.
Description: First edition. | New York : Alfred A. Knopf, 2020. | Includes index.
Identifiers: LCCN 2020002918 (print) | LCCN 2020002919 (ebook) |
ISBN 9780525658115 (hardcover) | ISBN 9780525658139 (ebook)
Subjects: LCSH: Archibald, John, 1963– | Men, White—
Alabama—Biography. | Alabama—Biography.
Classification: LCC CT275.A8125 A3 2020 (print) | LCC CT275.A8125 (ebook) |
DDC 976.1092 [B]—dc23
LC record available at https://lccn.loc.gov/2020002918
LC ebook record available at https://lccn.loc.gov/2020002919

Jacket images: (top and middle) Courtesy of the author;
(bottom) Alabama Department of Archives and History, AMG
Collection. Photo: Lankford, *The Birmingham News*
Jacket design by Jenny Carrow

Manufactured in the United States of America
First Edition

To family.

To Fire and Brimstone.

To change.

Give me one hundred preachers who fear nothing but sin and desire nothing but God; . . . such alone will shake the gates of hell.

—JOHN WESLEY, the founder of Methodism

Contents

II   The Prodigal's Ring

I

THE "RACE QUESTION"

The Letter

The people in this town who speak the most freely are usually those we dislike most.

—REV. ROBERT L. ARCHIBALD JR., March 2, 1968

I was born in the midst of revolution.

The son of a preacher, the grandson of preachers. The great-grandson of preachers, too. They were all Methodists—until you look beyond the Civil War. They preached on horseback and on foot and—in my dad's case—in a little white Fiat Spider. They preached of right and wrong and grace and goodness and believed it, I think, to their bones. They preached of stewardship—"pay up" in Methodist-speak—and dutifully passed the collection plate for missions in faraway places and building funds at home. In the name of God and something they called sanctifying grace, they preached in the Old South and longed for a New South, but were silent, too silent, on the complicit and conspiratorial South I never came to see until I was fully grown.

I was born in Alabaster, Alabama, a little crossroads outside Birmingham with a Methodist church and a Baptist church in those days, a stop sign, and a set of railroad tracks.

I was born on April 5, 1963, in the willful ignorance of the white South. I never knew, until much later, that as my mother went into labor, the foot soldiers of revolution gathered across the county line, that at the moment of my birth, Birmingham readied for a battle that was long overdue. The Reverend Dr. Martin Luther King Jr. had not yet put his Dream to words, but he had come to this town to change the world with another masterpiece.

Birmingham—white Birmingham—didn't like King's arrival. Not the merchants, who mourned the lost dollar, or the cops, who demanded obedience. Not the Klansmen, who longed for the way things used to be, or the preachers, who feared the noise and glare and shining incongruities, who wanted so badly to stuff the powder back in its keg that they never saw the explosion coming. Even as they lit its fuse.

I was born in the midst of revolution. And I didn't even know.

A week after my birth, eight clergy members, Christians and Jews, printed a letter in *The Birmingham News* asking for the demonstrations to stop in the name of law and order and "common sense." Eight white Birmingham men of God stood for the status quo.

King read their words and understood exactly what they meant. It was the past coming for the present, a call to do nothing, again, to slow the roll of justice in the name of peace. It was cowardice masquerading as reason. Silence in the guise of God.

Martin Luther King Jr. read that letter and decided he would march in Birmingham, even as friends advised against it. He was too important, they said. Tensions were too high, Birmingham was too hot. They warned him he could be hurt, or killed, or kept in jail for months by Eugene "Bull" Connor's police department. But he marched, and was arrested a few hours later. It was Good Friday—the day Jesus was hung to die after being betrayed by silver and silence. It was April 12. I was seven days old.

King was charged with parading without a permit, a crime deemed serious enough for solitary confinement. They put him in one cell and his colleague Rev. Ralph David Abernathy in another. And there they stayed. For days.

Connor, an active Methodist, thought Birmingham could keep King silent. Connor wanted him silent. Because silence is safe, and law-abiding, and powerless. Silence doesn't march, or demonstrate, or demand justice, or force you to see yourself. Silence vanishes. Into the night, like those men in hoods in their '57 Chevys with whip antennas bent double.

But what came out of that cell spoke louder than King ever had, up to then. What came out changed the city and the world and screamed with a voice that would not be silenced.

Legend has it King began his "Letter from a Birmingham Jail"—what many think of as the most powerful written document of the civil rights era—on the margins of newspaper scraps. It was the best recycling ever. He finished the rest in a legal pad somebody slipped him inside, and the pieces were assembled like a jigsaw puzzle by King's friend Wyatt Tee Walker.

The words were loud, and strong, and righteous.

I never read them. Not in Birmingham schools in the 1970s or my dad's churches or history classes at the University of Alabama in the 1980s. They were not assigned or recommended in classes I took. I never read them until I got my first newspaper job at *The Birmingham News* in 1986 and needed to know the story of the city's past.

The date of the letter was never lost on me. It was April 16, 1963. It was written eleven days after my birth, twenty-three miles from the hospital where I was born.

I came to love that letter, for it was bold and spoke in phrases I could pretend to claim, in the way a white person of privilege might foolishly want to do:

I am in Birmingham because injustice is here.

Yeah.

I cannot sit idly by in Atlanta and not be concerned about what happens in Birmingham. Injustice anywhere is a threat to justice everywhere.

Can I get an amen?

We are caught in an inescapable network of mutuality, tied in a single garment of destiny. Whatever affects one directly, affects all indirectly.

We are. It does.

I wanted it to be mine. I tried to claim it. It was my town, the time of my life. But it would take me a long time to find my place in it. And it would not be the way I thought. Because the point of the letter did not emanate from the lyrical phrases that would become memes for justice. The point of the letter was, in many ways, the rebuke.

For retreat, in the name of peace.

For obedience, in the name of law.

For silence, in the voice of God.

Birmingham firemen spraying demonstrators at the
Birmingham Children's Crusade in May 1963 captured
the world's attention, as had the words the Reverend
Dr. Martin Luther King Jr. wrote from Birmingham's
jail the month before.

The point of the letter was shame and disappointment, and
a truth so deep and ingrained that some people look at it for a
lifetime and never see it at all. The point of this letter was not a
message to Black people who lived the struggle and knew the barriers and blockades. It was a message to cautious and careful white
people, like those eight clergy members—the Waitful Eight, some
call them—to whom King addressed the letter. Like the members
of my family, who thought they understood. It was to people just
like mine, who tried to live like Jesus but turned the other cheek
only to look away.

King, in his letter, was direct:

The mug shot from the Reverend Dr. Martin Luther
King Jr.'s booking in the Birmingham Jail, April 1963

I must confess that over the past few years I have been gravely
disappointed with the white moderate. I have almost reached the
regrettable conclusion that the Negro's great stumbling block in
his stride toward freedom is not the White Citizen's Counciler
or the Ku Klux Klanner, but the white moderate, who is more
devoted to "order" than to justice. . . . Shallow understanding
from people of good will is more frustrating than absolute misunderstanding from people of ill will. Lukewarm acceptance is
much more bewildering than outright rejection.

You can see it today, as then, when protesters demonstrate against
police shootings or economic injustice or governmental neglect.
The racist or the closet racist clicks his or her tongue and speaks of
entitlement, and just how far we have come in the South and the
nation. The well-heeled moderate calls for order, and peace, and
caution until all the facts come in. I have done it myself. Shallow
understanding from people of goodwill causes them to wait, and
the silence persists.

It's easy to recognize that in a state where it is expected, where George Wallace stood in a schoolhouse door to keep education for the privileged. It's simple to spot in a town that is less explosive than it used to be but is in many ways as separate and segregated as it was when King was known as "Mike," when he came to stay with friends and confidants in the Birmingham neighborhood known as Dynamite Hill, where whites tried to control real estate with bombs. Misunderstanding is easy, and accidental, if careless.

But silence? Silence is something else. Silence, I always thought, was guilt. Silence was see no evil, acknowledge no evil, pretend there is no evil. Pretend we are post-evil. Silence is sinister, in a state and a region and a world that has long coaxed us to look away.

So when I was old enough to seek understanding, to question the most dedicated and humble and courageous and honest man I ever knew, I read King's letter again, for the fiftieth time, and wondered if my family owned—if I owned—that part of it I didn't want.

I was half a century old by then. My father, a preacher in the Birmingham area in the 1960s and that man I most admired, was now dead. King was almost fifty years gone, and my grandfather, also a preacher in Birmingham in the 1960s, had died a year after King.

My dad and granddad were legends of love and joy in my family and their communities, men of goodwill who believed in their God and their church in deep and profound ways. My parents hammered into their children that all people—all people—were entitled to the love and respect and the justice we took for granted. Dad quietly insisted I remain in public school in Decatur, Alabama, in 1970, the first year of court-ordered integration. He quietly met with Black preachers during those turbulent times, and quietly signed me up for a new, integrated Cub Scout pack at the Black Methodist church where his friend the Reverend Watt Washington preached.

He—along with my mother—quietly made me all I am, for good or for ill.

Quietly.

I struggled, though, to remember his words. I recalled none from the pulpit about race and justice and the sins that suffocated the South. I recalled no public acknowledgment of marches, no words about King or the Black ministers in Birmingham—the Reverend Fred Shuttlesworth or King's brother A. D. King, both of whom were bombed out of their houses for daring to claim that all men and women really were created equal in that American dream.

I believe Dad feared losing his congregation, that it was better to have subtle influence than outright rejection.

"Once you lose them, they're gone," he said once about another matter.

So the "racial issue," as he called it, the "race question," became a political matter, a secular query to be answered outside the sanctuary that was the church, if at all. In the back of my mind it haunted me. All that time I'd seen only the goodwill. I had never confronted what it meant. King cut deep:

> I felt that the white ministers, priests and rabbis of the South would be among our strongest allies. Instead, some have been outright opponents, refusing to understand the freedom movement and misrepresenting its leaders; all too many others have been more cautious than courageous and have remained silent behind the anesthetizing security of stained glass windows.

Silent.

I came to Birmingham with the hope that the white religious leadership of this community would see the justice of our cause and, with deep moral concern, would serve as the channel through which our just grievances could reach the power structure. I had hoped that each of you would understand. But again I have been disappointed.

I come from a family of ministers, in a state burdened by a history of injustice, in a region guided by those with the biggest Bibles and the loudest pulpits, and it took the death of my parents to make me question who I was.

I'd always pretended there was symmetry between me and King. I stayed in Birmingham, I told myself on my most haughty days, because injustice was here. What arrogance. What foolishness.

I had read all the inspiring parts of King's letter and committed many to memory. But I read right over the damning parts, those that charged my world like an indictment in the days after my birth. What if? What if, I had to ask, it charged my family, too?

They were people of goodwill, I was sure. What if that's not enough?

I thought, when I finally asked myself the question, that it was too late to know, with certainty. My father was gone, and memories fade. Until I found the file cabinets he left behind, with hundreds of sermons—every sermon he gave and some he gave many times—dated and noted and tucked away, in my own basement.

I knew this man. I knew his heart, and it was large. Now I could know where he put his words, in the crucible of Birmingham, in the cradle of the civil rights movement, at a turning point in history.

If only I dared.

2

A Serious Man

Never say something is too big to budge until you have asked your father to help you.

—REV. ROBERT L. ARCHIBALD JR., October 29, 1967

Dad always was a responsible man, so when it snowed a solid foot in Huntsville, Alabama, when I was two, he did not tie my sled to the back of his car as he did for my siblings and the other neighborhood children. He did not allow me to ride up Monte Sano Mountain, sliding, careening behind his Rambler station wagon in a long whipping train of sleds, screaming, like all those other kids, and praying only for life.

Nope. Dad was always a responsible man. He left me there on the side of the road. In the snow.

I was two.

Mother—Mary—came to rescue me, plucking me out of a drift.

"Honey!" she said to my dad later, after he towed the other children back up the side of Huntsville's steepest mountain and prepared to make another run.

"Oh, bless Patty, sweet!" he said. "I was coming right back."

Dad was always a responsible man. During that cold winter in Decatur in the seventies, when the Tennessee River froze as solid as a big river in the South can freeze, he insisted on walking out on the ice with us, so if we fell in, he'd be there to drown at our sides. When I slipped and fell, knocking myself senseless, he packed snow on my head to stop the bleeding while the other children scooted around on the ice.

It was only a concussion.

"Honey!" my mother said later. "Why didn't you bring him home?"

"Oh, for Pete's sake, Mary," Dad said. "He wasn't going to die!"

A whipping, sliding trail of danger on Monte Sano Mountain in Huntsville, Alabama, circa 1964

Dad was of the opinion that children needed a little adventure in their lives—that's why they healed so well. So he tied ropes in trees and took us on perilous hikes, on winding trails overlooking certain death.

"Do it. Just walk across."

We leapt from rock to rock on slippery waterfalls, and once he encouraged me to dive into a swimming hole in north Alabama, even as we watched what must have been half a dozen snakes swimming across the surface.

"Do it. They'll get away from you once you jump in," he said. "Don't be a mugwump, now. In or out."

A mugwump, as he told us, was an indecisive person, one who sits on a fence with his mug on one side and his wump on the other.

When we fell and scraped our knees, bumped our heads or stubbed our toes, he had the answer.

"Looks like I'm gonna have to cut it off," he'd say. And up we would fly.

I twisted my ankle on a hike up the Appalachian Trail when I was ten or eleven. He examined it.

"I think you'll live," he said. "Better walk it off. Go ahead, do it."

"Gosh, Dad," I said.

"Watch that mouth, son. Don't take God's name in vain."

"Sorry."

We were not permitted to say "gosh" or "gawd" or "golly." "My God," "for "God's sake" and "Lord a'mercy" were strictly forbidden as well, as were any derivatives thereof.

"I swanny" was expletive enough, or "Sam Hill," "bless Patty" or "for Pete's sake." As in: "What in the Sam Hill are you children waiting on?"

"I'm scared, Daddy."

"Oh, for Pete's sake, I've got you. Just do it! Jump off that cotton-pickin' log, and don't look down."

"One . . . two . . . three . . . go!"

"Well, bless Patty, you did it!"

I guess we all got a little bit of Dad's "Do it!" genes, the need for adventure and action, to push ourselves, and, more important, our companions, on to a little risk. We all got it, but my older brothers, Mark and Murray, got the most.

Like when Mark, who was three years older than me and closest to my age—found the snapping turtle:

"Stick your finger out, just to see if it will bite," he said. "Go ahead, do it! How bad can it be?"

Bad.

Or when he dared me to leap off the bluff above the river:

"Don't worry. Just do it! If you get knocked out, I'll save you."

And I'm sure he would.

Or when he told me I would have no problem, at the age of ten, carrying a thirty-pound boulder down the side of a mountain.

"You're strong—just do it! Just drop it if it gets too heavy. . . . Not on your fingers!"

But Murray, well, no one could coax or dare or cajole more effectively than Murray, the oldest of us four preacher's kids. Mary Beth—two years younger than Murray and seven years older than I—imitates him to this day, screwing up her face and spitting out the words, like the Wicked Witch of the West.

"Do it! Go ahead, do it, my pretty!"

He did it when he was ten, when he picked wild toadstools in the backyard, mixed them with dirt, spread it all on a saltine cracker and dared the girl next door to eat it.

"Do it! Come on, do it!"

He did it when he was fifty, too, when he gathered fat slugs from Mother and Dad's front sidewalk, and urged his nephews to eat them.

"Do it! It's not so bad. Have you ever had escargot? It's a delicacy! Just do it!"

"God, Murray, what are you feeding them?"

"Watch your mouth, son. Don't take God's name in vain."

"Sorry, Dad."

But Murray was always hard to resist, and just as hard to stop, whether he was heaving rotten eggs into the neighbor's yard, feeding slimy slugs to children or putting on one of the many elaborate plays and spectacles he created even as a child. He was quite the producer, Murray, and one did not easily say no to his casting.

My debut in his plays came in 1963, or so family legend has me believe. Of course, my debut in life came that year, too, so I had no opportunity to turn down the part. I was eight months old.

Still, I had the title role—a starring role—in a play produced, written and directed by Murray, and also starring him in multiple parts, including the heroic father and the sinister old villain. I would appear as the Baby New Year, in a play called—and this should have been a warning—*The Year Without a New Year*.

All my siblings played roles, for no one could resist Murray's charms, or his urging.

"Do it. Come on, do it! We need you!"

Everything Murray has ever done has been a production, like the way he feng-shuis any hotel room he checks into, rearranging furniture, re-draping drapes, substituting the art on the walls, even if he plans to stay only overnight. He carries extra lighting in case the room, or part of it, needs brightening, and fabric to hang over lamps if the bulbs are too harsh. At Christmas, he arranges the mountain of gifts under the tree so only those with the most

appealing wrapping—those wrapped by himself or Mary Beth—
are visible from the front. Murray once repainted all the figures in
Mother's Nativity scene because the shepherd's expression was "too
dour" and the wise men's robes looked "dull and lifeless, anything
but wise."

"There," he said when he was finished. "Now that's how you
want to look when you go to greet the son of God!"

It was the same then. All in, all the way, all the time. He built a set
in the basement with plywood and cardboard, painting it carefully
for just the right effect. He stitched together costumes from old
Halloween-wear and cloaks from the Christmas pageant at church.
He painted my name—Baby New Year—on a red satin sash that
once belonged to the wise man Melchior. He gathered props. A
broom and a mop, a caldron and an old china barrel Dad used to
pack the dishes when we moved from parsonage to parsonage.

We practiced, or they did. I was only eight months old, like I
said, so it was not really a speaking part. Then Murray did what
any good producer would do. He set a date and a time, and he sold
tickets. Or so goes the family legend.

And people came. It was hard, even then, to tell him no.

The curtain opened and there we were, a happy family celebrating the coming of a New Year. Murray played the father. Mary Beth
the demure mother. She had already grown a little wary of these
productions, having been forced in a recent play to deliver a baby
onstage—a big round-headed baby doll. Mother and Dad and the
grandparents burst out laughing in that scene, and my shy sister
was mortified. She was sure they were laughing at her and not the
role, and she cried.

Mark was three, and he stood scowling on the edge of the stage
from the moment the curtain rose—if there had been an actual
curtain. He was dressed in a long blond wig and a red skirt, his lips

Murray, far left, always had a way of making us siblings perform in his plays, as in this one with neighbors in Jacksonville, Alabama, in the mid-1960s.

bright with red lipstick, his cheeks caked with rouge. Mark was the daughter. He had fallen for Murray's charm, the power of "Do it! Do it!" But he was not happy about it. He never moved. He simply glowered.

As the play progressed it was revealed that an evil old man—Murray—hoped to stop his advancing years by kidnapping the Baby New Year. Even then, Murray recognized the importance of keeping one's youth. He swept across the stage, laughing cruelly, "Ha, ha, ha ha." He scooped me from my crib and ran offstage to end Act I, shrieking: "There will never be another New Year!"

I must acknowledge that a few of these details are in dispute, like any oral history passed down across the decades. When I asked my father to sort out fact from fiction, he bit his lip and simply looked perplexed. So I am left to assemble all the pieces. It is a duty. From what I gathered, Act II began in the villain's lair, with Murray pacing back and forth in front of the china barrel, a metal-rimmed cylinder the color of cardboard that stood about four feet tall and snapped airtight.

Murray gave a soliloquy, telling the audience his plan to hold the baby captive so he could live forever, locked in eternal youth, although it looked more like middle age, with that mustache.

The muttering in the audience had already begun.

"Where is John?"

"I don't see John."

But the play went on, Mark still standing on the side of the stage, scowling, even though he was not in this scene, Murray earnestly, precisely reciting his lines.

"As long as I have the Baby New Year locked safely away in this barrel, I will remain young and beautiful . . . forever! Ha, ha, ha, ha!"

The audience again:

"You don't think!"

"Oh, my stars!"

"What in the Sam Hill?"

"Bless Patty!"

It's quite possible, I suppose, that I slept through the entire second act, and possibly the whole play, deep in the womb of that barrel. But family legend has it that all hell broke loose.

The whispers turned to murmurs and the murmurs to shouts. Dad leapt from his chair, bounding to the stage and ripping the lid off the barrel. He pulled me out blinking and slobbering, and held me high for the crowd—specifically my mother—to see.

And the crowd cheered.

But Murray was crushed. His play was ruined. To make matters worse, the production was canceled, even the next day's matinee. And if that injury needed more insult, Dad made him give refunds.

"Do it, son. Go ahead, do it!"

Murray is indignant about that even today, more than a half century after his play was unceremoniously shut down. It would have been something truly special, he knows. It was far less dangerous than chugging up the mountain behind a Rambler station wagon, or leaping from rock to rock above some mountain waterfall. That was the real injustice of it.

"There was plenty of air in that barrel," he says, as he did just before Dad died a few years back. "Why did you have to do that, Daddy?"

Dad just stared, still dumbfounded after all those years.

"Oh, for Pete's sake, son . . ."

Like I said, Dad always has been a responsible man.

3

Bombingham

I spoke to God last night. With him I shared my dreams. A living sacrifice, I want to be wholly accepted, Lord, to thee. But instead, to my weary soul it seems weakness and failure follow me.

—REV. ROBERT L. ARCHIBALD JR., journal entry, March 25, 1963

Most people think Birmingham got its nickname, "Bombingham," after four little girls were killed in an explosion on a September Sunday morning at Sixteenth Street Baptist Church. But that's not true. As many as forty bombs, some lit with fuses and others detonated with timers rigged from fishing bobbers in leaky buckets, exploded across the city between the end of World War II and the Sixteenth Street blast in 1963.

Birmingham was exploding as I was born.

I know this not from Alabama schoolteachers, for they taught me none of it. At least not officially. Nor did I learn it at home. My family left the Birmingham area a few months after I was born, moving to larger and more prestigious churches across north Alabama, and would not return for a decade. But for years to come, the mere mention of the "Birmingham problem" drew little more than faraway looks of sadness from my mother and father.

It was turmoil and meanness from a past no one wanted to see, and it might as well have been the Civil War. It was as if all the violence and injustice in centuries of slavery and racism could be tied up in a bow and dismissed as "Birmingham."

All that was too hard to comprehend. So it was common for reputable and important people to simply shake their heads grimly, to talk instead of just how far we'd come.

Look how far we've come.

Just look where we're going!

Yeah, right.

So I grew up, the son of reputable and important people of goodwill, with no real idea that the state of Alabama was at war with itself, that its most prominent city was ruled by terror for decades. Birmingham and Atlanta were roughly the same size in the 1950s. Atlanta was moving forward, though, while Birmingham looked back. Atlanta called itself the city "too busy to hate." Birmingham, as the world would learn, was not that busy.

But I didn't know that growing up. I didn't know how housing laws in the 1940s separated Black people from white, how failure to abide by the strictures of that rule brought Klansmen out to enforce it. I could not comprehend a world where, even after the U.S. Supreme Court struck down laws allowing housing discrimination, segregationists kept their version of order with dynamite—which was easy to find in a mining town like Birmingham—and the impunity that only collusion with the local police could bring.

The Reverend Fred Shuttlesworth, a young civil rights leader and pastor of the Bethel Baptist Church in northern Birmingham, was blown from his own bed in the Christmas Day bombing of

1956. His church was bombed again and again, but the fire burned in him as much as around him.

It was Shuttlesworth who talked Dr. King into coming to Birmingham in the year of my birth. It was Shuttlesworth who saw that the hatred in Birmingham was so barbaric it would shock the world into attention. It was Shuttlesworth who knew what would take place.

Birmingham was exploding all around, and I never knew.

Not as a child. Not of bombs or demonstrations or corrupt governments that did all in their power, and the power they claimed but did not deserve, to keep Black people in their place of disadvantage. I did not know of sit-ins at downtown department stores on the day I was born, or Shuttlesworth's march to city hall the next day, or the arrests that would follow. I did not know of King's incarceration or his letter from jail or a summer so intense its shocking

The Reverend Fred Shuttlesworth, kneeling, in tie, led marchers in Birmingham, Alabama, on April 6, 1963, the day after I was born.

images of snarling dogs and bludgeoning fire hoses would be seen on television screens around the world.

Only much later, when I read the words of Harrison Salisbury in *The New York Times*—they were considered fighting words in Birmingham back in 1960—did I begin to see.

"From Red Mountain, where a cast-iron Vulcan looks down 500 feet to the sprawling city, Birmingham seems veiled in the poisonous fumes of distant battles," he began under the headline FEAR AND HATRED GRIP BIRMINGHAM.

It speaks to me like poetry. It paints a masterpiece of a place I love and live and shines a light on all its flaws. It makes me fear the past, for if I look too deeply into it, I'm afraid of what I'll see:

> On a fine April day, however, it is only the haze of acid fog belched from the stacks of the Tennessee Coal and Iron Company's Fairfield and Ensley works that lies over the city.
>
> But more than a few citizens, both white and Negro, harbor growing fear that the hour will strike when the smoke of civil strife will mingle with that of the hearths and forges.

It speaks to me like poetry and truth and pain and premonition. Because I know now what will come for this city that tore itself apart. I read it, I can see it now. I can almost live it. And I dread where this journey will lead.

Salisbury's story was legendary when I went to work in the newspaper business in Birmingham much later. It said the things few locals were willing to say, in a way that embarrassed chamber-of-commerce types and prompted the powerful to decry "outside agitators." It said what could not or would not be said in civic clubs or between the stained-glass windows of white churches. It told truths that dared not be spoken in the oppressive censorship of the mid-century South:

Every channel of communication, every medium of mutual interest, every reasoned approach, every inch of middle ground has been fragmented by the emotional dynamite of racism, reinforced by the whip, the razor, the gun, the bomb, the torch, the club, the knife, the mob, the police and many branches of the state's apparatus.

In Birmingham neither blacks nor whites talk freely. A pastor carefully closes the door before he speaks. A Negro keeps an eye on the sidewalk outside his house. A lawyer talks in the language of conspiracy.

Telephones are tapped, or there is fear of tapping. Mail has been intercepted and opened. Sometimes it does not reach its destination. The eavesdropper, the informer, the spy have become a fact of life.

I always wondered how so many otherwise courageous, decent men and women could look away, blind or oblivious or numb to the injustice surrounding them. It never dawned on me to look at my own home.

Salisbury's thunderbolt of a story appeared in the *Times* on April 12, 1960. A few weeks later, my dad climbed into his pulpit at Alabaster Central Methodist Church, as it was then known, and preached a sermon about the horrors of the world.

His sermon was called "Where Is God?" and was based on a psalmist's cry. He began by relaying a conversation:

Some time ago a group of men were talking. They were not talking about the bills and inventories that they had. They were not talking about the problems of their respective jobs. They were talking about the problems of the world—Katanga, Cuba, Vietnam and the many other problems that face the world. Finally one of the men just burst forth with the agonizing cry: "Where is God? Where has God gone?"

In the margins he scribbled notes. "Near East. Cambodia. Korea. Guatemala."

Not Birmingham. Not among the bombs, or the whips, or the blades, or the politicians pandering in the name of God to a confused and hateful population. Not so close to home.

"Where is God?" I cannot help but think it a good question, for God is not in a sermon spoken from a pulpit in the shadow of Bombingham in the age of hatred and fear. Not even with the words of the Psalms and the great theologians. There is no mention of rights or race or wrongs in this church a half hour from Bull Connor's office in Birmingham's city hall. No mention of beatings or lynchings or the inhumanity of racism.

"Problems" are easier when they are foreign and far away, the sins simpler to hate when they are academic and theoretical. The omissions are glaring and the references, if they exist at all, veiled and vague.

The real problems were never foreign and far away. They were there in the courthouses that denied Black people the right to vote, there in the pews, where uncomfortable silence apologized for the hate of the Klansmen, who proclaimed it "Christian" to stand against equality for all. It was there in Birmingham, where powerful men argued that church was no place for integration. It was there in Alabaster, in my father's own church, and at his alma mater, Birmingham-Southern College.

Salisbury talked about BSC in his story, too. And it surely would have struck home with my father, for Birmingham-Southern was like a friend to him. It is a Methodist liberal arts college and headquarters of the North Alabama Conference of the Methodist

Church, the regional ruling body of the church to which he was so committed. He loved the rolling hills of that campus, and took his family there every chance he got. He sang for the bishop's choir there, and attended conference sessions in its arena. He parked there to walk to Alabama football games at Legion Field, the old gray lady once known as the "Football Capital of the South."

The president of Birmingham-Southern College in 1960, Henry King Stanford, was under intense pressure then to expel a young white student who dared to participate in sit-ins supporting the civil rights of Black people, Salisbury wrote. Stanford refused to rush to judgment, and stood by Thomas Reeves, the twenty-one-year-old student and part-time preacher.

"In Birmingham this kind of courage does not come cheaply," Salisbury wrote.

He went on to quote an anonymous Birmingham citizen about the pressures to remain silent.

"You weigh the situation. You take the counsels of caution. You listen to the voices which say don't rock the boat," the unnamed person said. "But finally the time comes when a man has to stand up and be counted."

If not then, well, when? If not from a pulpit, then where?

The words of Dr. King ring in my head:

I came to Birmingham with the hope that the white religious leadership of this community would see the justice of our cause and, with deep moral concern, would serve as the channel through which our just grievances could reach the power structure. I had hoped that each of you would understand. But again I have been disappointed.

Disappointed. Again.

4

Closer to God

> The lives we live when we are unconscious of being watched by others reveals to them our faith—or lack of it.
>
> —REV. ROBERT L. ARCHIBALD JR., February 20, 1966

Dad was not a tall man. Five feet eight, tops, with a crooked smile and sparkling eyes and a head that was bald on top long before I was born.

People remember the sparkle of his eyes. And the way he'd stand behind the pulpit beaming, belting out the old Methodist hymns and bouncing—bouncing up and down on his tiptoes—as if he could not contain the spirit inside.

He might have done that because of his height, to seem somehow larger before his flock, but I don't think so. I think it was pure joy. He was in his place, in his space, carrying on the family business in a life that seemed predestined. When he sang of his God and grace and faith, he was home, where the rules were clear and goodness was written in a book validated by all of his favorite philosophers and theologians. And his heart. In his pulpit he could be sure, and never more than when he sang the jubilant hymns of Charles Wesley, the prolific brother of John Wesley, who founded Methodism:

> O for a thousand tongues to sing
> My great Redeemer's praise,
> The glories of my God and King,
> The triumphs of His grace!

When I close my eyes I can see him in that pulpit, oblivious and joyful. And loud. Because that's where all the worries of his life were stripped away. That's where he could forget the illness of his wife or the missteps of his children. In that moment he did not have to be burdened with the sick and the dying in his congregation, or the demands of the bishop, or the Pastor-Parish Relations Committee, or the gossips who might stop by the parsonage just to see if our new Saint Bernard, Bubbles, was too hard on the furniture.

But when I really think of Dad, he is not in church. He is at home, picking chords on a baritone ukulele, singing old cowboy folk songs to my mother:

> Come sit by my side if you love me,
> Do not hasten to bid me adieu,
> Just remember the Red River Valley,
> And the cowboy who loved you so true.

I remember him with a harmonica in his mouth and a grin somehow still on his face. I think of him standing on the sidelines at Banks High School in Birmingham, watching me practice with my football team, interested but not interfering. I think of him

With my father, the Reverend Robert L. Archibald Jr., at Cane Creek Falls at Camp Glisson in northern Georgia. At the time, in the early 1990s, Dad grappled with the issue of gay rights and acceptance in the church.

coming to me after a brawl in which another boy got the worst of it, saying, "I don't want you to fight, but if you do, I'm glad you won."

I think of him marching into the bathroom at my sister's high school with cleaning supplies to erase her name and number scrawled in a stall by some teenage punk. I think of him as a scoutmaster who remained for all his days an Eagle Scout. I think of him loving and accepting his children even when all four of them did things that caused him agony. I remember him showing up, unannounced and uninvited, to a court hearing I did not think he knew about, in which I had to cop out loud to stealing a box of condoms from Big "B" Drugs. I threw myself on the mercy of the court. And the mercy of Dad.

He patted my knee, in a silence I welcomed, and appreciated. The only thing I remember him saying that day came after the hearing.

"You know stealing is wrong," he said, and I nodded. "Right now we're not even going to talk about what you took."

For that I was grateful.

Mostly I think of my dad in the outdoors, identifying birds and writing them down in a little spiral notebook he carried in his pocket. I think of him camping in a big blue tent, for he did not believe in hotels. He came from the same school of Methodism as the Finches in *To Kill a Mockingbird,* after all. The ones, as Harper Lee put it, wary of "doing what . . . was not for the glory of God, as the putting on of gold and costly apparel." Or staying in extravagant lodgings when a tent was closer to nature anyway, and nature was—it went without saying, as so many things did—closer to God.

Where I was closest to Dad, where I prefer to think of him most, is on a smooth little lake in the north Georgia mountains, with songbirds singing and dawn breaking to burn away the mist. Lake Hale sits on the property of Camp Glisson, a Methodist campground my mother's father helped found in the 1930s. We fly-fished there, nearly every year, in a canoe that he, most often, paddled silently as I fished.

Dad taught me with a chartreuse popping bug, a little wooden fly with rubber bands for wings. He taught me as a child—patiently—how to tie the fly onto the leader, how to draw out my line and whip it, all in the wrist, so it swept over the water like a flying insect and dropped, gently, inches from the bank, where the little bass and bream gathered. If the flight is right, the fish will take notice before it even hits the water. And then with a little tug and a little shake, you make it judder through water until—*whoosh!*—the surface explodes with fish and fins and fury.

Fly-fishing on a lake is far different from what you see in rushing water, as in the *River Runs Through It* ballet of trout and waders and baskets and hand-tied flies. It is less of an art, perhaps, but there is rhythm to the dance of fly-fishing from a boat. Dad—like Norman Maclean—said fly-fishing was like life. Patience and persistence and attention to detail and peace—and a thrill you cannot imagine.

In the South, most anglers like to fish for large bass with a spinning rod, which can be tricky. You must feel the fish, be one with the fish, keep your line taut and set the hook at just the right moment, or the bass will make you look a fool. With fly-fishing, though, there's no mistaking the intent of the fish. When it strikes, crashing the surface of a mirrored lake, the moment is obvious and unforgettable and heart-racing.

It's a burst of adrenaline and a shock to the system. Oh, you still need patience, or you will, as the fish breaks the water, react so violently that you will snatch the bug right out of its hungry mouth, sending it—and the hook—like a heat-seeking missile in the opposite direction.

One of the first times Dad taught me fly-fishing I yanked my line out of the water too soon, and, to make matters worse, jerked it straight toward my father. It soared over his head. When I realized my mistake I whipped the tip of the rod forward again. The line changed direction and whistled through the air until the hook landed—*thwack*—right in the middle of Dad's bald spot. A big, bloody, bald bull's-eye.

I don't recall exactly what he said. "For Pete's sake," probably. Or "Bless Patty." Not much more, I think, for he was a taciturn man. But he paddled to the bank to assess the damage. He told me to push the hook through the scalp and cut off the barb with the pair of dirty needle-nosed pliers he kept in his tackle box. I could not do it, and I cried.

Because I hurt him. Because I didn't have the strength to help him. Because I feared this thing we shared would be ruined by my own ineptitude.

He laughed, and scobbed my knob, as he called it, grabbing me by the neck and running his fist playfully through my hair. He told me not to worry, that there were still fish to catch. Sometimes you get stuck and sometimes you do the sticking, but you don't stop. He handed me a new chartreuse fly and watched as I tied it to my line just so. He paddled silently back out onto the lake, smiling, with my fly still embedded in his head.

I don't know how he got it out. I presume he stood in front of a mirror when we got home and pushed the barb on through the skin of his scalp, but I don't know. Maybe he got my mom to do it. All I know is it wasn't the last time I hit him with a fly, or stuck him with a hook. He didn't stop paddling me around the lake, but he did start wearing hats.

Nothing mattered in those moments but the moments themselves. We were there, communicating without words, talking without speech, understanding each other in ways we never did anywhere else, with anyone else.

It was silent, and spiritual. We rose early in the morning, at dawn, and slipped the canoe into the water without a sound. I'd climb in the front and he in the back, and without the need for instruction, we'd make our way through the fog and around the little lake.

He'd see turtles on a log, and point, or birds of prey in the sky, and gesture excitedly toward them. Nothing thrilled him more than spotting a rare species or an animal outside its normal habitat. We'd smile and nod to each other at the sight of snakes, or butterflies, or neon dragonflies. He'd stop sometimes and paddle silently to the bank to examine a fern, or wildflower, or a tree he could not instantly identify, which was rare.

When I caught all the fish I needed to catch, we'd switch places so I could paddle him around a time or two, so he could do some fishing himself. He could place a fly on a dime six inches from the bank. He could make it dance across the surface of the water. He could set the hook and pull a fish effortlessly into the boat. He was never as excited, though, as he was when I pulled a big fish, flipping and flopping and banging against the side of the gunwale, into the canoe.

I used to think Dad loved fishing. And I suppose he did. It was only later—after I had my own kids—that I realized it was not the whole truth. What he really loved was fishing with *me*.

In those moments there was no need for talking, or preaching, or questioning, or worrying about school or sermons or family or bills or any of the things that sometimes got in the way in real life. There were no worries but the fish, and where they might gather, and the perfect cast, and perhaps hurtling hooks, thanks to me. In the end, it did not matter if we caught fish. We mostly let them go, anyway. It was simply understood.

There are moments when you can say more in silence than you can ever say in words.

There are other moments, though, when the world requires a voice.

5

Silence and Dynamite

In a world that is so filled with hatred, it is easy for us to fall into step with it and become hate-mongers ourselves.

—REV. ROBERT L. ARCHIBALD JR., July 7, 1963

Silence, in the South, is like the air of an Alabama summer. Oppressive. Sticky and heavy and palpable, even though you cannot see it.

Perhaps the silence pours down from the clouds of Civil War, and the hardship of Reconstruction. Perhaps it comes from institutionalized fear of the Ku Klux Klan, which re-formed early in the twentieth century under the direction of a failed Methodist preacher named William J. Simmons and—for a while, anyway—terrorized those who would say the slightest word against racism, and segregation, and the way things had always been.

But I think it comes more likely as a direct descendant of the "Lost Cause," the effort across the South at the turn of the twentieth century to recast the nature of the war, to proclaim the effort just, and gallant, and godly.

Confederate statues were built all over the region. They tell the world, and the white Southerner, that slavery was not the cause of the "War Between the States," that the real culprit was economic espionage and Northern aggression. It worked, in the long run. It allowed white Southerners to remain proud, and convinced many not to question the history, or the sin.

The Lost Cause narrative was told in every Southern state to make the descendants of slave owners feel less guilty as they continued to build their lives on the foundation of bondage. It was a story told to pit poor whites against poor Blacks, to ensure, for as long as possible, that Southern elites who profited most from the practice of slavery could stay safely above the fray. If the poor fought among themselves, they would have no strength or resources or will to fight the real powers.

The Lost Cause was a story told on park lands, in families, in some white churches, and in school textbooks like *Know Alabama,* the history book all fourth graders in the state studied for generations.

One version of that textbook describes the antebellum South this way:

> The Southerners had a right under the law to own slaves, and the Southern states had a right under the law to leave the United States. Many Southerners did not want to leave the Union. But when Abraham Lincoln was elected president in 1860, the South felt that they had to leave the Union to keep their rights.

That book served as an apologist for the Ku Klux Klan and ignored the violence—the routine lynching and flogging of Black people, the terror, the intimidation of those who maintained "friendly relations" with people of different races. There was no mention of how the Klan grew tens of thousands strong in our state in the 1920s, patrolling the roads as if they were the police, storming businesses as if they were SWAT. Alabama children, into the 1960s, at least, were taught this:

> The loyal white men of Alabama saw they could not depend on the laws or the state government to protect their families. They knew they had to do something to bring back law and order, to get the government back in the hands of honest men who knew how to run it.
>
> They held their courts in the dark forests at night; they passed sentence on the criminals and they carried out the sentence. Sometimes the sentence would be to leave the state.
>
> After a while the Klan struck fear in the hearts of the "carpetbaggers" and other lawless men who had taken control of the state. . . . The Negroes who had been fooled by the false promises of the "carpetbaggers" decided to get themselves jobs and settle down to make an honest living.
>
> Many of the Negroes in the South remained loyal to the white Southerners. Even though they had lately been freed from slavery, even though they had no education, they knew who their friends were.

Alabama schoolchildren, Black and white, were taught to revere those *loyal white men of Alabama*. And to not think much more about it.

The history of the South, really, was a case study in deception, and fear, and retribution, and the rewriting, reshaping of history itself. In 1901, Alabama based the whole drafting of its constitution on white supremacy, and used the document to diminish the power of Blacks and preserve the authority of whites.

David Vann, a lawyer and politician, was among those who
worked for a change in Birmingham government to remove
Bull Connor from power in the 1960s. Vann was elected mayor
of Birmingham in 1975. Here, at work at his notoriously messy
mayor's office.

John B. Knox, the president of that constitutional convention, opened discussion by demeaning Black people, saying, "The
Negro . . . is descended from a race lowest in intelligence and moral
precipitations of all the races of men."

The question was not white supremacy. It was how to incorpo-
rate white supremacy into the foundations of law, into the very
fiber of the state, so that all laws, all decisions, all facets of life
would be based on the state philosophy that all men were definitely
not created equal.

"But if we would have white supremacy," Knox said, "we must
establish it by law—not by force or fraud."

So by 1963, after Rosa Parks and *Brown v. Board of Education of
Topeka* and World War II and the Tuskegee Airmen and Supreme

Court rulings that reminded America that Black people deserved rights, too, enough was enough. Black people looked at Birmingham and saw an all-white police department—the last one in America among larger cities—and a police commissioner who used it like the weapon it was. That Bull Connor was a favorite both of the Klan and the White Citizens' Councils was reason to stand, and march, and shout, and risk the consequences in hope of a long-suffering reward. A very few progressive white people looked and saw the same thing, and even fewer took action.

One of those white progressives was David Vann, a lawyer who would later become mayor of Birmingham; he moved to change the city's form of government in 1962, successfully ending the reign of Bull Connor the next year.

But most whites in the South did nothing. They looked away. Looked away. Looked away, Dixieland, because of pressure, fear of losing status or saying the wrong thing, or because they forgot just how things were done around here. Or simply because they felt pride in the place they loved, because they grew resentful of the nation's ridicule. Because they wanted to believe the South was no more racist than Boston or Chicago or anywhere else in the world, that it had dealt with its demons as well as any could.

The long, turbulent spring of 1963 stretched into a summer so scorching the city was close to spontaneous combustion. The A.G. Gaston Motel in downtown Birmingham, where Dr. King and others in the movement frequently stayed on trips to the city because they were not allowed in white hotels, was bombed in May. The city seethed.

The next day President John F. Kennedy deployed troops to Alabama to quell riots, should they occur. Demonstrations across the state grew more threatening, and by June police and state troopers used cattle prods and batons on hundreds of Black protesters gathered on the Etowah County Courthouse lawn, about an hour from Birmingham.

Through it all, my father, like many white ministers in the South, failed to hear or heed the words of Dr. King, or to use his own pulpit for justice. My father preached of love, and devotion, and the need for Jesus and study and repentance.

As Fred Shuttlesworth and Dr. King gathered in Birmingham to begin the campaign, Dad preached in Alabaster on the "Steps in Finding Jesus." I read his sermons, which he fastidiously kept in a cabinet, with citations and references and dates and notes on all the scholars and theologians he used to build his lessons in Alabama.

They are careful and true to his beliefs. They hint at goodness and mercy with scripture and academic ambiguity, but offer the people of Birmingham no pumping blood, no heartbeat in a time

Police officers and two other men, the one in front thought to be Bull Connor, restrain a civil rights demonstrator during a protest at Kelly Ingram Park in Birmingham on April 7, 1963.

of passion. In the spring of 1963 my father stood in a pulpit in the Bombingham metropolitan area and offered words without resonance or relevance to the people who needed it most. And it breaks my heart.

How do you find Jesus? "Remember," he told his congregation. "The first step is to remember."

Remember Moses, he said, and Saint Peter, and Jesus himself. Remember the home from which you came and parents who set such a *grand* example. They weren't perfect, sure. "But they had a faith in God that was beautiful."

Beautiful. Just beautiful.

I can barely read it now. I know this man was thoughtful, and genuine, and deeply concerned about the state of the world and humanity. I saw him, countless times, bring homeless people, Black and white, to the kitchen table or the diner up the street. Yet he stood at the rocking cradle of the civil rights movement and told sleepwalking white churchgoers to find Jesus in the old-time religion of their Jim Crow parents and Confederate grandparents.

He spoke of his own ancestors:

My mother was raised in the mountains of Virginia. Her father and mother were simple, yet devout, people. I remember going to visit Grandfather and Grandmother Hillman. I remember the big fireplace with its roaring fire in the winter time. I remember the old wood stove and the safe in the kitchen, a place where a person could always find a biscuit and some syrup or honey. I remember the spring house with its crocks of milk and butter. I remember the smoke house. I remember the ash pit. I remember the big feather beds. But most of all I remember Grandfather Hillman sitting by the fire with his glasses down on his nose reading God's Holy Word and praying for his family.

"I remember the only two times in my life that I ever saw my Daddy cry," he went on, in a rare and brief personal reverie from the pulpit. "One was when his own mother graduated into that home eternal. The other was when he saw his only son, me, answer a call in a revival and dedicate his life to God and the Christian ministry. The second time they were tears of joy."

Reading it brings tears to my eyes, too. And they are not tears of joy. It makes me wonder, for the first time in my life, if there was pressure on my dad to remain in the family business, if comfort and approval and his father's acceptance were as important as the zeal of justice and the voice of conscience.

I don't know that I will ever understand how a good and decent man can tell his followers to look inward and backward at a time in history when they most need to look outward and forward.

Remember, yes, remember. Remember the things you were never allowed to see, if you were lucky. The beatings and lynchings, the Jim Crow laws that kept people poor and powerless for no reason but the color of their skin, the assaults and murders and governments that turned a blind eye to lawlessness. To a state and a region that made laws to perpetuate oppression. In the land of the free. And the home of the brave.

I saw my father cry only a few times myself. Once was when his aunt died, and he held her by the face, looking at her with frightening intensity, as if trying to burn her memory into his brain.

Another was later, when he was old, after his stroke, and cancer, and the effects of Parkinson's disease and sporadic dementia. He reached out to me, crying.

"I couldn't save them," he said. "There was nothing I could do."

He told me of two women, drowning. Somewhere. He was high above, and they were down below. Too far below, perhaps. Or the current was too swift, or the danger too great. I never knew if the women were a delusion in his confused brain, or if they were real, and the tears were part of a confessional.

To him in that moment they were real. To him—always in his eyes and mine a lifeguard and a saver—he had failed them, and they had perished. Whoever they were. If they were. Because he lacked the courage. So he cried.

I cried, too. Because I never imagined a time when my father, still the bravest man I had known, would lack for courage.

This was a man who tackled a burglar who broke into the church and assaulted a staff member in Decatur in the seventies, who held on to him as long as he could before help arrived, but didn't hit him because—well, hitting was wrong. This was a trained lifeguard, a man who would walk into a tornado. This was a man who, to me, embodied the most famous words of John Wesley as they were taught to me, though there is some dispute as to whether Wesley said them at all: "Do all the good you can, in all the ways you can, to all the souls you can, in every place you can, at all the times you can, with all the zeal you can, as long as ever you can."

What on earth could make him afraid?

It's getting to me now. It's killing me. Why have a pulpit if you will not use your voice in all the ways you can? How, by looking to the stars or the heavens or the pages of an old book, and not outside your front door, can you do the good you intend?

6

Camp

Forgiveness does a great deal for man. It cleanses him. Sin is drabness and dirt. Forgiveness does the same as the tea advertisement claims to do—it brightens us up.

—REV. ROBERT L. ARCHIBALD JR., July 15, 1956

Methodist preachers' kids are like army brats. Itinerant. Transient. Nomadic. You move not where Uncle Sam demands, but where the bishop and his cabinet of district superintendents point.

That's the one rule above all others in the drafted army of Methodist preachers' kids, the one law passed down as if from the mouth of Francis Asbury himself, the first Methodist bishop in America. It might as well be an eleventh commandment.

Where the bishop sends, you go.

You go. Without wailing or flailing or curses or complaints. At least publicly. Forget about those tryouts for next year's football team, or that girl who seemed like she was just starting to like you. Forget her. Or the fort in the woods you were going to build with those friends who will in time become nothing but faceless, nameless memories. I wonder, now, if they found what they needed to build it on their own.

My family left Alabaster in the summer of 1963. We moved to Huntsville, where my father would serve as pastor of Monte Sano Methodist Church, atop the mountain overlooking the city that would help put a man on the moon.

It wasn't a choice. In the Methodist Church, preachers move regularly, especially when they are young, and serving small congregations. If you do a good job, avoid scandal or controversy and don't make too many waves, you go to larger congregations with nicer parsonages and better pay, like Dad did.

It was the way Wesley intended, we were told. Itinerancy, so it goes, keeps a preacher from saying the same things over and over to the same crowd, and allows the pastor to speak truths that need speaking, to wear out welcomes when welcomes need wearing. That's the point. But that doesn't make it any easier for the children, who don't accept some divine call or take a sacred vow. They just live their lives, oblivious, until springtime comes and conference appointments are made.

That's when Methodist preachers' kids sit down at the kitchen table and learn their fate. You might get to stay, granted a reprieve for another year. Praise the Lord and pass the potatoes. Or you might have to leave, and you get until June to do it. So you go. In the middle of summer. So you'll never get a chance to say goodbye to those kids you know only from school. You'll never see them again, to say those things you could never find the will or the way or the reason to say.

You'll pack, and move to a house you don't choose in a town you don't know. You'll enroll in a new school with new classmates and classes, and teachers you'll have to charm from scratch. You'll learn to make new friends. Just in time to do it all over again. You'll learn to make a new you. Whenever the old one gets tired.

You go. The eleventh commandment. And don't look back. That's the twelfth.

So in a long line of preachers and preachers' kids, you hold on to the things that are constant. In my family that constant was camp. Or camps.

In the 1930s my grandfather on my mother's side, Grandfather Holland, helped found Camp Glisson for the North Georgia Conference of the Methodist Church outside a little town called Dahlonega—the site of the first gold rush in the United States. He died long before I was born, but he was said to be a gentle man. The camp named an auditorium after him—the Harvey C. Holland Activities Building—and he built a cabin on camp property.

From the sound of it, Grandfather Holland must have learned a lot of things from Jesus. But carpentry was not one of them. So the foundation of that cabin slipped and Cane Creek floods warped the floors and weather and time separated the chimney from the walls. The roof sagged and there was no heat and if you wanted a hot bath you took an old teapot and heated it on the stove and filled the old claw-footed tub. Or you just mixed it with tap water in an old ceramic bowl and poured it on your head over the kitchen sink. That thought horrified some people, but it was always the most precious place in the world to me, a living time capsule from those who came before.

We thought the whole place belonged to us. It was Granddaddy's building, Granddaddy's camp. It was the constant, the permanence in our gypsy lives. But it was not the only camp that called and claimed a part of us.

My dad and his dad—the grandfather we called "Pop"—were

almost as involved in the beginnings of the North Alabama Conference Methodist camp, a mountain retreat called Camp Sumatanga.

And it is just as much home. I spent a week there each summer, swimming and hiking and climbing Chandler Mountain, singing the songs of Jesus, hearing how he loved every single one of us. Red and yellow, Black and white.

I can't say that I felt Camp Sumatanga belonged to my family in the way I thought Camp Glisson did, but it was clear I belonged to Camp Sumatanga.

It's where I caught my first bass, chased blue-tailed skinks until they vanished under rocks and captured my first snake—a green snake that curled around my wrist like jewelry. We caught snapping turtles there and pancake turtles and brought them home to live in a little pond Dad and Mark built from a blue plastic boat outside the parsonage. Camp Sumatanga is where I lay on my back and learned the constellations in the night sky, where I smashed the

The family cabin at Camp Glisson, begun by my maternal grandfather, the Reverend Harvey C. Holland, in the 1930s, a time capsule and a place of refuge for generations of Archibalds and Hollands

tips of my fingers with a rock so that one is forever shorter than the other. It is where I had my first kiss, where I fell in love forever—every year—a week at a time. It's where I learned to tell the story of the wide-mouthed frog—*the wiiiiiiiiide-moooooouuuuuuthed froooooooooog*—that made little old church ladies laugh, and drove Mark insane. It's where I learned to sing, over and over again:

> This is the song that never ends.
> Yes it goes on and on, my friends.
> Some people started singing it, not knowing what it was,
> And they'll continue singing it forever just because . . .

Dad, like the rest of us, was never happier than at camp. He saw wonder in the stars and the plants and the birds. He ran, gasping and out of breath, into the dining hall when I was young, yelling for my mother.

"Sweet! Sweet! Come here!"

She thought one of us had fallen, or disappeared, or died.

"No," he said. "It's a pileated woodpecker!"

He stopped, on walks, to simply stare. At mountain laurel or jack-in-the-pulpit or at birds only he saw. He stopped every time he saw sweet shrub—a little wild bush with woody, reddish brown blossoms—to say, "Mary loves sweet shrub." He'd gaze at the trees, gently rubbing the leaves between his thumb and forefinger.

"What kind of tree is this?" he'd ask, out of the blue, as a pop quiz.

"Oak?"

"How do you know?"

"Um. It has acorns. And those—you know—leaves."

"What kind of oak is it?"

"White? Red? Black?" It was a crapshoot for me. There were a lot of oaks.

He preached a sermon once about his own youth, how he cut down an oak tree and hauled it back home to make baskets. He had been mortified to learn that he lugged a red oak back home, but the baskets called for white oak. He thought everybody should know the difference.

I never saw my father as distraught as I did when he got the call, sometime in the late sixties or early seventies, telling him a building at Camp Sumatanga was on fire. He put us kids in the back of the station wagon and rushed to camp. But there was nothing left, nothing to do. It was simply gone. All that was left was smoke and ruin and acrid sadness.

We stood there, Dad and I, staring into darkness. There were rumors, later, that the fire was started by the KKK, though it was never proven. But that would explain a lot. I can smell it. I can feel it, still hot from the embers. We stood there doing nothing, saying nothing, for what seemed too long. Dad pursed his lips, like he did when he was thinking hard thoughts he did not wish to share. The moment is framed in my head like a painting. Only now does it occur to me that this is the first time I saw my father as helpless.

As a young minister, Dad served as head of the conference youth council, which had some responsibility over the camp. In that role he worked with conference youth director Nina Reeves—pronounced *"Nine-uh"*—who had been an institution there since the 1950s, when Sumatanga was practically brand new.

I came to Nina in her ninety-third year to ask about her memories of Dad and my grandfather. I told her of my search, of my concern for what I had found in all those sermons, or, more important, what I had not found. I understood differences in time and place in history. I understood tact and tactic and consequences. I understood the pressure from peers and the powers of the church. I understood the urge to preach the gospel from the pulpit and to leave the messier parts of humanity outside the chapel doors. I understood the BS, that you had to raise money to exist as a church, that you had to meet goals to send missionaries across the world when you couldn't bear to coexist with your neighbors across the street. I understood the fine lines and broad highways that so often separated the words of the church from its realities. What I couldn't understand, I told Nina, was having a good heart and a pulpit and an inability to use it.

"I know," she said in a weary way that proved she did. "I know."

But Nina wanted to ease my mind. She was almost desperate to ease my mind, so she told me things I already knew. Dad was not a vocal proponent of civil rights or any other cause that might be construed as political, but he was always on the right side of history. In times of grief or trial or trouble, he inevitably stood up, and that's how she said she remembers him: standing up.

No, he wasn't much of a talker, she acknowledged. But if the time came, he'd speak up about whatever he needed to speak up about, and that's more important, she insisted, than someone running around saying empty words.

I'd heard it before. I'd heard it a thousand times and twice that week. I'd heard it that day from an Alabama preacher who said dad kept him from being fired in 1992 after he spoke up for gay rights.

I'd heard it a thousand ways, a thousand days, and it still didn't add up. I'd met a man the day before who swore to high heaven Dad changed his life sixty years ago. Different story—this one involved chickens—but same conclusion.

The man—Allen Montgomery—approached me unsolicited, saying he just wanted me to know. He'd been a Boy Scout in Alabaster in the days just before I was born, and Dad had been the scoutmaster. Montgomery was trying his best to earn his poultry-keeping merit badge, an endeavor that required him to keep and raise chickens, to rear them and feed them, to candle the eggs and pack them, to ultimately kill the birds and dress them for market.

But Montgomery couldn't do it. Oh, raising the chickens and packing eggs wasn't the problem. The problem was killing the chickens. He told Dad he was going to do it the coming Saturday, but he was having second thoughts. Montgomery recruited his family's housekeeper, Katherine, to help him do the dirty work, and in his mind he could already see Katherine swinging the ax.

The two of them were in the yard when Dad drove up unexpectedly, and it was clear he saw exactly what was going on. Montgomery remembered it like it was yesterday, like one of those old memories saved to the brain as a flickering black-and-white short. Dad pulled him aside and asked him the first point of the Scout Law.

"A scout is trustworthy," he said. They talked about the truth, and the importance of keeping promises, and how doing your duty to God and country can't mean sloughing it off on Katherine. That was not honor. It was privilege.

Butchery was the rule. It was the requirement. There would be no dickering or dithering or debate, which sounds a lot like Dad. If Montgomery wanted his merit badge, a chicken would have to die, and Montgomery would have to do the deed. Life was harsh, and in it you had to do the tough things at tough times.

So he killed his chickens, and never forgot it, he said.

For the rest of his life, decades and decades now, he thought about that lesson in the rough spots. Not the harshness of life. Not the need to swing the hatchet, but the importance of trust, and truth, of being dependable.

"There are only a few people you remember forever," he said. "I remember Bob Archibald."

But Nina had a different sort of story. It was directly related to my questions, directly linked to my quest, she thought. My dad, she said, stood up for her early in her career when she was sure she would be fired. Because of a Black man. She wanted me to know.

My grandfather—Robert Lambuth Archibald Sr. to the world, and Pop to me—had a part to play as well, she said. I was eager to hear. Finally, a story of race and voice and action all tied together into one, from the days when Dad and the civil rights movement were young. Maybe, as Nina seemed to think at the start, I would feel better.

Her story began in 1954, when she was still new to her job. She'd gotten her master's degree and set out to be a teacher, but wasn't able to land a teaching job right away. She was offered the Methodist Church job as conference director of youth work, and decided to take it for a while. She'd end up being there four decades, touching the lives of more young Methodists in Alabama than perhaps any woman in history. It wouldn't have happened if not for Dad, she insisted. With help from Pop.

Reeves—devious and innocent all at the same time—decided she wanted to invite a friend to speak to a youth group at Camp Sumatanga. He was a scholar and a preacher, a man named Dr. Julius S. Scott, who would go on to run colleges and direct higher-education programs for the entire Methodist Church. He was brilliant, she said. Fun and funny and smart. And he was a friend. Oh, and he was Black. In Alabama. In 1954.

Reeves asked Dad about bringing him in, and Dad said it was fine by him, but said they better make it official and ask the confer-

Nina Reeves has told stories to generations of young Methodist campers in Alabama. She did not see herself as an activist when she invited a Black man to speak to the youth at Camp Sumatanga in the 1950s. She was doing what she thought was right.

ence's Board of Christian Education for permission, just to be safe. Just to be . . . *safe*. Pop was a member of that board.

I'd never heard this story and was eager as it rolled out to me in Nina's soft drawl. This was history from the heart of the South in the waking hours of the movement. It was 1954, just weeks after *Brown v. Board of Education,* six years before Harrison Salisbury wrote of fear and hatred in Birmingham, nine years before Dr. King sat in a Birmingham jail cell and excoriated white ministers across the South for their silence, for their inaction, for their hypocrisy and their weakness.

In truth I was shocked to learn the conference board agreed to let Julius Scott come to camp in the first place. But it was hardly an enlightened decision. It was a concession to Nina, and perhaps my father, but it was as safe and backward and insulting as the racism that allowed Jim Crow to dominate the South. The board ruled Scott would be allowed to come to camp if, and only if, he agreed to certain conditions.

Scott would have to sleep in the infirmary, away from all the little white campers and the white staff. He would be allowed to take meals in the dining hall, but he had to sit at a table by himself. Jesus loves the little children, they agreed. As long as they know their place.

I asked Scott about it after my conversation with Nina. It was sixty-five years after the fact and, at ninety-four, he still remembered it like gospel.

"There were some vicious racists in Alabama, and they weren't all Baptist," he said.

Reeves just about gave up. It wasn't worth the pain, or the shame. There was no reason to bring Scott to hide him away, no excuse to put a friend through the humiliation of church-sponsored segregation. She told Scott to forget the whole thing. She told him not to come.

But Scott decided that if Nina had the nerve to ask, and if the church had the audacity to hide him away like a leper, he'd come on down. So come he did, ready for battle and rebuke and possible danger in the Heart of Dixie. But he remembered the trip for its success.

A white friend stayed with him in his segregated room, and at his first meal the camp posted a sign on his dining table warning that the spot was reserved for the singular Julius S. Scott. It lasted but a day. For when Scott walked into the dining room for his second meal he didn't see the sign at all. He didn't see much of the table, for it was filled with young people from the Methodist Youth Fellowship, or the "MYFers," as he called them. They wanted to eat with him. They wanted to talk to him. They wanted to be with him so badly there was no room left for him at the table.

"Sumatanga was a complete success," Scott said. "Because of Nina Reeves and her toughness."

This made it all seem a wonderful story of camaraderie over conflict, the power of youth over stale convention, humanity over hate. But, I would come to learn, there was far more to this story.

Those white teenagers got so used to talking and eating and actually living alongside a Black man, that they began to simply treat him like a human. And that was unexpected. Those students didn't merely resist by daring to sit with him as he ate food. They talked to him in chapel and they walked with him in the woods that made it a camp.

The problem came when a twelve-year-old girl—the daughter of a conference official named Rev. E. Hobson Clark—dared to talk to Scott outside the building, to walk with him on the trails surrounding the lodge. Prying, suspicious eyes saw Scott and the little girl strolling along the vesper trail, an area of contemplation and grace and introspection and closeness to God.

And the shit hit the fan.

Somebody called the conference to complain that "he's out there walking with a white girl," and it pushed—"mashed," as we say in the South—all the Southern red-hot buttons. White people across the conference lost their minds, the more conservative elements of the church shouting for Nina to be fired. Dad said that was absurd, that everybody knew Scott was coming to camp and their board had given its stamp of approval. But reason and race have long been segregated in the South, so Nina was again called before the Board of Christian Education, her job on the line. She had to stand before those educated, pious white men, including my grandfather, and explain how a Black man was allowed to behave like a human being on church property.

Dad spoke on her behalf, she said. My grandfather sat mostly silent throughout the whole meeting, though Nina was sure he used his ample influence to keep her employed.

This was supposed to make me feel better, I know. It was supposed to make me understand silent goodness and grace and that song about how Jesus loves all the little children of the world. But there was more. There was so much more, and it was more telling than the story was meant to be.

Members of the board—the board that included Pop and had pre-cleared Scott to come to Camp Sumatanga in the first place—decided Reeves should be allowed to keep her job.

Thanks, guys. That's mighty . . . *Christian* of you. They also decided that a line had been crossed that should not be crossed again. It decided no more Black people should come to Camp Sumatanga. In fact, no more Black people should be there at all.

So they let Reeves stay. And they fired all the Black cooks.

Camp had always given me hope, and peace. But I was stunned now. Shocked. Shaken.

"I don't feel better," I told Nina.

"I know," she said. "I know."

7

Too Late

Are we going to play around with our own little pettiness, prejudice and pride until it is too late to understand the significant things that are happening in the world?

—REV. ROBERT L. ARCHIBALD JR., September 15, 1963

I began in 1963. So it's no wonder I think it all began in 1963. It's the greatest and most horrible year, the epicenter of all I know and love and loathe. Especially in the South. Especially in Alabama. It is the beginning and the end, the year of life and death. It took only two weeks of January before the newly elected governor, George Wallace, infamously took his oath of office dripping with indignation and the absurd language of the white oppressed, vowing segregation forever:

Today I have stood, where once Jefferson Davis stood, and took an oath to my people. It is very appropriate then that from this Cradle of the Confederacy, this very Heart of the Great Anglo-

Saxon Southland, that today we sound the drum for freedom as have our generations of forebears before us done, time and again through history. Let us rise to the call of freedom-loving blood that is in us and send our answer to the tyranny that clanks its chains upon the South. In the name of the greatest people that have ever trod this earth, I draw the line in the dust and toss the gauntlet before the feet of tyranny . . . and I say . . . segregation now . . . segregation tomorrow . . . segregation forever.

Fuck you.

It is hard to believe, impossible to comprehend all that happened in the opening weeks and months of 1963 alone. By Good Friday, King was arrested and taken to jail. It was just April, and Birmingham's police dogs had already had their way with marchers leaving a Black Methodist church. Voters in the city had already rejected Bull Connor after a change in government and a disputed election—but he refused to leave office. Demonstrators came and sit-ins followed and by May thousands of students took to the streets of Birmingham in what became known as the Children's Crusade. Almost a thousand children were arrested on May 2, and the city came apart. Connor brought out the dogs and the fire hoses that would be seen around the world as weapons of hate. Within days those things became synonymous with Birmingham.

It was, perhaps ironically, Children's Sunday at Alabaster Central Methodist Church on the following Sunday, May 5, 1963, as thousands of children sat in jail in nearby Birmingham. Dad's sermon on that morning was titled "Of Such Is the Kingdom."

There would be no mention of arrested children in that message, no acknowledgment of crusades and retribution, or protest, or inequality, or the fact that any of those things were in debate. There was only the notion that good Christians "must become like little children in many ways. Christ does not mean for us to be childish, but he does mean for us to be childlike."

Christians should be childlike in their candor, their willingness to speak truth without fear of offense, he said. They must be childlike in the way they come to trust.

"We are living in an age when nobody trusts anyone else. That is bad," he said. "We must have the trustfulness of a little child. Murray trusted me to catch him when he jumped to me from on top of the car. He didn't ask, 'What would happen if Daddy didn't catch me?' He said, 'I know he will.'"

I'd be more likely to trust this theology and these words if there was just a hint in them that great and horrible things were happening outside the doors of every church in Alabama. I'd be more likely to trust my father's strength if there was some recognition that the South smoldered even as he said these things, that the fuse had been lit by active Methodists like Bull Connor and George Wallace, that time was short and the times explosive and all those people who looked just like all those people in the pews of Dad's churches could change the world. If only they could stop pretending nothing was happening. Nothing at all.

Outside the sanctuaries, the world was changing. Especially in Birmingham. The protests were working. The insistent peacefulness of marchers, juxtaposed against the brutality of the city's police force, shaped global opinion and put pressure on those who wanted to change the city for the better, or those—there were more of them—who simply wanted the trouble, and the spotlight, to go away.

The following Friday—May 10—business leaders in Birmingham met with Shuttlesworth and King and other leaders of the movement and mapped out an agreement to end the demonstrations. It was a win for civil rights, a concession in the heart of hate.

Birmingham vowed to get rid of separate drinking fountains, to desegregate lunch counters and bathrooms at downtown department stores, and to hire Black people for jobs that weren't simply menial labor.

But reaction was swift in Alabama, where the governor railed against godless government, where churchgoing white people sat in pews, nodding at the parable of the Good Samaritan and plodding through the irony, where people of goodwill did all in their power to pretend nothing was happening. Until they were forced to see.

The day after that agreement was hatched and victory seemingly in reach—it was May 11—Klansmen offered up their reply. Bombs blew up at the home of King's brother, and at the A.G. Gaston Motel. Three people were hurt in that explosion, which sounded, according to a witness, "like the world was coming to an end."

Cops, complaining more about the anger of Black crowds than the bombers, gravely put out word they were looking for perps "in a 1962 automobile," which didn't narrow it down. Dr. King spoke at New Pilgrim Baptist Church on May 12, the day after the bombing. He warned Black people to be safe, and peaceful, to avoid gathering in groups that could be seen as targets.

The Birmingham News wrote that "white pastors also made appeals from pulpits" that Sunday. But you wouldn't see any in my dad's sermon. At least not the written version. Dad preached again about family and the "Christian home," about the great joys of his youth, of sitting around the kitchen table with his father, drinking a glass of milk and talking of his dates and school and the highlights of his day.

"A sense of belonging is needed by all people," he said. "We belong to the earthly families, but more importantly we belong to God's family."

Perhaps it was a metaphor. Perhaps it was a reference, however vague, to a world in which some are denied a seat around the table because of what they look like, or where they come from, or whom they love. Perhaps in the delivery he did emphasize *all people* and *God's family* in a way that made his meaning clearer to his congregation than it now seems. I do not know. Perhaps it is just milk. Spilled on the table of the *Christian home.*

The next week—May 19 was Stewardship Sunday—Dad preached about the church budget, and stewardship, and how the "joy of life does not come from having something done for you, but in doing something for someone else." If everybody in church tithed like they ought to, the church would have another ninety to a hundred thousand dollars a year "for the kingdom of God," he said.

Children and teenagers marching in Birmingham in the spring of 1963. The response by Birmingham public safety commissioner Eugene "Bull" Connor was exactly as Dr. King predicted: violent and dramatic. Here, demonstrators are sprayed with fire hoses at Birmingham's Kelly Ingram Park on May 8.

Not a word about bombing or beating or burning. Not a syllable about fairness or justice. Or the impending desegregation of schools that made the fires of hatred outside grow hotter. And 1963 churned on.

The next week Birmingham's school system expelled more than a thousand students for taking part in the marches. By early June, federal troops were sent to Tuscaloosa as Gov. Wallace made his stand in the schoolhouse door at the University of Alabama, a hollow show of blocking the admission of Black students James Hood and Vivian Malone, until Deputy Attorney General Nicholas Katzenbach told him to get out of the way.

The world watched that moment. And on the following Sunday—June 16—my dad preached, in one of his last sermons at Alabaster as he began to climb to bigger and more active congregations, about Christian growth and discipline.

"Probably the greatest danger of the church today is that it has lost its disciplined spirit," he said. "Our present danger is that of laxity, self-indulgence, and the rejection of all authority and discipline. And the plain truth is, only the disciplined change the world."

Yet he urged members to bear witness to their God.

"Most church people shrink from any kind of personal testimony," he concluded. "But Christ said, 'Ye shall be my witnesses.' We are called to tell others what Christ does for us. And if we do not tell others, we will lose the experience."

Can I get a witness? Well, can I? Ever?

I know it is harsh to judge a man in another place, another age, but I allowed myself to hope for better, to expect better. Dad was always one to seek refuge from the news of man in the word of God, I tell myself. And I know he was tired, from church and scouts and weddings and funerals and knowing he was about to move his

family to a new church in a new city in the coming days. All that
and a postpartum wife and four children to look after, including
me, a brand-new baby. I tell myself all of it, and it doesn't help.
Because I can hear his voice saying these things—calling for testi-
monies and discipline and tithes—but not what I want, or need,
to hear. It is not sin of hatred or intent. It is the sin of oblivious-
ness, of self-absorption and privilege. It is everything wrong with
the church, and with people of goodwill and shallow understanding. It is hypocritical and impotent and passive and silent, so I am
angry.

I am angry, for I have met people like James Armstrong, who lived
with the consequences of hatred, which was allowed to flourish in
the silence of white pulpits and boardrooms.

Armstrong was a barber in Birmingham, a man who served his
country and had seen a freer world as a soldier in Patton's army
than he did at home in Alabama. He was brave and quiet, and in
the spring of 1963, as my dad spent his days preaching of stewardship, Armstrong spent his nights on his front porch watching, waiting, with his grandfather's .30-.30 Winchester rifle ready across his
knees, just in case. Armstrong expected the worst, and he got it.

Armstrong was at the center of Birmingham's school desegregation efforts. He had filed suit to integrate the schools, and his
two sons—eleven-year-old Dwight and nine-year-old Floyd—were
among five Black students chosen to enroll in white schools.

I first spoke to Armstrong in 2001, long before he died in 2009
and decades after this remarkable year. He spoke of the fear he
felt in the days leading up to his sons' first classes at Graymont
Elementary School. It's one thing to worry for yourself, to go to
war to fight Nazis and risk only your life. It's another to put your

children in harm's way, to fear for them, to know that through your words and actions—no matter how just—you have put them at risk. Armstrong gambled on a better world, a freer world for his children and children like them, and he put Floyd and Dwight up as his ante.

Threats would come, from a voice on the phone:

How would you like to see all your kids lying in a casket?

Somebody smashed the window of his Buick with a rock. Somebody poisoned the family dog. Somebody drove up and down the street in front of his home reminding, warning, threatening silently that the dog was just the beginning. Armstrong got the message. Loud as dynamite. So he sat, upright on his porch with a rifle on his lap, and waited for the start of school.

Armstrong heard the blast about 9:30 p.m. on August 20, coming from the nearby neighborhood known as Dynamite Hill. Klansmen had set off a bomb under a tree at the corner of civil rights lawyer Arthur Shores's home. It exploded, but Shores was at the other end of the house, and unhurt. The newspaper that gave me my career devoted far more ink to the hundreds of angry residents who met police outside the Shores house—the "Negro mob," as the paper called it—than to the bombers.

A frenzied front-page editorial on August 21 did as it always seemed to do in those days. It used the law to condemn civil disobedience. It focused on extremes so everyone else could wash their hands of responsibility:

> If we are to have a community where men, women and children can walk in safety, we must have law and order.
>
> We cannot have Negroes running riot, violating laws they don't like.
>
> We can't have whites, even a handful of misguided zealots,

deciding for themselves when they will resort to violence, law violation, to stop processes of courts.

All that white leaders of Birmingham have been asking all along is for everyone to abide by the law. . . .

Just a week after that bombing, on August 28, 1963, the voice of Dr. King rang loud and true across the nation:

> I have a dream that one day in Alabama, with its vicious racists, with its governor having his lips dripping with the words of interposition and nullification, one day right there in Alabama little black boys and black girls will be able to join hands with little white boys and white girls as sisters and brothers.

A week later, on September 4, Armstrong sought to live that dream. He registered Dwight and Floyd at Graymont as white protesters hurled insults and unfurled Confederate flags. The mob chanted, "Two, four, six, eight, we don't want to integrate," and clashed with police. That night, Arthur Shores's home was bombed again, his wife, Theodora, injured. Riots erupted and police fired tommy guns and shotguns over the crowd. Cops shot twenty-year-old John Coley in the side, neck and head. He fell dead. They said he had burst through a door with a gun. That was all. That was it. A Black man. A dead man.

I have a nightmare. In it I can see little Helen Shores, the daughter of Arthur Shores. In this dream she is a child, scared and angry and sick of threats and of white people. Before she died in 2018, she told me the story of her childhood. She knew nothing of white silence, for she could not fathom a world in which white people might have something to say that was not a threat or a rebuke or a curse. All she had ever seen from white people was hatred and dynamite. Just bombs and threats and white teenagers who drove up and down Center Street taunting her and her sister and her mom and dad. It wasn't a normal childhood; it was insane.

Dynamite Hill, the ten-block neighborhood punished by explosions as Black families achieved middle class, would produce activists like Angela Davis, and Black doctors and lawyers and judges—including Alabama's first Black supreme court justice, Oscar Adams. But Helen could not see the future. She could not see through her rage. So at thirteen she took a Colt .45—she said she slept with it under her pillow—and went outside to shoot those teenagers.

And why not? It couldn't go on, and the police didn't stop a thing. They just came by after homes were bombed to cause more trouble, so she would do it herself.

She raised the gun and prepared to fire until, at the last moment, her father appeared and knocked the gun away, saying, "Chicka-dee, don't you know if you hit one of those people, there would be nothing I could do to keep you from going to prison for the rest of your life?"

Helen shot no one, for all her trying. Instead she grew up to be a judge and a civil rights figure known as Helen Shores Lee, a voice for reconciliation, and truth, and understanding.

I have a nightmare. And I can't wake up. Much of America couldn't wake up before September 15, 1963.

On that day my father, still in the first few sermons at Monte Sano Methodist in Huntsville, preached a sermon entitled "Too Late." Too. Late. It was built on a theme of "missing the boat," and if there is any statement at all in that sermon about that remarkable time in history it came in this unremarkable passage:

As I look at the complex problems of life around us, I wonder if we are not missing the boat in our understanding of these things. Are we going to play around with our own little pettiness, prejudice and pride until it is too late to understand the significant things that are happening in the world?

Too little. Too late. There is no way Dad could have known, as he gave that sermon that morning, that just before 10:30 a.m.—it must have been the same time he took the pulpit, or close to it—churchgoers at Sixteenth Street Baptist in Birmingham heard a click loud enough for a Sunday school teacher to stop to ask what it was. Seconds later the answer would come from ten sticks of dynamite that shook Birmingham and the world, that killed four little girls and shattered the eye and the future of a fifth. The bombing of that church that morning killed fourteen-year-olds Addie Mae Collins, Cynthia Wesley and Carole Robertson, and eleven-year-old Denise McNair, who had gathered in the basement's ladies' lounge to freshen up.

Sarah Collins—now Sarah Collins Rudolph—was just twelve. She was the fifth little girl, the one who lived. She washed her hands as the bomb went off. The other girls, the older girls, were standing by a window talking. Sarah's sister, Addie Mae, helped Denise tie a sash on her dress. And then—*boom!*—the world turned upside down and nothing would be the same. Because Robert Chambliss, Bobby Frank Cherry, Tommy Blanton and perhaps other hateful little men were whipped up by George Wallace and abetted by Bull Connor's police department and emboldened by the silence of otherwise good people.

It is not just the hatred that kills. Not just leaders who capitalize on fear and incite the mobs to violence. It is the silence. None of the demagogues or racists could thrive without the silence.

Charles Morgan Jr. saw that. Too late for those little girls, but not too late to tell truth. Morgan, a white Birmingham lawyer, was scheduled to speak at the Young Men's Business Club on Monday, the day after the Sixteenth Street bombing. He was righteously angry after the blast, filled with frustration and despair and guilt. And what he wrote that morning, what he said to that group in a speech that was later published nationally, hit Alabama's smug and silent majority right between their pious eyes:

Four little girls were killed in Birmingham yesterday.

A mad, remorseful worried community asks, "Who did it? Who threw that bomb? Was it a Negro or a white?" The answer should be, "We all did it." Every last one of us is condemned for that crime and the bombing before it and a decade ago. . . .

And all across Alabama, an angry, guilty people cry out their mocking shouts of indignity and say they wonder, "Why?" "Who?" Everyone then "deplores" the "dastardly" act.

But you know the "who" of "Who did it" is really rather simple. The "who" is every little individual who talks about the "niggers" and spreads the seeds of his hate to his neighbor and his son. The jokester, the crude oaf whose racial jokes rock the party with laughter.

The "who" is every governor who ever shouted for lawlessness and became a law violator.

It is every senator and every representative who in the halls of Congress stands and with mock humility tells the world that things back home aren't really like they are.

It is courts that move ever so slowly, and newspapers that timorously defend the law.

It is all the Christians and all their ministers who spoke too late in anguished cries against violence. It is the coward in each of us who clucks admonitions.

We have 10 years of lawless preachments, 10 years of criticism of law, of courts, of our fellow man, a decade of telling school children the opposite of what the civics books say.

We are a mass of intolerance and bigotry and stand indicted before our young. We are cursed by the failure of each of us to accept responsibility, by our defense of an already dead institution.

Yesterday while Birmingham, which prides itself on the number of its churches, was attending worship services, a bomb went

The bomb that exploded September 15, 1963, at Sixteenth Street Baptist Church in Birmingham killed four girls—Denise McNair, Carole Robertson, Addie Mae Collins and Cynthia Wesley, and wounded Sarah Collins. Their deaths shook the world, and the city, into seeing the realities of injustice.

off and an all-white police force moved into action, a police force which has been praised by city officials and others at least once a day for a month or so. A police force which has solved no bombings. A police force which many Negroes feel is perpetrating the very evils we decry. . . .

Birmingham is the only city in America where the police chief and the sheriff in the school crisis had to call our local ministers together to tell them to do their duty. The ministers of Birmingham who have done so little for Christianity call for prayer at high noon in a city of lawlessness, and in the same breath, speak of our city's "image." . . .

Those four little Negro girls were human beings. They have their 14 years in a leaderless city; a city where no one accepts responsibility; where everybody wants to blame somebody else. A city with a reward fund which grew like Topsy as a sort of sacrificial offering, a balm for the conscience of the "good people." . . .

Birmingham is a city . . . where four little Negro girls can be born into a second-class school system, live a segregated life, ghettoed into their own little neighborhoods, restricted to Negro churches, destined to ride in Negro ambulances, to Negro wards of hospitals or to a Negro cemetery. Local papers, on their front and editorial pages, call for order and then exclude their names from obituary columns.

And who is really guilty? Each of us. Each citizen who has not consciously attempted to bring about peaceful compliance with the decisions of the Supreme Court of the United States, . . . every citizen and every school board member and schoolteacher and principal and businessman and judge and lawyer who has corrupted the minds of our youth; every person in this community who has in any way contributed during the past several years to the popularity of hatred, is at least as guilty, or more so, than the demented fool who threw that bomb.

On the day of the Sixteenth Street Baptist Church bombing, Dad preached an ironic sermon called "Too Late," a tepid treatise on missing the boat, which itself missed the boat. The next day Chuck Morgan spoke of being too late, a condemnation of himself and of politicians and ministers and all who could have made the difference. He looked at himself and at the world around him and said the thing his conscience demanded, no matter the reaction or the cost. And it would cost him.

Morgan later told *The Atlantic* the threats came almost immediately. He was awakened the next morning before sunrise by a caller who warned there would be bodies all over his front yard. He feared for his family. The intimidation continued through the fall, as President Kennedy was killed in Dallas and vows of violence seemed to come from everywhere. Anything seemed possible in this world of hate and dreams. And nightmares. Morgan closed his law office and left Alabama. The conspiracy of Southern silence was strong.

Morgan spoke, and Morgan suffered. But I can't help but see that Morgan stayed true to himself. He would go on, as a civil rights lawyer, the first head of the ACLU's Southern Regional office, to become a critical voice in the South who argued important cases about voting rights and districting. His work helped put Black people in office and challenged the way Southern states kept Blacks and women off juries.

It was largely because of Birmingham. He felt he found his voice too late. But what he really learned—what he really taught all of those who struggled to find their voice—was that it is never too late.

8

Angels Unawares

This is life's marketplace, and all of these people are angels unawares.

—REV. ROBERT L. ARCHIBALD JR., June 18, 1972

I was eight, maybe nine, sound asleep upstairs in the little parsonage across Canal Street from First United Methodist Church in old Decatur, the fourth church in my young life. It must have been a Saturday. I feel like it was a Saturday, because the knocking on the back door seemed like an intrusion, an imposition. It was loud, and persistent, and unwelcome. It jerked me awake and frightened me all at the same time. People don't knock like that on a Saturday morning unless something is terribly wrong. People don't knock like that at all unless something is wrong. Or something is wrong with them.

I lay awake for a while, waiting, listening. I heard Dad scramble to the door and I heard a caustic voice I could not identify. I could not make out the words, but they scraped across my eardrums and

I didn't like the feel. I couldn't tell if it was male or female but the voice frightened me in ways that left a sort of scar. I waited for the disturber to go away. *Leave,* I thought. *Leave.* But it didn't go. I didn't hear it again—not the voice, not the way I'd heard it at first—for the longest time. But I knew it was there. I could sense it. And there was activity downstairs. I could feel it from the flurry in the kitchen. Mother was up, banging pots and pans in a way that sounded exasperated. Or maybe it was just a little overeager, like she got when she tried too hard to make people feel comfortable. She tried so hard sometimes that it had the opposite effect. But whatever the reason, the banging soon stopped and the smell of bacon and eggs filtered upstairs and into my nose. The sounds that had seemed so frantic and frightening before seemed like muffled conversation now. Maybe I found my nerve. Maybe it was just the bacon. Either way, I got out of bed, changed out of my pajamas and crept downstairs to see what was happening in my kitchen. I reached the bottom and stuck my head through the doorway and knew immediately it was a terrible mistake. My face must have shown exactly what I felt inside because, before I could take a single step back, Dad knew I was in retreat and his voice snapped like a belt.

"Son," he said. "Have a seat."

It was not the voice to argue with. Not a multiple-choice question, not a question at all. It was simply a calm command. He said sit, so I sat.

I don't know what he said after that. It must have been along the lines of "This is Mr. So-and-So and he is joining us for breakfast this morning. Say hello."

Dad was smiling. Friendly but formal, as if welcoming an ambassador, or the Indian princess, as she called herself, who had come from Oklahoma to stay with us a year or so before. But the man

across the table from Dad was the dirtiest person I'd ever seen in
my life, and I knew a thing or two about getting dirty. I have no
memory of what he was wearing but I recall the smell. It hit like
a wave, a wall. I had never smelled anything like that in my life,
to that point, and perhaps I never did again, even though I played
every afternoon at the slaughterhouse by the Tennessee River, keeping track of a single fish that swam in a puddle of water and hog's
blood. Hell, I worked as an incinerator operator at a hospital after
high school. I had a summer job at a circus theme park, cleaning
up after tigers and catching elephant poop before it hit the ground.
But the smell of elephants is musky and alive. This was something
else.

The man, I think, was white, though his skin was black, crusted
and filthy in ways that seemed unnatural. He said hello to me, and
I'm sure I shrank away, afraid he would extend an infectious hand
to shake. But he did not. He simply ate, ravenous, without the
grace or manners my mother demanded of her children, without
concern for what others thought, without concern for anything.
He was finishing off the eggs and the bacon as I sat, but Mother was
cooking more. I didn't want them. I just wanted to go upstairs and
wash. She gave Mr. So-and-So a second pile of eggs, then she gave
me a look and a little nervous smile and a small helping. I looked
at the eggs, and I looked at the man.

He was old, I think. He must have been old. But what was old?
Thirty? Fifty? A hundred? I have no context anymore. You'd think
I'd be able to smell him in my memory. Smells are like that. They
stick with you and remind you of things your brain can't find on
its own. But when I think of him now, I just smell black pepper.
Perhaps as a defense mechanism. Perhaps because he poured it on
his eggs like I poured sugar on my Cheerios. More than a shake, it
must have been teaspoons full. When he finished dumping it on,

he mixed it with his fork, aggressively, the same way he'd knocked on the door, until his eggs looked gray, like ash. He finished them, wiping the plate with his toast, and was gone.

Dad said he probably went back up across Bank Street to the railroad tracks that made Decatur a town in the first place back in 1821, two years after Alabama became a state. That's probably how he had come to town, and it was no doubt how he would leave, Dad said. He would jump a train and set off to find other doors to knock on, in other cities in counties that didn't prohibit the sale of alcohol. I guess Dad was right. I never saw Mr. So-and-So again. But he would become a lesson to me. He would become a lesson for me.

Dad wanted him to be a lesson. For this man was proof of all his warnings, all his harrumphing when Budweiser commercials interrupted football games. This man was evidence that was used time and again to demonstrate what happened to a soul when alcohol had its way with you. He was the pain the partier could never see, the inevitable conclusion to a life seduced by the sirens of spirits and debauchery.

Dad despised alcohol. He never spoke of hell, but if he did, the devil would tend the bar. He mourned for families he said were torn apart by booze, and preached of them in nameless examples. I waited in the car as he visited a young man in jail in Decatur. He used that as a lesson, too. The fellow had gotten drunk on bootleg beer and run from the cops. He'd have to spend a year in jail, away from his family. That's what booze will do, Dad said. It drives people away from the church and their children and those who depend on them. It fools them into selfishness and allows them to suppress their shame, to forget themselves.

"Remember who you are," he said to me every time I left the house. "Remember who you are."

He hated alcohol, and would not allow anything resembling it into the house. He discovered a bottle of white wine vinegar my mother bought for a recipe and threw it out unopened, over protests from everyone.

"Not in this house!"

Once, at the University of Georgia Creamery, where Mother and I went often for frozen raspberry yogurt when on visits to see my grandmother in Athens, the student stuck the wrong label on the carton. It said CHAMPAGNE ICE, and didn't make it to our freezer at home before it found the trash. We told Dad about the misleading label, but it didn't matter.

"Not in this house!"

I saw men, bums, hoboes—we call them homeless people now—stop Dad on the street and ask for money. He never gave it to them, not a dime, for he feared they would take the cash and spend it on drugs or alcohol, that they would feed their addiction instead of their hunger. But if they told him they were hungry, he invariably offered them food. At the house, if he had to. But more often, in later years, he'd take them to a diner and order breakfast, or lunch, or dinner. He didn't take them to save their souls or get them into church or lecture them about drugs or alcohol. He took them to eat because they were hungry. He took them because he believed the thing they needed most was to be treated like people, to be seen beneath the soot. They are lost, he said once. They just need to know that sometimes, some days, they are found.

Other men would come to the house over the years—the parsonage was just two blocks from the railroad tracks—and I wonder if Dad got a reputation as an easy mark. Perhaps in the boxcars, over a bottle of bootleg whiskey, men spoke of a preacher who always opened his door, even on Saturday mornings. Or perhaps their parents, like mine, told them that if they ever got too hungry, or too tired, or too troubled to handle the magnitude of the world all by themselves, they should find the nearest Methodist church and ask for the preacher.

"Tell them who you are," Dad said. "They'll help you."

I believed it for a long time. Perhaps I believe it still.

I learned more lessons from Dad and those men than I ever learned in a service, in any one of his sermons. But it wasn't the lesson he was pushing, the moral he was selling. It never did convince me alcohol was the devil, but it taught me things I never could comprehend in a sanctuary, like all those kinds of grace John Wesley passed down and Dad talked about from the pulpit. Methodists aren't much on damnation but they talk a lot about grace. On and on about grace, and it always seemed about as useful as algebra. What is grace? Solve for *x*. *Prevenient* grace, they say, covers you like some kind of security blanket before you even know it is there, and *justifying* grace somehow settles in when you give up trying to prove how much you deserve it. *Sanctifying* grace seems to me like the one at play here. It's the one that helps you love God, and yourself, and your neighbor, which does not just mean the old lady next door or the Baptists down the street, but men who climb on trains and wind up in little towns, hungry and smelly and banging on doors at ungodly hours for just a bite to eat.

I rarely saw Dad practicing his sermons, in front of a mirror or otherwise. I often saw him visiting the sick and the dying in hospitals. I have the physical and emotional scars and stories to prove it. Once he left me alone, reading biographies of famous Americans, in his white Fiat in a hospital parking lot, as he made his rounds. Don't touch anything, he warned, and don't get out of the car. But he was gone forever, and my book—on Davy Crockett or Thomas

Edison or one like it—was done. I pushed the cigarette lighter in the car, pulled it out and examined it. I watched as the little metal coil faded from orange to black. I did it again and again. Then I touched the black center of the coil with my index finger, just to see what it was like. I still have the scar, small and round and spiral.

Dad got excited about visiting people. The Reverend Mike Harper, who served as Dad's associate pastor in Decatur, said Dad developed a plan to divide up the congregation and have one of the preachers visit every member of the church at home. They weren't to ask about coming to church, or about money, or service, he said. They were there only to show they cared, and to help if they could.

My brother Mark and I went together on Dad's rounds some-times, playing in hospital waiting rooms or on nursing-home grounds. In the lobby at Decatur General Hospital I played with the pay phone, and found that when I pressed the coin return, money fell out like from a slot machine. The more I pushed, the more poured out, and Mark grew madder and madder. It was wrong, he said, after more than three dollars fell out. It didn't belong to me and he was going to tell on me and then I would surely get what was coming to me, and it wasn't all those dimes. Mark did not lie. Ever. So when he saw Dad returning down the hall, he ran to him, eager to bear witness to my misdeeds.

Dad considered his complaint, and decided that I must do my due diligence before he could render a decision. He told me to talk to the lady in admissions behind the glass. Mark was sure justice would prevail.

I approached the woman shyly, my hands out and full of change. I told her what happened and asked if I must return it, and how.

She shrugged and smiled, and said: "Well, I guess it's your lucky day."

In the late 1960s, Dad was appointed pastor of Decatur First United Methodist Church, where he began to be more vocal about civil rights.

She told my dad she had no idea who to call about that money, that I was such a good boy for telling her that I ought to get to keep it anyway. Dad said okay, and patted me on the head. Mark was outraged. He still is.

Some days it seems I remember more about Dad in hospitals and funeral homes and jails than I do in the pulpit. Oh, I can see him singing, and smiling, and bouncing up and down on the balls of his feet, and that brings a smile. But the sermons seem impenetrable, irrelevant and almost preposterous. I heard a thousand of them, and heard nothing.

When we lived in Decatur I went home from church often with my friend David Reed, a transplant from Chicago who loved the Cubs and came to indulge my enthusiasm for the University of Alabama's football team, the Crimson Tide. We caught big bullfrogs behind his barn—Hooker and Luther, after characters from *The Sting*—that won first and second prize in a Mark Twain–style frog-jumping contest at Decatur's Fourth of July festival, the Spirit of America. David and Hooker finished first. Luther and I settled for second. We got trophies, and a story in *The Decatur Daily*, which I delivered on my bicycle. David and I made up superheroes and drew comic books. We wrote and sang song parodies, like the ode to Alabama quarterback Richard Todd, number 14, my favorite player. We sang it out loud to the tune and intonation of Tanya Tucker's "Delta Dawn":

> Richard Todd, what's that jersey you've got on,
> Could it be a faded red from days gone by,
> And did I hear you say Bear was a-meetin' you here today,
> To take you to that end zone in the sky?

David's mom, Winnie, cooked Sunday lunch while his dad, Jerry, talked to us about the dismal Cubs and David's favorite basketball player, Knicks power forward Willis Reed. But to get dessert we had to pass a test. Each Sunday Jerry asked the same question:

"Name one word Brother Bob said in his sermon."

One word. That was all, for pie or cake or pudding. In retrospect I should have just told Mr. Reed "grace." I'm sure it was in there in some form or other, if I could solve for x. But I couldn't name a single word. Not the first time he asked, or second. Oh, I tried all the tricks. "It," I'd say. Or "of" or "the." There had to be a "the" in the sermon, right, Mr. Reed? I was sure I had him, but he was nobody's fool. He made me use those words in a sentence from the sermon, or at least explain the context, and I couldn't do it. No matter how many times he asked or how many weeks I knew it was coming, no matter how many times Dad read the scripture for his sermon at Sunday breakfast as my head nodded into my oatmeal, I couldn't process the words of Dad's sermons or commit them to memory. It's like they flew over my head and shattered against a nagging wall of doubt. Maybe it was just a preacher's kid thing, the familiarity of this man in this pulpit speaking words about impossible concepts like three different kinds of grace. It was just Dad up there, talking to people who didn't really know him, in words and ways I didn't recognize.

There is a lot I do remember about church. I remember old women wearing fox stoles with the head and feet still attached, the marble eyes glaring like those of their owners, warning visitors that this pew was *taken*. I remember the Sunday morning my brother Mark hit Skipper Stewart over the head with the Methodist hymnal. It sounded like a cannon, right there in the front row. I remember when Dad warned me, from the pulpit, to behave myself or else. I remember sitting in the balcony in Birmingham, holding my watch up so my father, in the pulpit, would know it

With the Fiat that Dad drove to hospitals and weddings and funerals

was 12:15, a critical time if all the good Methodists were to beat the Baptists to the Pioneer Cafeteria. It was an effort appreciated by the choir, if not by my father. I remember the baptisms of my children, Dad holding Drew, and then Ramsey, and then Mamie against his shoulder—just like he did when he calmed them in my own home. I remember Drew's cheer after a rousing rendition of the Hallelujah Chorus from Handel's "Messiah," when all church members stand for what my mother-in-law calls the "Christian National Anthem." The sanctuary went dead silent and Drew filled it with an exuberant "Yaaaaay!" I remember my youngest nephew, Max, taking a first communion.

"Mmm," he said after sampling the body of Christ. "Tastes just like Jesus!"

But I don't remember the words of Dad's sermons. It is as if they are behind a curtain. I know they are there. I can hear the sounds, like those of that man downstairs at the parsonage in Decatur, but I cannot hear the words. Even when I read them now, even when they are spelled out to me, I have trouble grasping the threads, for I cannot reconcile the actions with the sermons, the man with the message. It doesn't seem real.

Those men in the diner. They were real. All those people in hospitals and jails and along the streets. I know they were real. I saw them. That man in the kitchen. He was real.

I find a reference to that man, the one who knocked on our door, in a sermon Dad gave in the summer of 1972. He spoke of those people you meet in the marketplace of life, the sick and the hurting, the imprisoned and the outcast. He spoke of angels, an exhortation from Hebrews to "Let brotherly love continue. Do not neglect to show hospitality to strangers, for thereby some have entertained angels unawares."

This is the way my dad told the story:

An old man came to our back door. He had been riding the rails, and the dust and grime of the railroad was on his face and neck. He said, "I'm hungry. I haven't eaten in three days." I watched him as he wolfed down the eggs and toast and jelly my wife cooked for him. I noticed the cloud of black pepper he showered on his eggs, and I knew he had had too much alcohol in his life and needed as much spice as possible to bring back the flavor of food. I sat beside him and asked, "Tell me about your family." Holding a piece of toast in one hand and the fork poised in the other, he said with sad eyes, "I ain't got no family. They all left me." This is life's marketplace.

All this time and I did not understand the lesson. I thought it was about booze, and bad behavior. I thought it was about pepper and taste buds and consequences. I thought it was about this man, this visitor, this angel unawares. And that's the story Dad told. But it's not the lesson I learned.

That man might well have been an angel unawares. But so was Dad.

9

Conspiracy of Silence

We profess, "Love one another," but we live the philosophy of "to the strong belong the spoils." And when a minister dares to speak out in the pulpit, there is the cry, "Tell the preacher to quit meddling and preach the simple gospel."

—REV. ROBERT L. ARCHIBALD JR., June 15, 1958

I was supposed to be Andy. Andy Archibald. It sounds like a cartoon character, like some fifties cowboy with red hair and freckles and a Howdy Doody grin.

Andy Archibald. It had been discussed and decided. Murray had been named for my great-grandfather, the right Reverend Robert Murray Archibald, and Mary Beth was more formally Mary Elizabeth, both biblical and family names, the best of both worlds. Mark was Charles Mark. I always assumed he was named for Charles Wesley, who wrote the joyful hymns that made Dad bounce most enthusiastically behind the pulpit, and for Saint Mark, writer of that spartan gospel.

I was to be John Andrew Archibald, and I would be called Andy. Like Raggedy Andy. Until April 5, 1963. Until my mother handed me to Dad in that maternity ward at Shelby Memorial Hospital, until he looked down and clamped his jaw the way he did as he pondered before pronouncement, until he held me up like Rafiki would to Simba in the opening of *The Lion King* and proclaimed, in his most clerical voice: "His name is John."

Dramatic. Biblical. Maybe a little pretentious. *His name is John.* How many times have I heard that story? I knew it came from one of the gospels—Luke, it is. I knew it described the origin story of John the Baptist, that terrifying prophet sent to prepare his world for his cousin Jesus. He was the guy who ate bugs, who looked like a madman and dressed like a wild man and still expected people to listen to him when he told them to repent. He was the man who baptized Jesus, the voice crying in the wilderness. And when he was born, his dad, Zechariah, proclaimed, "His name is John." I got it. I got enough of it.

But the biblical version was only half my origin story. The other half, according to my mother, is that I was really named for the Reverend John Rutland, a Methodist preacher a few years older than my dad who bridged the gap between my father's and his father's generations. He was a friend and a role model and an inspiration, in ways I never really understood.

I know I met John Rutland as a child. He was as legendary in my household as people like Bishop Kenneth Goodson or family friend Bill Miles. Rutland was my namesake, after all, a larger-than-life figure I heard about forever, but without any of the detail that would explain why. I met Rutland again late in his life, before he died in 2002. I said, "They tell me I was named after you." He just looked at me funny.

I didn't know then that Rutland was larger than life in the real world, too. I didn't know the stories at all. I didn't know how Rutland had become a sort of hero of white progressives during the civil rights movement in Birmingham, a stone in the shoe of the white supremacists. I didn't know the stories of how Rutland was the preacher at Woodlawn Methodist Church in Birmingham in the late fifties and early sixties, when Woodlawn was the home church to none other than that good Methodist Eugene "Bull" Connor.

I am reminded that Methodists are all over the place, all over the political and theological spectrum. George W. Bush and Hillary Clinton are both Methodist, and so was George Lucas, once. Which changes everything.

May the Force be with you. And also with you.

Harriet Tubman and Stephen Crane were Methodists, and Atticus Finch and Clark Kent. That's right, Superman. I grew up thinking Methodists were better, more evolved, than the Baptists we liked to joke about:

Why are you a Methodist?

My family's been Methodist for generations.

Well, if your family had been idiots, what would you be?

Baptist.

Yeah, yeah, yeah. My wife, Alecia, always liked to tell my dad she was Baptist until she was saved. He laughed at that one. But the difference between Methodists and Baptists, as the Whiskey-palians say in the South, is that Methodists are Baptists who can read. Maybe they're on to something. But it was always a shock to see people like Bull Connor on the Methodist rolls, or George Wallace in his racist heyday. It's enough to make you question the whole thing.

I never heard the sordid side, maybe because Dad liked to preach about how Methodism began over concern for others, that the "great fault of preachers is that we preach too much on the negative side."

So somehow, some way, I never heard how Rutland—this man

who as much as John the Baptist gave me his name—preached of racial inclusion in a church that included the most vile figure in Birmingham political history, the man who stands as a symbol for American racial bigotry not just in Alabama but across the world. He did it in an explosive Birmingham, in Woodlawn, of all places, in a church just down from the old brick building that served as home to the notorious Eastview 13 Klavern of the Ku Klux Klan, a group of thugs that included Bobby Frank Cherry, Tommy Blanton and Robert Chambliss, men who would only much later be convicted of bombing Sixteenth Street Baptist. That group included Herman Cash, who would die before he could be judged on earth for his part in those murders. It was a band of cowards, scared of losing all they knew. Its members beat Black people on a whim, as long as they had the numbers, and called on the phone to threaten whites who dared say anything about it.

Eastview members beat Freedom Riders at a downtown Birmingham bus station after they learned Connor would give them fifteen minutes of free time before the cops showed up. That was in May 1961, when Rutland was at ground zero of Birmingham hate.

But I never heard about that. Not from Mother or Dad, anyway. I didn't hear tales of how Rutland said his piece from the pulpit and how Connor stood up in church and stomped away, saying, "I'm not going to sit here and listen to that nigger-preaching."

I never heard tell of how Connor stood outside the church one Sunday morning, guarding the doors to make sure no Black people tried to come in, or how Rutland, as he described it in his own book, threatened to swear out a warrant for Connor's arrest. I was, they tell me, named after this man. And I never knew, until after my parents died, how Rutland and his wife, Mary, got some of those late-night calls that were the hallmark of that Klavern, or how a cross was left burning on the lawn of their parsonage.

I certainly never heard how his bishop in the late fifties—Bishop Bachman Hodge—responded to the cross burning not with strong words or action but with a question for Rutland:

"Why, why, John, do you have to keep preaching about this race question?"

The *race question*. There's that phrase again. It's the one my father always used, along with the *race problem*. It's the phrase I keep reading from preachers in books about the sixties. It always seemed wrong. It always seemed antiquated and duplicitous. Because there isn't a race question. There isn't a question at all. There is only right. And wrong. The question is what you're going to do about it, what you are going to say.

That's pretty much what Rutland told Hodge. He put it this way in his book, *Mary and Me*:

> My answer to the bishop was, "The question is not, 'Why did I do it?' The question is, 'Why don't you, Bishop, take the lead in speaking out for Christian brotherhood?'" His heart was willing but his feet would not stand.

Willing hearts are like thoughts and prayers after a mass shooting: useless and impotent and empty. Willing hearts are a waste of time and space, like a car with no combustion or a dog that won't hunt. But that's not true. A dog that won't hunt has plenty of redeeming qualities. Thoughts and prayers are bullshit. Without action, willing hearts paint the stripes on the road to hell. Willing hearts are like those talents the guy in the parable buried in his backyard.

The way that story goes, a master gave three of his servants money while he went on a trip, and expected them to invest it wisely. The first two servants put their cash to work and made the

Birmingham public safety commissioner Eugene "Bull" Connor during a civil rights protest march in downtown Birmingham, Alabama, in 1963

master a profit. They were rewarded. The third guy, though, poor sap, buried his bag of money in the yard. He was afraid to lose it, afraid the master would be upset if he squandered it on a bad land deal or a Ponzi scheme. So when the master returned, the servant gave him the same bag he had left. Safe and sound. But the master was pissed. He had the guy thrown into "the outer darkness," where—he coined the phrase—"there will be weeping and gnashing of teeth."

Harsh. But willing hearts have always been easy, and safe, and useless. It's the words and the actions that actually change things and get you into trouble. There are plenty of stories about that. I heard the first one from my mom, who was a preacher's kid herself, a Georgia Peach who was as entrenched in the Methodist family as I was.

She grew up idolizing her father, the Reverend Harvey C. Holland, as she did until her death. I never knew Grandfather Holland, but to listen to my mother, he was tall and quiet and strong and kind and all the things a loving daughter would say about a dad who died too young. In the early fifties, Mother was a psych major at Agnes Scott College, a highly regarded women's liberal arts school outside Atlanta, but she was naïve, and sheltered. She didn't think much about it when several young Black ladies visited her father's church in suburban Atlanta. It was in some ways a more progressive era than what waited just down the road. The war was over, and anything could happen. This was before *Brown v. Board of Education,* before the worst of the beatings and bombings, before Lester Maddox and George Wallace learned to turn hate into successful campaign strategy, before people like the goons at Eastview 13 Klavern in Woodlawn spread their fear and poison.

Mama was so trusting. She had no reason to disbelieve all that stuff she kept hearing in church about loving one another, about doing all the good you can, all the ways you can, all the days you can. She thought they really meant it. So she never imagined the reaction she would get when she welcomed those young ladies into the church.

I don't know what happened, exactly. I don't know if they were met at the door by some Bull Connor body double with his arms crossed. I don't know if they were allowed to come inside and given the illusion of welcome. I just know, the way my mother told the story, that she brought them in and her dad said, "Seat them." So they sat.

He stood with her—and for those young ladies—during the whole thing. He hugged her in a way that made her understand, for the rest of her life, that she had done right. Even if nobody else could see it.

Grandfather Holland was moved from that church a short time later. The move was sudden, and unexpected, and completely out of the blue. It was not explicit. Nobody, as far as I could ever find out, told him he was no longer welcome because he and his daughter let *those people* into their house of God. They didn't have to. To my mother, anyway, it was obvious.

For years she felt guilt. She thought she had made waves that had caused her father grief. She became convinced she had cost her father a good appointment at a good church. Good, my eye. For decades she believed her mother, Grandmother Holland, blamed her for it.

It was only in her later years, after maturity had settled in, but before dementia took it away, that Mother was confident enough to understand she was not the one who ought to feel guilt. She was just the one who, without thinking or planning or trying, practiced the thing her dad and everybody else preached about, if only in parables. It was only then that Mother realized she was the one who should be indignant. And she was.

Like John Rutland, if not as loud. Righteous. Right. You can make 'em pay, but you can't make 'em wrong.

I grew up in it. In churches and parsonages where fine people came to hear fine words and sing fine songs about *every kindred, every tribe on this terrestrial ball,* to later profess their faith by renouncing injustice and oppression. I grew up with the lineage and the background noise, the Wesley soundtrack and the kinship and the questions, but I never knew the church. Not really.

I didn't understand the history, or the consequences. I didn't fully realize how segregation was assured in the Methodist Church before the 1960s, that a merger in 1939 created a convenient separate-but-unequal Central Jurisdiction, where all the Black people would go. I didn't even know Alabama had an all-Black conference—the Central Alabama Conference. I knew that in 1968 there was another merger that created the United Methodist Church, the body that finally integrated in the name of God.

It was only fourteen years after *Brown v. Board of Education,* a decade and a half after the U.S. Supreme Court showed more humanity and decency than all the Southeastern bishops combined. It had taken the church almost a decade and a half longer to decide to integrate its sanctuaries than it took the courts to move to desegregate the secular world.

There were many good, active people in the Methodist Church in Alabama at the time. Rutland. Nina Reeves. Civil rights activist Joseph Lowery, who, with Dr. King, founded the Southern Christian Leadership Conference and helped pull off the Montgomery bus boycott. Bishop Kenneth Goodson would arrive in Alabama in 1964, giving progressive Methodist preachers a green light and a little cover, but I see now they had gotten little of that before.

Crosses burned in the yards of preachers like Rutland, and of Rev. Daniel Whitsett, the preacher at First Methodist Church of Sylacauga, a town in Alabama's Talladega County about an hour east of Birmingham.

A cross burned at a church school across from Rev. Ennis G. Sellers's home in Tuskegee, too. He got little support from the church. Certainly not from his boss, the district superintendent. Sellers had to go to a diner and tell a Klansman he better not find a burning cross in his yard because he'd be waiting with a twelve-gauge automatic Remington shotgun loaded with number-one buckshot.

There were consequences for speaking out against segregation, or hate, or injustice. They were real and scary and I keep hearing how you would have to be a fool to ignore them. Bill Nicholas is a retired Birmingham-Southern College professor who studied the era and wrote the book *Go and Be Reconciled: Alabama Methodists Confront Racial Injustice: 1954–1974.*

He's not a Methodist, and laughs at the way Methodist preachers and the whole Methodist system likes to pretend it stays out of politics. It's one of the most political organizations he's ever seen, he said; to progress, preachers have to make friends and not waves. They can't make enemies, or they will rarely move up the clerical corporate ladder. Methodists talk about the folly of mixing politics with the gospel from the pulpit, and wind up making their choice. They mix in politics by simply going along with the system. In silence.

In the fifties and early sixties, in those days before King unloaded on the inaction of all those wait-and-see clergy, leaders of the church worried more about losing membership than they did about right and wrong. So there were consequences. Whitsett and others were run out of town, out of the state. Vocal preachers were relegated to tiny churches in tiny towns, or were stuck for too long as associate pastors—the second string—in churches run by senior ministers.

I asked Nicholas about them, and about my father, my grandfather. He talked about a "conspiracy of silence" that was forced on them and other preachers.

"Your dad was aware of how much he could lose if he did deliver sermons on this topic," he said, in a way that was supposed to make me feel better. "Those who dared to speak out were banished from the conference or the ministry. The consequences could be terrible. You could be exiled. Your family would be in jeopardy even though [you] were [a minister] of faith."

Nicholas told of Bill Davis, a moderate preacher at the time, who had explained that "if you spoke out on behalf of integration, you'd be looking for a new church the next Sunday."

And I keep hearing it, over and over, on and on, from preachers, contemporaries of my father and those who came after, Black and white, from big churches and small, from his peers and his protégés, from those who worked alongside him and those who worked under him.

Dad couldn't preach about integration, about the "race question," because of us, because of me, because of his family. Because he would be branded a rabble-rouser and barred from the bigger, better, more prestigious and more lucrative appointments.

I keep hearing it, and it is supposed to make me feel better.

He had to do what he had to do so his family would survive.

Okay.

He had to feed his family. He was worried about you.

I understand.

Don't beat him up too much. You don't know what blowback he received.

I don't. I don't. And I get all that, I understand it, even as the images of real sacrifice run through my head in black-and-white newsreels. I see Shuttlesworth getting the hell beat out of him in Birmingham, and Emmett Till's face after his Mississippi murder. Unrecognizable. I see the blood spatter from MLK and Malcolm X, from Jimmie Lee Jackson and the Reverend James Reeb in Selma, and Viola Liuzzo after the march from Selma to Montgomery. Nobody—no family—should have to sacrifice like that. But I keep that to myself and tell Nina and Nicholas and so many others that I appreciate their assurances, that I get it when they warn me to understand the depth and breadth and gravity of this conspiracy of silence. I ask them all the same question, the one that nags when I wonder if it is too harsh of me to go back in time and judge a man by the standards of this day.

"But how," I say, "how do you have a pulpit and not use it?"

They never have an answer.

I wish Ennis Sellers were alive. I wish I could talk to him. I can't help but think of him, that man who told a Klansman it didn't matter that he was a preacher, that he had three children under the age of eight and if they were threatened, he'd shoot first and take his chances in court.

Sellers went to Emory University's Candler School of Theology with my dad and considered him a friend and peer and a quiet but consistent warrior in the push for equality. Ennis and his wife, Jule, called me years ago to talk race and equality and the rights of gay people and immigrants, issues I'd written about in columns they'd read in the Mobile *Press Register*.

Jule was in the middle of writing me a note on December 28, 2017, on lined yellow paper. It was the day after their sixty-fifth wedding anniversary and Ennis was on the point of death, she wrote. But in mid-sentence the ink changed, from a dark blue to a lighter one. There was a dash, and suddenly the cursive was thinner, and just a little shakier.

At present, he is at the point of death—in fact, died this very morning, after our 65th wedding anniversary on the 27th. He wanted me to tell you that he knew your parents and grandparents are very proud of you. With all the Methodist preachers in your family the whole Annual Conference is proud of you—including him (Ennis).

She underlined *Annual Conference* like that. For emphasis. I don't know. I doubted the entirety of the conference felt that way then. I certainly doubt it now. But I can't think of that, I can't think of him, without thinking of something else Sellers wrote, and sent to me, about those turbulent days of early 1960s desegregation in

Tuskegee, the home of George Washington Carver and the Tuskegee Airmen and the horrific Tuskegee experiments by the U.S. Public Health Service that left hundreds of Black men untreated for syphilis. Which, too, could happen only if white people in positions of authority said nothing.

Sellers was vocal. Sellers was firmly insistent. Sellers was threatened with bodily harm and warned that he would find his name on the conservative Methodist Layman's Union's list of undesirables, that his failure to hold his tongue was career suicide. This is what he wrote:

> I did get on the list and there were churches that were closed to me. So what? I did what I thought was the right thing to do, and I sleep well at night! My call to the ministry was to preach the Gospel and be a pastor to the people wherever I was appointed—not to big or small churches—and I did my best wherever I was appointed.

I ask why a person would have a pulpit and fail to use it. Sellers was the one with the answer.

10

Hush

Whatever your need or problem, your conscience is dealing you fits about it. It keeps blaring in your soul like an automobile horn that is stuck, and you can't get out of earshot of it.

—REV. ROBERT L. ARCHIBALD JR., April 20, 1969

Fly-fishing is life. Right, Dad?

You can't just lumber over to the water and drop a line with a splash and expect anything to eat it up. You taught me that. You can't bang on the side of the boat and believe they'll bite. You gotta hush now and hold your rod just so, at the vertical. *Shhhush.* Start the motion—it's all in the wrist—and let her fly. Back and forth, now, never past ten and two o'clock. Back and forth over the water, smooth and easy, until it draws their attention, until the sight and sound of it is hypnotizing. Back and forth and back and forth like music, until their mouths start to water and you drop that little bug—*plop*—where they can't help but see it as a big, fat, juicy steak on a cartoon plate. Not right on top of them. Not so obvious it spooks 'em, but close enough where they can't look away.

Close enough where they'll stay with you. Close enough where they'll . . . *bite.*

Who am I?

I mean, who the fuck am I?

You're out there trying to reel them in to a little goodness, Dad, to coax them and lure them and love them into being something, seeing something better for themselves and this whole pond, and I'm splashing around banging on the gunwale. You walked it and I'm whining because you didn't talk it the way I want. You didn't say it plain, and blunt, and simple. You lived it and I'm over here questioning your damn technique. I can't even do the one thing you asked. I can't even remember who I am, because I'm still trying to figure it out. I'm still trying to prove I'm a tough guy, that I don't give a damn. I don't give a damn.

But I do. I do. You were out there telling them about three different kinds of confusing grace and I'm out at night, in Birmingham in high school trying to forget who I am and make people think I'm somebody else. I'm out looking for trouble, so I laugh when my friend walks up to a stranger's table outside McDonald's, reaches down, picks up the dude's hamburger and takes a bite. Just like that. Chomp. Then he spits it out. On the table. In front of the guy's girlfriend and everything.

Hilarious. Economical, at least. No wasted time between meeting and fighting. Which was the whole point anyway.

Who am I? How dare I?

You were out there trying to make people act right, Dad, trusting that if you gently dropped some hope and humanity on them they'd take the bait. You had so much more confidence in them than I ever did. You believed you could talk about how Jesus loved tax collectors and foreigners and lepers and hookers and beggars, and rich young assholes and skeezy Pharisees and they'd make the connection, they'd look around and see that this faith they claimed demanded they love, or at least tolerate, people different from them.

You were out there quietly trying to live in a way that gave them something to strive for, that made them see what they didn't want to see. And I can't see. I never could. I was always too worried about what people might say, or think. An older kid once told me to punch another kid for acting weird, for being different. And I did. He pointed, and I punched. To prove I was strong. Proving that I was weak.

And what is this guilt? Huh? Tell me. We're not Catholic. We're not supposed to have all that, to drag it around like carry-on luggage with broken wheels. Why the hell do you have three different kinds of grace if you're still going to get stuck with guilt? It's like having a retirement plan and a death wish, all at the same time. Spend it now or save it for later. Pick one.

Who am I? Pompous, self-righteous little shit. Ungrateful ass. I don't know, man. I don't know.

Hell, my favorite memory from childhood is sitting with my sister, Mary Beth, on the ground in the front yard under the oak trees—I have no idea what kind. I'm in second, third grade, tops, and Mary Beth is teaching me how to shoot a bird. "Like that," she says, laughing, and flicks her long fingers in an elegant "fuck you."

But I can't make my little, ring and index fingers bend and keep the middle finger straight at the same time. Mary Beth is supportive, as she always has been, and teaches me things a kid has to know. She tells me to bite down on my middle finger, which will give me the needed leverage to bend the ones on either side. So I do it. First the left hand and then the right, and it works! I'm so proud I hold both hands high, running 'round and 'round the parsonage lawn, right across Canal Street from Decatur First United Methodist Church, flipping off the world. I don't have a happier memory.

Who am I?

Shooting those birds doesn't bother me, Dad. Not a bit. I don't even think it would have bothered you all that much. Oh, you would not approve. You would scowl, and scold, and tsk. But you were more interested in real birds, live birds, like the kind you spotted and cataloged in your notebook. You'd stop dead still at the distant *thwat-a-tat-tat* of a woodpecker. You'd stare at your cedar waxwings and eastern towhees and the tufted titmice, whose name always did and always will make me laugh because I am forever in eighth grade. You loved the sparrows and mourning doves as much as the flickers or finches or the Carolina wrens that came to your feeders. And of course the cardinals. You told me not to shoot those birds when you gave me my Daisy BB gun, and I can't help but think of Atticus Finch now. How can I not? You were always Atticus. But your birds were never an allegory. Not for you. Your mockingbirds were not a metaphor, not some symbol for justice or a stand-in for the weak. They were joy enough for you just being birds. I knew that even then. I had to know, but it didn't stop me.

When you were gone, visiting sick people in a hospital or buying some hobo lunch, I rolled open the window of my bedroom in Birmingham and waited until a bright-red male cardinal landed on your bird feeder. And then I pulled the trigger. *Pop.* The red down exploded like a red dawn, like the blood mist in a Quentin Tarantino film, and when I think of it I can't help but see it, and I wish I couldn't. Just a harmless, beautiful bird, lured to a feeder with premium sunflower and safflower seeds, with all the bits guaranteed to draw him in and win his trust. Just so I could roll open the window and shoot at damn near point-blank range. Not hunt-

ing over a baited field, exactly. That would be too generous. It was
an execution, an extermination over dinner and hors d'oeuvres.
Welcome, have a seat, *bam!* I ran to the bird feeder and stared at
what I'd done. Senseless. Stupid. I picked the little bird up with a
napkin—it weighed nothing—ran to the back fence and hurled it
into the woods.

I cleaned up the feathers under the feeder. I put up the gun and
I washed my hands over and over again as if what I'd done would
leave a stain. Would you miss it? I couldn't stop thinking about it.
You watched those birds so closely. It beat in my head like a telltale heart and I wondered for weeks—I wonder still—if you ever
missed that cardinal.

Who am I? I mean who the hell am I?

It's like I spent my whole youth trying to push you, to prove you
couldn't get to me. I'm the guy who, at twelve, took hungry friends
into your inner sanctum at the church for an afternoon snack of
Welch's grape juice and communion wafers. Nothing like the body
and blood of Christ to tide a kid over until dinner.

I'm the guy who smuggled beer onto the church bus in sixty-
four-ounce soda bottles while you—you, of all people—were driving us to St. Louis. Yeah, that was me, knowing exactly how you felt
about alcohol. I got half the youth group drunk and then mooned
the youth director out the back window of the bus. Proud? That
ain't the half of it.

You and Mother went out of town and left sixteen-year-old me
in charge of the parsonage. So I had a three-day party where some
asshole I didn't really know got so wasted he ate your tropical fish.
Neon tetras, barbs, whatever. I don't remember how I explained
that. I did clean the place up before you came home, but my so-
called friends, who told me they'd get rid of all those trash bags,

tossed them on our next-door neighbor's lawn instead. I know you heard all about that.

You preached about the wickedness of drugs and alcohol and I worshipped at their altar. Mother drove me home from school one afternoon and I dropped a little bong—brass and clear acrylic, as orange as the 1970s—as I got out of the car. It clattered onto the parsonage driveway and rolled down toward Ridge Road. I panicked. I ran after it, and grabbed it before it crossed the street.

"What is that?" Mother asked.

I flung it, with all my teenage jock strength, into the woods. Like a dead cardinal.

"It was—just a piece of the car," I said.

She looked puzzled.

"Well, why did you throw it into the woods?"

Like I said. I panicked.

Who am I?

I'm the kid who stole that box of condoms from Big "B" Drugs because I was too embarrassed to buy them. And let's face it, because I was too broke, too. I'm the guy who realized that the courtroom bailiff was an usher at your church, Dad. He recognized me. I'm the guy who didn't know whether to cry for joy or for help when you walked in unexpectedly and sat down beside me. I'm the preacher's kid who rebelled so hard growing up that I grew up indignant, like some kind of reformed smoker.

Hell, my mother asked me one thing, just one thing when it became clear I was going to write for a living.

"If you ever write a book, please don't use bad words," she said.

I can't get one fucking thing right.

Sorry, Mother.

Who am I to question you?

Everything I've ever done, everything I've ever said, everything

I've ever *not* said, comes at me like an assault now, like an affront to you and me and our very name.

But it's not the things I did as a child that bother me. It's not the things I did at all, for we are nothing if not the sum total of our mistakes, and my regrets are few. It's the things I didn't say, the words I couldn't find or find the strength to use. Lord, the things I didn't say, the courage I could not muster. I can't even imagine my youth. If you're asshole enough to punch a guy in the face to satisfy some other asshole, what wouldn't you fail to question? Anything? Everything? Probably.

But it is the adult silence that stays and sticks and stings, because it feels like more than weakness. Silence is like betrayal, like Judas's kiss. Like denial, like Peter before the cock crowed. Before all my cocky crowing.

Who am I?

I met my wife, Alecia, in college in 1985 at the University of Alabama. She was a sorority girl, a Phi Mu, with pink ribbons in her hair and Greek letters around her neck. I was a GDI, a God Damned Independent, on a campus where you had to have some letter by your name or God forbid nobody would know who you are. She was *soooo* not my type at that moment, and vice versa. Everybody said so. So on our first date it was clear to both of us we were going to be married. We told each other almost everything, spent days and nights and work and school together, said all that needed saying and a lot of things that didn't. It was half a year later, I guess, that she met Mary Beth, who rarely suffers from reticence.

It was the eighties, the U.S.A. was singing for Africa and AIDS was scary as hell, and Murray was living in New York City with his partner, Steve. Mary Beth and her husband, Bob, were visiting from Florida and we sat in the swing set at Snow Hinton Park in Tuscaloosa, smoking Vantage Ultra Lights, which I did for a while in college, because we all smoked in college when we drank, which meant we smoked a lot. I remember it like it was last week. I remember it like it was a test.

We were sitting, swinging, smoking.

"I'm going to quit soon," Mary Beth said. "You know Murray already quit. You know, those gay men in New York are so fit."

Silence. Evaluation.

Mary Beth put her hand to her mouth as if she'd spoken out of turn.

"Oh!" she said to Alecia. "John did tell you Murray is gay, didn't he?"

"Of course," Alecia said. "So how did he quit?"

It was always a test. For the longest time I thought of it as a test of Alecia, that she passed. But that's not it. It was a test I failed. Because *I had never told Alecia that Murray was gay.* It had never come up.

The real truth is I'd never told anyone Murray was gay. Not because I was trying to keep it secret. I just never found reason to talk about it. I told myself anybody who ever met Murray knew he was gay anyway, from the plays and productions he put on as a child to the knee-high leather boots. If you had to ask about Murray you didn't know what you were asking about.

But that's the way silence works, I guess. You find good reasons, fine reasons, perfectly reasonable reasons to say nothing at all, to stand for the way things are, to avoid division or confrontation or judgment or unnecessary bullshit. It's obvious or it wouldn't do any good anyway. It's nobody's business or it's not worth it. There might be repercussions, or there might be a better way or a different strat-

With Alecia at *The Crimson White,* the student newspaper at the University of Alabama, where we met in 1985

egy. What would people think? What would people think I think? Better to simply be, to live and let live and let others—like Mary Beth—fight the fights out loud. Whatever whatever whatever.

It is so easy to go silently. Especially in the South. You hardly even know you're being suffocated until you start to fade to gray, until you can't find the breath to say that thing you always meant to say. So you keep it to yourself, like they want. Don't ask, don't tell, don't say it out loud, don't let them in on more than they need to know. Smile, and nod, and don't let them in at all.

Who am I? I'm a goddamn fraud. They pay me to say what I think, and call me *courageous*. Bullshit. I'm a coward. My pulpit is a pen. It is meant to provoke and to question, but it does not depend on tithes and diplomacy and butts in the pews.

And yet I still anguish over the things I've left unsaid. I can live with saying the wrong thing. When you take a stand, you risk being wrong. Every time. You own it and are rightly judged. I write words, with opinions, and some are better than others. But silence is something else. Weakness. Denial. Betrayal. And the cock crows.

Those times I sat around a table and heard the jokes, or lamentations about the good old days, when people knew their place.

Those times when friends or friends of friends presumed my white skin gave them permission to use the n-word, when all I said was *nothing*. There is always a reason, an excuse to keep your mouth shut. Because they are my hosts. Because I don't want to make trouble. Because it is not my place.

And the cock crows again.

Silence is always easier. And more treacherous. I finally learned to speak and write openly about my brother's sexuality, about my love for him and how he and Steve opened my own mind and heart. It only took decades. People pat me on the back for bravery, for my willingness to share. But I am not open. I am careful, and guarded, and selective. I seldom say out loud the things that truly matter to me, like the fact that I have LGBTQ children of my own, and I love 'em like air. But I am silent, unless asked. Because it never comes up, because it's nobody's business, because it's not *my* business, because they deserve their privacy, because *don't mess with my children*. Or because I'm a hypocrite, maybe. Because I fear, in my weakest moments, that it will simply be too much for some. And then they will no longer listen. Once you lose 'em, they're gone. Right, Dad? Like fly-fishing.

Cock-a-doodle-fucking-doo.

This song has been playing in my head now for weeks, months, like a theme that just won't stop. I try to think on my own but the song by Lee Bains III & the Glory Fires says everything, about the South and the silence and the fear of being absent. It plays in a loop:

> I don't want to be a whitewash.
> I don't want to be an absence.
> I don't want to be the great silence.
> I want to be—

Alabama state troopers shoving civil rights marchers on Bloody Sunday, March 7, 1965, in Selma, Alabama. John Lewis, with backpack, would suffer a fractured skull when beaten by the troopers.

I don't want to be a whitewash.

It's child's play for me to focus on issues of race because it's easy, for anyone who takes time to look, to see the right side of racial history. I live in Alabama, for God's sake, where music and art and food and words are beautiful because of how this history unfolded. I live in the South, where everything there is and everything there ever was is charged and tinted by slavery and war and Reconstruction and cheap labor and lynching and exploitation and bitterness and Jim Crow and poverty and oppression and gerrymandering and segregation today and tomorrow and forever and bombs and scars and wounds that will never heal. It is easy to stand outside Sixteenth Street Baptist Church and decide who was on the right side of history. It is easy to stand inside the National Memorial for Peace and Justice in Montgomery—the lynching museum—and separate

Birmingham civil rights leader Rev. Fred Shuttlesworth was beaten and his church and home repeatedly bombed as he demanded change in Birmingham in the 1950s and 1960s. The parsonage next to Bethel Baptist Church—where Shuttlesworth and his family lived—was leveled in a bombing Christmas night, 1956.

wrong from the righteousness. You'd have to be a psychopath not to see it. It's easy to see the injustice of a city where Black people hold a political and physical majority and hold desperately to economic scraps. It's easy to look back and pick the comfortable, comforting side of history. People like John Lewis and Fred Shuttlesworth got their heads beaten in to make it easy for future generations to see the evil that's still out there. It's harder to look forward, harder still to look at yourself right now, in this moment, and ask what you have to say. What do you have left to say? Better to say it wrong than to wonder later why you didn't have anything to say at all. About race or religion or gender issues or LGBTQ issues or women's rights or #MeToo or politics, or your own feelings or failings.

Who am I? History will decide that for me, I guess. Like everybody else. Let it judge me on what I say, and not on words I dared not speak.

I look back and I look forward and there's that familiar rhythm, back and forth and back and forth, and life is like fly-fishing again. Rod vertical, never past ten and two o'clock. I keep thinking about that bug flying over water, about coaxing and cajoling and setting it down gently on the surface, about the shake and skitter that will lure them right onto my hook. Maybe I'm missing something. Maybe I've got it all wrong and it's not about the rhythm at all. Maybe what really matters is deciding to cast that line in the first place. Right, Dad?

11

For All in Tents and Porpoises

Leave your campsite cleaner than you found it.

—REV. ROBERT L. ARCHIBALD JR.

Sometimes I wonder if Dad might have been happier in another line of work. As a forester or a mineralogist, a park ranger or a herpetologist. Especially a herpetologist. He had a thing about snakes.

It's blasphemy, of course, to say Dad would have been happier doing something else. Preaching was in his genes, in his dreams. He believed he helped people over the roughest spots in their lives, the sickness and the funerals and the mistakes that haunted them. He was faithful and earnest and committed, with principle and conscience and that thing preachers refer to as the *Calling*. He was called to the ministry by God, by gum. At an Alabama tent revival. And there was never a question he would do anything else.

I thought I got that call once, but it was the wrong number. I determined it was just the DNA talking, the faith of my fathers trickling from the wellspring of my gene pool. Like the way I mist up when I hear bagpipes at a funeral. Like the way I'm instantly, instinctively at home when I see the mountains of north Georgia, or Virginia, or the abandoned old roads of Alabama's Black Belt, an agricultural region with rich dark soil, a *Gone with the Wind* history, and many lingering sins. I would have been disastrous as a preacher, a scandal waiting to happen. I have a filthy mouth and a faulty filter, and while I try to live by the stuff Jesus said was important, nobody ever really latches on to his love and peace and turn-the-cheek stuff. Many would rather listen only to Saint Paul to justify ways to limit love. Besides, I'd never be able to stand on a stage and tell people with surety how a guy died and came back to life and floated off into the sky, where he sitteth at the right hand of his father, who apparently wanted him killedeth in the first place.

One preacher told me then that everybody has doubts. Even John Wesley had them. You just preach faith until you find it.

But that sounded a lot like lying to me. I would have been tortured and conflicted and disastrous.

I wonder sometimes if Dad ever felt that way, if he ever had doubts or second thoughts. It's another thing I never had the will or the thought to ask until it was too late for an answer. But I know if he ever lacked for faith, he found it restored in the woods or on the water, in the peace of the morning fog in the quiet hollows of north Georgia, or the fields and forests wherever his tent was pitched.

He was a Boy Scout forever, an Eagle Scout until death. "Be prepared" wasn't just the scout motto, it was a manifesto for his life. He made sure we all knew we were expected, scout or not, to be trustworthy, loyal, helpful, friendly, courteous, kind, obedient, cheerful, thrifty, brave, clean and reverent: those characteristics passed down through Scout Law. On a good day I'd go 8-4.

I'd been a Cub Scout in the early seventies. Dad, along with the

Reverend Watt T. Washington, the Black pastor of King's Memorial United Methodist Church in Decatur, conspired to integrate the scouts, and started Pack 19, Den 1. It was groundbreaking at the time, a phenomenon. But I don't know if it was successful as far as integration goes. If there was a white kid other than me, I don't recall him. We met at Washington's church, under the watchful eye of our den mother, Emmie Washington, Mrs. Washington to us. Our group met maybe six blocks northwest of my house, five blocks from Dad's church. It was across the railroad tracks in that part of Decatur where I delivered *The Decatur Daily,* that part of town where I went to school after desegregation finally reached Decatur in 1970, that part which for generations had been marked off and largely reserved for Black people. I didn't know that. I just went to scouts because it was like going to church. That's what Archibalds did.

We didn't do a lot of camping as Cub Scouts, not at Pack 19, but we cleaned up vacant lots and collected household items—alarm clocks and shampoo, deodorant and sweaters—in boxes for patients at Bryce Hospital in Tuscaloosa, the old and maybe haunted place they used to call the Alabama State Hospital for the Insane, or simply the "insane hospital." It was the creepiest place in the world to a ten-year-old. Actually it was just the creepiest place in the world.

Pack 19 had programs on Malcolm X and Marcus Garvey, because one of the young leaders—Frederick Outlaw—thought we might not learn those things elsewhere. Outlaw would later become the Reverend Frederick Outlaw, after Dad and Washington again conspired to help him get a scholarship to a state college, which kickstarted his education. Outlaw—who was aptly named, and was told later his blunt style "made white folk uncomfortable"—never got over the absurdity of George Wallace's signature being on his diploma when he graduated in 1976.

My brother Mark was a Boy Scout, a member of the Order of the Arrow, an honor reserved for the best scouts, the ones who live the oath and preserve the camping traditions like Dad used to teach. I joined the Boy Scouts after we moved back to Birmingham, but I wanted to play football instead. Besides, the scouts in that new troop—a bunch of white kids who didn't know Marcus Garvey from poison ivy, started campfires with flaming Lysol cans, and sent newcomers on humiliating snipe hunts. It didn't seem like a camping tradition worthy of my father.

It was with Dad that I learned to respect nature and to find solace in it. He was always so much happier in places like that, watching the sun rise over Pamlico Sound on Ocracoke Island on North Carolina's Outer Banks, or hiking the Appalachian Trail, even the stretch of Springer Mountain in Georgia where he had to carry me on his shoulders. He wanted all his children to see swamps and deserts and bayous and mountains, the piedmont and the plain, lakes and rivers, highlands and lowlands, and all the secrets they held. Not just for life's lessons but for the wonder of it. He wanted us to see bears and gators and wolves and roadrunners and all, as he would say, the *creatures of the earth*. He spoke often in the lyrics of hymns, or phrases of the Bible. It was language familiar to him, a part of him.

He spoke in puns, too. He loved a pun almost as much as a proverb. Especially in those places, in those wild spaces.

How can you identify a dogwood tree? . . . Its bark is worse than its bite.

Daaaaaad!

Each year, starting in the spring, after conference appointments, after we knew if we were going to have to get busy and move or not, Dad carefully planned a two-week summer vacation to sites of natural or historical significance, to wildlife refuges and Revolutionary War or Civil War battlefields, to caverns and national parks and forts that held off the British or held in Geronimo. We visited Williamsburg on July 4, 1975, the year before the bicentennial, when it was like a patriot's Disneyland. We saw the HemisFair in San Antonio in 1968, the World's Fair celebrating the many peoples who settled the Southwest. Native Americans—Native Mexicans, perhaps—spun by their feet on treelike poles. The Alamo was tiny. That's what I remember.

Dad mapped out campgrounds where we could pitch the big blue six-person tent, because he wouldn't waste the money or time at a hotel. It was a process, drilled into us since birth, a science of making or breaking down the campsite. Dad found a flat spot and Mark and I picked up rocks or sticks within its perimeter. Dad rolled the tent out carefully and set up the poles. Murray and Mark hammered spikes and Dad tied it off, with square knots and clove hitches he described with every loop. Mark set up the tarp over the aluminum camp table, and Mary Beth and I lugged the Coleman stove and the plywood box filled with camp silverware—Dad even built plywood drawers for it—to the table. When everything else was in place, Dad hung the placard he had made from an old board, with all our names burned on: THE ARCHIBALDS: BOB, MARY, MURRAY, MARY BETH, MARK AND JOHN.

Everybody had a job, everybody had a duty, everybody had an edict: Carry your weight, and leave the campsite cleaner than you found it.

Later in life I started to think of that as Dad's motto and his creed, his primary message to humanity. Leave your campsite cleaner, the world better, than it was before you arrived. That—as much as money—was what he meant by stewardship.

Sometimes I feel like I learned everything worth knowing on those trips. We discovered a world outside Alabama, and learned of cultures and histories our schools never taught. Those vacations opened our eyes and minds to things we'd never have known if we spent all our vacations at Disney or only on the Gulf beaches, as my friends' families often did. They taught us to appreciate a smooth patch of ground and cool breeze, the sweet smell of honeysuckle, of damp canvas and fresh dirt and bacon on the camp stove first thing in the morning. We learned to seek the curious and the strange with a sense of adventure and a pretense of fearlessness. We learned survival. We learned self-reliance, and that we could rely on one another.

I close my eyes and still see myself as a child, walking barefoot through sandspurs toward the beach or the bathhouse, tagging along behind Murray and Mary Beth and Mark, trusting to go anywhere they might lead. Even when it inevitably led to trouble.

Dad taught us wild things. He taught us how to dig up sassafras root—the root beer root, which is delicious, though now considered carcinogenic—and brew it into tea. It's easy to identify because sassafras has three different kinds of leaves, like mittens with one or two or three fingers. He taught us in springtime, when the sap flows, to find a young hickory tree and cut off a small branch, to carve a notch in it and slide the bark over the slippery interior wood to make a hickory whistle. He taught us to play it. Badly.

He laughed, and said one of those old chants that was passed down, probably from camps or the scouts, along with his religion:

> I bought a wooden whistle, but it wooden whistle,
> So I bought a steel whistle. It steel wooden whistle,
> So I bought a lead whistle. It steel wooden lead me whistle.

That summed up Dad. Bad puns and whittling, the outdoors and whistling. All of his favorite things. I could never make a hick-

ory whistle that worked, but it didn't matter. It was enough to recognize the hickory by its vertical bark, from the sharp leaves that
grew on a sort of stalk. It was enough to smell the freshness of the
sap to know, at the very least, it was the right time of year to make
a working whistle.

At least I was good at the puns.

ME: Are there snakes around here?
DAD: I don't know the hissstory.
ME: That's cold-blooded.
DAD: Fangs. Fangs a lot.

My own sons would take it way farther, but that was much later.

RAMSEY: Did you hear about the fire at the underwater circus?
DAD: What? No.
RAMSEY: It was chaos for all in tents and porpoises.

There is nothing I can do about Ramsey or Drew. I blame their
mamba.

We treasured all those things in our youth, until we got too old
and too cool and too busy to care about them. And when they lived
only in memory we treasured them again. We watched the slides
together year after year, and lived them again. We played alongside
decaying hulls of shipwrecks at Cape Hatteras, the Graveyard of
the Atlantic. We ate BLTs and caught horseshoe crabs on a deserted
driftwood beach near Port St. Joe in Florida. We lay on an Atlantic
beach in 1974, counting shooting stars and listening on a transistor
radio to Richard Nixon resign the presidency. We sat in stocks at
Williamsburg and ran Pickett's Charge at Gettysburg and camped
on Roanoke Island, falling asleep on the tent floor with the mys-

terious stories of the Lost Colony creeping through our heads. We hiked the wooden boardwalks over the Okefenokee Swamp, with alligators below and eagles overhead, with Spanish moss like beards of ghosts in the trees and a sign in the middle of the swamp, adorned with human skulls, that warned:

> We were once alive like you are now.
> But we complained and hollered anyhow.
> So love each day, don't pass it by,
> Sooner or later you too will die!

We learned—I was crushed by this—that roadrunners were rather drab birds, and they could fly. We saw poverty in rural Mississippi like we'd never seen, lives on Oklahoma reservations that seemed as harsh as any we'd known in Alabama.

We saw the Smithsonian and Kill Devil Hills and the Gateway Arch and learned early that the world was bigger than we lived, wider than Birmingham and Alabama and the highway back and forth to the Alabama beaches.

But mostly what we learned—what I took away, at least—was that life's great memories were the ones with the greatest risk, the greatest fear. The moments that stood out were not sunbathing or eating or history lessons or hickory whistles or phosphorescent fox fire burning in the trees at night. Oh, no. The moments that stood out were the ones where somebody almost died.

Somebody almost died on every one of our camping trips. In fact that's how we remember them, my brothers and sister and I. There was the time in the Great Smoky Mountains the black bear tore up our campground and we had to hide in the car, and the time in Florida when a tornado hopped right over the big blue tent.

As a paperboy for *The Decatur Daily,* hawking papers in front of Decatur First United Methodist Church in the early 1970s

It has been a long time since we watched the old vacation slides together. The projectors don't work so well anymore and the inlaws—the "Outlaws," as Mary Beth's husband, Bob Ramsey, called them—don't have as much patience for our vanity as they once did.

But one look at those slides and it brings it all flooding back. It started, years ago now, with a picture of the roadway, a tunnel of the variety Wile E. Coyote would paint on a sheer rock face, with majestic purple mountains in the distance.

"Oh-oh-oh," Mary Beth says. "It's the Big Bend trip. Wasn't that the trip Murray got lost in the sandstorm?"

"I wasn't lost," Murray says. "I just wanted that handsome park ranger to find me."

"Like when you got stuck in the quicksand?" I say.

"That was somewhere else. But maybe."

But Mother was back to Big Bend.

We traveled the country, to forts and national parks and near disasters, camping in the big blue tent. Here at Stone Mountain, Georgia, in the late 1960s. Left to right: me, Mark, Mary Beth and Murray.

"This was the trip Murray got meningitis on the way home. He was so grumpy. And we thought he was just being a teenager."

And that's the way it goes from slide to slide, and a picture of the blue tent pops up, pitched in the sand.

"That was the trip when Murray got stuck in quicksand."

"No, that was in the Okefenokee Swamp. This was the trip when the swarm of bees attacked John."

"No, that was in Kentucky, where we saw the white squirrels and the bluegrass that was green. This was the trip when bears stole our food and we had to hide in the car."

"No, that was in North Carolina. We'd come from the beach where Murray got stung by that stingray."

"No, that was later. This was when he was stung by a school of jellyfish."

"Yeah, but Murray was stung by the stingray on the trip when John fell off Geronimo's jail cell."

"That was Fort Pickens, and I fell off a cannon."

"And for the record, none of us were even there when Murray got stung by the stingray."

"I bet there was a handsome lifeguard there."

And on it goes, until we return to the Big Bend photos with a picture of Murray in those *awkward* teenage years. He leans against a park entrance, tired and surly in a red and white shirt striped like a convict's.

"Oh, that was the year Murray bleached his hair and it turned green," Mother said. "That was the best vacation ever."

I try to remember all these things when life inevitably goes bad, in those moments when it all comes crashing down, when you think it's all over and it's hard to fathom a life beyond the pain, or the shame. The things that stay with you, the things worth remembering, are the things that make you feel, the ones that make you fear. Because your life is your story, and everything you do and everything you feel is the arc of that story, and who wants to live a story that is boring?

12

Change

We look at the racial demonstrations which make us so uncomfortable, and there is the tendency to long for the antebellum splendor of the Old South, where people knew their place. But we cannot live in the past, and we must not try. We must do something today about the bias and prejudice in our hearts now.

—REV. ROBERT L. ARCHIBALD JR., April 26, 1964

John F. Kennedy was dead. And those four girls in a Birmingham church. And Medgar Evers in Mississippi. He was shot in the back.

King had shared his Dream, that even down in Alabama, little Black boys and girls would be able to join hands with their white counterparts. Wallace shared his dream, too. That it would never happen.

It was in this time, in April 1964, when I was barely more than a year old, that I find my father's first overt reference to race from the pulpit. It was clear he was not the only preacher struggling to find his voice, stuck between the Bible and a hot place. Methodist ministers like Rutland and Sellers had spoken out, and had been tolerated at best. Others like Andrew Turnipseed, who worked for integration with King himself, were all but banished from the state. But the church was in conflict nationally. The bishops a year before had issued a resolution declaring that all people had a right to worship, no matter their race, and called on Methodist preachers to "speak and live so as to deepen by word or deed the brotherhood of man."

Alabama Methodists fought that like the truth, of course. The Alabama-Northwest Florida Conference in 1964 rejected the bishops' resolution and urged instead that individual churches should be able to decide their level of racial tolerance. It was the church version of the states' rights cry, the foundation of the segregationist argument. Alabama Methodists also condemned preachers who dared to participate in civil rights demonstrations, saying it wasn't their place.

But the world was changing. You'd have to be blind as a biblical beggar not to see it. Congress had begun debate on what would become the Civil Rights Act, which ultimately would make it illegal to discriminate against people in the workforce because of their race, color, gender, religion or national origin. Senators from the South launched a filibuster to kill it. It was clear that preachers were going to have to decide who they would be.

On April 19 *The Birmingham News* led its opinion page with a column opining on the plight of preachers. It was written by editorial-page editor E. L. Holland Jr., under the headline OUR PREACHERS, OUR TROUBLES . . . :

Some ministers have faced very difficult times in assessing their own consciences, evaluating what it is they ought, or ought not say from the pulpit. Sometimes ministers announce that they are answering calls to other pastorates. News accounts do not always say why. Occasionally, it is because the minister of a given church has preached what his congregation thought went too far.

Not infrequently you may hear a minister seeking in sermons to address himself to what we call "touchy issues." In this there may seem to be a good deal of beating around the bush. But the meaning gets through. Some ministers might say it sometimes gets through too well. . . .

We suspect a minister can be a very lonely man as he searches his conscience for decisions which affect the "here." . . . It is a troublesome time for all men, but troublesome probably to few as to the preacher. We need to think of him as a man who is not immune from the world's tugging, but indeed may be most punished by it.

It was the following week, in Huntsville, that Dad addressed those "touchy issues" head on for the first time. Or more directly than he had thus far. Senators in Washington were still debating the civil rights bill, bickering over a jury-trial amendment, and Dad preached on a passage from Acts, written by Luke, in which Jesus tells his disciples they must go into all the world to tell what they have seen.

Dad began with a story about a young couple who went to be married at their church in the north Alabama town of Gadsden. The preacher pronounced them man and wife. The groom kissed his bride and the bride kissed him back and they stood, husband and wife, in front of God and everybody who was anybody in Gadsden. The clueless new husband said, loud enough for the whole church to hear, "Well, what do we do now, Preacher?"

What do we do now?

Dad spoke of scripture, and Roman soldiers, and unanswered

questions. He cited theologians, with their pointy-headed inter-pretations about how the disciples wondered what to do next. But then he did the thing he hadn't done in previous years: He acknowl-edged, out loud, that the words were directly relevant to the way the people in his congregation must meet their world.

> We have a tendency to do the same thing. When times are hard, it is always a temptation to some people to dream about the future, and to project into the future all the things they long for, yet lack in the present.
>
> We speculate about the future of our world, of our nation, of our church, and of our families. We would like to think that in the future men will love each other, but we have to live a life of love in the midst of the cold war of today's world. Jesus says, "Quit speculating about the future. Be a witness for me in the present."
>
> Take the effort to restore the past. Some people, when they face times of difficulty, turn to the effort to bring back the past. When the disciples asked about the kingdom, they were think-ing of the sort of kingdom of Israel which King David had established some 1,000 years earlier. But there is no way back. Jesus says that our task is to transform the present by witnessing to it.
>
> We look at the racial demonstrations which make us so un-comfortable, and there is the tendency to long for the antebel-lum splendor of the Old South, where people knew their place. But we cannot live in the past, and we must not try. We must do something today about the bias and prejudice in our hearts now.

He went on to talk about the role of witnesses, in a courtroom and in life, and said, "I am afraid that too many of us have perjured ourselves on the witness stand of life, in that the lives we live are conflicting reports to the things we say."

He ends with Jesus, as he almost always did, and with a command.

"We are under orders," he said, "to tell what we have seen and heard."

I cringe at the tone of futile inevitability, at the thought of longing for antebellum splendor. My gut physically hurts at the phrase "where people knew their place," but I tell myself he was using a device, playing off his audience's worst impulses to make his point. I tell myself it's his first time, that it is, in 1964, a brave act for a young man who found safety in the words of the Bible and the words of others, and uncertainty with his own. It was tepid. Careful. But it was a start. The country was starting to see it. Preachers were starting to see it. Dad was starting to say it. In a South that was still insane.

In Georgia, Lester Maddox chased Black people out of his restaurant at gunpoint, or at the end of an ax handle. White people loved it so much they elected him governor in 1966. Maddox proclaimed that God had been his campaign manager. That was a year *Time* asked if God was dead. If so, God must have rolled over in his grave.

Change came slow, and halting. The Civil Rights Act—letters in *The Birmingham News* called it the "Civil Wrongs" bill—passed on July 2, 1964, and two days later, on the Fourth of July, whites claiming to stand for God and country used folding chairs to beat Black people who tried to enter a states' rights rally in a Georgia amusement park where George Wallace was to screech.

Alabama newspapers reacted to the passage of the Civil Rights Act with a tired, exasperated tone, and urged readers—as was their calling card—to obey the law. *The Birmingham News* urged Black people to exercise care, to "tolerate no willful exploitation of the

Dr. Martin Luther King Jr. and Ralph David Abernathy (behind King) in Senatobia, Mississippi, during the March Against Fear in June 1966. The march was begun by James Meredith.

new condition, and reject the impulse of the professional few who would make of this very law itself an occasion for a public circus." *The Huntsville Times* bent over backward on its editorial page not to take a real position, saying: "President Johnson has just signed something—maybe a Magna Carta and maybe a monstrosity. History will tell us which—that is, unless a long, hot summer has made it abundantly clear which it is before history can get its hooks on the matter."

Wait and see, time will tell, history will reveal. The words of the cautious. The words of a coward. They were everywhere. In newspapers that cried for law over justice, like the Pharisees did with Jesus, in pulpits that preached ironic gospel over genuine goodness.

Horrors were still unfolding all across the South. Bombs still went off in Birmingham, and the men who killed those four little girls remained at large. Three civil rights workers in Mississippi were still missing, and had been since June, since they were pulled over for speeding and then detained, only to be released into the arms of the Klan. It would be another month until the bodies of James Chaney, Andrew Goodman and Michael Schwerner were found, buried in a dam of dirt.

Dad was still cautious, preaching of love and acceptance in parable rather than the palpable, how "Jesus was the perfect example of perfect love. He loved all people, regardless of who they were." Change was so slow. In the church, and in the world. And from my father's pulpit.

By early 1965 the country was watching Selma, in southern Alabama, in that shattered Black Belt region that holds so many ghosts of Alabama's oppressive past. By February, King and Abernathy had been jailed in Selma, just as they had in Birmingham, and Wallace sent seventy-five state troopers there and to surrounding communities to keep Black people from protesting at night. It was clear Selma was heading toward violence, and for the first time, in his words from the pulpit, Dad saw it coming and said so. On February 14, Valentine's Day, he preached with a searching sadness that was atypical of him. The sermon was called "Christ's Affirmation of Faith," and included this reflection:

> I think that a Christian philosophy of history must think of God as speaking to man through human events. I believe that God is trying to reach our dull minds and hearts through the chaotic jumble of events of modern history. A shadow has fallen across the face of the earth. We look at it and it looks like a giant mushroom cloud. Again we look at it, and it looks like the face of a man of color. It could be either Saigon or Selma.

Saigon or Selma. Not so far away, after all. Not always.

Four days later, Alabama state trooper James Fowler shot Jimmie Lee Jackson in Marion, about a half hour west of Selma. He died eight days later. It was the killing that birthed the Selma-to-Montgomery marches, a killing that would not be prosecuted for four decades.

Bloody Sunday would come, the first attempt on March 7, 1965, when John Lewis and Hosea Williams tried to lead a throng of six hundred people on the fifty-four-mile trek to unwelcoming Montgomery. They were stopped before they started, met by Alabama troopers at Selma's Edmund Pettus Bridge—named for a Confederate officer and Klansman—beaten and gassed and bloodied. The State of Alabama sent fifty-eight people to the hospital that day. One of them was Lewis. A trooper hit him in the head with a billy club and fractured his skull.

Bloody Sunday again focused the nation's attention on Alabama, on Selma and Wallace and on those who would fight for change against those who fought to hold on to their powers and fears and privileges. President Johnson would ultimately send troops to protect marchers as they tried again. The world moved on from Selma, but not until Unitarian Universalist minister James Reeb was beaten to death, until Viola Liuzzo was shot dead, until federal judge Frank M. Johnson Jr. stood for justice instead of his own safety.

President Johnson pushed for a voting rights act then, and would get it later in the year.

Dad preached that summer that "hate is deadly," that calling yourself a Christian doesn't make you one, that the sinners who were most denounced by Jesus were the ones who did *nothing*.

He was gaining strength. He was finding a voice, even if it was as halting and hesitant as racial progress in the South. He found role

Hosea Williams (front left) and John Lewis (front right) lead marchers across Selma's Edmund Pettus Bridge on Bloody Sunday.

Marchers, including Dr. Martin Luther King Jr., Coretta Scott King, James Bevel, F. D. Reese, and Hosea Williams leave the City of St. Jude in Montgomery, Alabama, on the final day of the Selma-to-Montgomery march.

President Lyndon B. Johnson
speaks on a visit to Staten Island
to campaign for Congressman
John Murphy in 1966.

models in Rutland and the Reverend Denson Franklin Sr., the pastor of Birmingham First Methodist who opposed the segregationist elements in the church. He welcomed the new bishop, Kenneth Goodson, who made it clear that Methodist preachers in Alabama would be allowed and encouraged to speak from their hearts.

You can almost sense an awakening in his words: "The Christian is committed to do what Christ would do, feed the hungry, heal the sick, befriend the friendless, teach the seeking, and preach the gospel *to all*."

He was gaining confidence and courage. And then, in a flash, everything he had known was upside down. He was ripped from the world and the world ripped from him. He couldn't think or feel or see beyond himself. He could not laugh, for a time, and he could not cry.

His mother and father—the grandparents we called Mom and Pop—had gone to a Methodist camp for a conference, and got in a car accident on a mountain road on the way home. They were coming home from Lake Junaluska, a beautiful place in North Carolina I recognize from the family slides. My family went there often before I was born, or when I was too young to really remember. We didn't go back after August 20, 1965. It was too painful.

Dad got the call on that Friday night. He left for Chattanooga at once. *The Decatur Daily* wrote the story like this:

H'selle Church Pastor's Wife Dies in Wreck

The Rev. Robert L. Archibald, minister of the First Methodist Church in Hartselle, was critically injured and his wife, Alyce Archibald, was killed Friday in a three-car collision on rain-slick U.S. 411 near Benton, Tenn.

The Rev. Mr. Archibald, 63, was reportedly in critical condition Friday night in the intensive care unit of Erlanger Hospital in Chattanooga, Tenn.

The Rev. Mr. Archibald has been pastor of the First Methodist Church in Hartselle since June. He was pastor of Central Methodist Church in Decatur several years ago.

A second fatality in the wreck was identified as Frank L. Kersey, 47, of Cleveland, Tenn.

State Troopers said the accident apparently happened when the driver of a third car attempted to pass the truck Kersey was driving, found he couldn't make it and cut back into Kersey's vehicle.

The Kersey truck rebounded, hitting the rear of the third car and swinging . . . into the path of the oncoming Archibald automobile.

Troopers said none of the passengers in the third car were injured. One of the three young boys riding with Kersey suffered slight injuries.

Mom was dead, and Pop forever damaged. Dad went to Chattanooga and sat with his father that weekend. He paced in the waiting room at Erlanger, and prayed with a Black family from northern Alabama and a white family from southern Tennessee as they awaited word on their own loved ones. The families ached together when the news was bad, and rejoiced when it was good. He thought of them always.

He took the pulpit the following week and preached a sermon. He asked, a year before *Time* magazine did, "Is God Dead?"

13

The Wreck

It has been out of the depths that my own soul has cried.

—REV. ROBERT L. ARCHIBALD JR., August 29, 1965

My grandmother, Mom, died on the spot. On a highway an hour east of Chattanooga. Coming home from camp, on roads winding through the southern tip of the Smoky Mountains.

She loved the mountains. She was a highlander, after all, a Hillman, a native of the Holston hills in the Blue Ridge Mountains. It was in her name and in her veins. She was born Alyce Hillman, of the Virginia Hillmans, who settled in the hills and hollers that stood as vestigial reminders of the old country. She was born Alyce Drucilla Hillman, but she hated that. So she called herself Alyce Dear. And so did the world.

Alyce went to Hiwassee College in the hills of Tennessee, and to Emory & Henry in the hills of Virginia, where she met that jolly little man Lambuth, named for the nineteenth-century Methodist bishop Walter Russell Lambuth, who built schools and hospitals across Asia. Her Lambuth went on to seminary at Candler School of Theology at Emory University in Atlanta, while Alyce went back to Tennessee to teach high school English and chemistry. But the chemistry was already working, so Lambuth would not let go. He wrote her long and lyrical letters of impish innuendo and veiled seduction, and lamented his love for her with a twinkle in his eye. He called her Buddy, and she him. He signed his name Archie, and begged for kisses, and perhaps more.

"Buddy Dearest, please kiss your little preacher boy for he is so lonesome and so hungry for a kiss," he wrote her from seminary in 1928. "He has tried to be good and not think too much of you, for that would be disastrous for his school work, but thus far he has been unable to do it and you come in for nearly all of the Archie that should be at work on Hebrew etc. I am going to play like you are in your Buddy's arms and he is holding you, ever so close to him and telling that little story of three words that he has told you before."

She gave as good as she got, and Lambuth finally got up the nerve to ask her to marry him. He gathered himself to send a letter to her father, Henderson Kedron Hillman, not so much to ask for her hand in marriage as to ask for his blessing.

Old father Hillman got around to answering a few weeks later, to "acknowledge receipt" of it after the crops came in. He stiffly apologized for the delay, pointing out that "since the event to which you refer is still several months away I saw no immediate exigency demanding undue haste, so I have taken the liberty to be deliberate."

But by the end he grudgingly offered his validation. Alyce Dear and Archie married in 1928, and Archie dragged his bride to a flatter part of the world: Alabama.

Lambuth wooed her with stories about "Dreamy Alabama," with its watermelon and possum grapes and all the sweet peaches she could pick up off the ground. He told stories about the blossom of the sweet pea plants grown to enormous heights in the warm, wet Alabama soil, and he brought her home to see them all.

He felt a twinge of guilt about that his whole life, about bringing her down from the mountaintops. She had followed him like a star. He said always that he would get her back one day, that he would take her home to her mountains.

We remember that story, I suppose, to give us comfort. Mom went home in 1965. To her hills.

I have no memory of her, or her death or funeral. I was two, so I make my own memories, patched from family slides and stories, from letters and newspaper clippings and a book of her poetry. And from those kind people—they grow fewer with every year that passes—who write to tell me they knew my grandmother as a radiant woman of faith and compassion. She is everywhere, in Alabama. In the words of my father and the reverent memories of my siblings, in the furniture passed down through generations and the fading mark she left on Birmingham and Florence and Decatur and Hartselle and all those churches they served. A friend found a silver loving cup in the basement of a house she'd bought outside Birmingham, forty-five years after Mom's death, and gave it to me. It was engraved to Mom:

In honor of Mrs. R.L. Archibald
Wesleyan Service Guild
December 1956

She was the child of a Methodist preacher. Like the rest of us. Two of her brothers became Methodist ministers and a sister married one. Like Dad used to say, "We had enough Methodist ministers in the family to start our own conference."

Since I have no clear memory of Mom on my own, my impression grows from a void. I can hardly say it, I can barely think it, but I am scared of her, afraid to disappoint. It's the black-and-white film, the severe cat-eye horn-rimmed glasses and the weight of all that expectation. She was exalted in memory, like many who die suddenly and unexpectedly. She was legendary for her spirited spirituality and rigorous religion. I heard all my life how beautifully her words fell together, but I can't follow her poetry. Oh, there is heartache there, about losing a child, and joy, and the love of her husband. But it is overwhelmed by religion. I hear it like I heard my father's voice from the pulpit as a child. I want to know of her life. There is so much God there, in those verses, and not enough flesh to make me feel. There is so much heaven, and not enough earth. Not enough grit and grime and mud to make me believe they are real. They are like songs hauled out for a week at camp, with nothing for the rest of the year. I learn more, I feel more, from the introduction Mom wrote for her book—called simply *Poems,* and bound the year after she died:

> May each one who reads these lines find some word to ease the pain; to quicken a pulse; to comfort a broken heart, strengthen a binding love, make merry a heart in need of laughter, or increase a waning faith, inspire a patriotic lift, or merely open a door in a cloistered soul. Whatever good there may be found here-in, we send it forth with gladness.

That I grasp, or it grasps me. That touches me in my soul, in places that make me ache and make me smile and make me solemn and serious and sentimental. That makes me want to know her, to understand her. I am angry that I don't recall her voice or her touch, her smell or laugh or presence. The her in my head is not her at all, but a puzzle fitted together with bits and pieces to form an image that was only described to me in one dimension. I am bitter that she was taken away before I could see her and know her full form. It is not fair that she was gone, and I was left only with fears I could not understand.

There are worse things, though, than to go as she did. The Wreck, as it was simply known in my home, then as now, took 90 percent of Pop's brain function, and he required twenty-four-hour care. After about a month in Chattanooga, he was moved to Tuscaloosa, where his daughter, Mary Alyce Mize—sweet Aunt May, who didn't even merit a mention by name in Mom's *Decatur Daily* news story—cared for him in the hospital and 'round the clock at her home afterward.

Mom's niece Sue Angel moved to Alabama to help, and never left. Sue was one of the few who wasn't a preacher's kid. Her dad had married Mom's sister and Great-Grandfather Hillman famously summed it up this way: "All my daughters married preachers, except for the one who married an Angel."

That was Sue's mom, Vassie. But Sue, as far as I can figure, was the angel of the family.

Sue came at once to Tuscaloosa and looked after my young cousins—Chad, Alyce and Lou Lou—as Aunt May cared for her dad. But it became clear quickly that even with Sue's help the demands were too high for the family to bear. Pop went to a nursing home in Northport, outside Tuscaloosa, and that—sadly—is where he lives in my memory.

I have two profound memories of him. The first is vivid and bright and splashed across my consciousness in Technicolor. He is in the nursing home, in a place smelling of urine and ammonia, in the shadow of death and dementia and demands that I be on my best behavior. Pop is in bed, mewling like a child, or an animal, and I stand beside it—it is a hospital bed in my mind, stark and white and foreboding. I wish I were somewhere else, anywhere else. I'm afraid of this place and these sounds and smells, afraid to talk or to move. I am terrified of this man I am supposed to know and to love, afraid of this stranger, who is supposed to love me, and who, so I am told, is the last person on the planet who should cause me fear. I am five, maybe six, and I lean in to the bed as I grow restless. The bed is on my right side. I can see it. I can see myself. I lean in and I touch it, just brush it is all, I promise. But it slips on the slick tile floor and slides a fraction of a millimeter and jostles Pop so he begins to wail, to cry out loud like he's been assaulted by demons.

I shrink away, mortified. I am the demon. Horrified. Wracked with guilt and shame. I cry, and my brain snaps the permanent photograph that will never leave when I want to remember him fondly, that will always flash on the damned screen when I think of my grandfather. I want desperately to go, to run, to fly.

Dad gives me a little pat and tells me to wait, to be patient. I must be a big boy, and he must calm his father before we can go.

That's the second thing I remember, the wonders and mysteries of the mind. The curious way the brain works, some would say the way the spirit works, the way things that are important to us are held so deeply they cannot be removed, even by an oncoming truck spinning into your lane on the way home from camp. My dad—I guess he had seen it before—knew what to say to his father.

"Do you want to pray?"

Pop stopped. Calm. Serious. Grown, and as dignified as a man can be after a paroxysm in a backless hospital gown. He reached out a hand and clasped it in my father's, held it, like both of them demanded as they said grace around the table three meals a day, whether at home or at McDonald's. Pop didn't wait for Dad to pray; he did it himself. Out loud, in clear words, and complete sentences. Amen.

They say—Mother and Dad and Aunt May and Sue and the cousins and everybody—he did it often, with family or friends or preachers who stopped to see him in the nursing home. They were not always traditional prayers, like you'd have heard in his churches. Like the time he began his prayer: "Our Father, it says here, enjoy America's leading pipe tobacco—Half and Half." And then he stopped.

Those in the room wondered what to do, uncomfortable in the silence. Then Pop continued: "But, Father, we don't come to you half and half. We come to you in the name of Jesus Christ."

Pop might, on a good day, be able to say halting words of confused conversation, but in prayer he reached deep into all that was left of him and found something solid. He spoke beautiful and sometimes unconventional phrases, usually without stuttering or stammering or searching for words. The skeptic in me says it is merely a riddle of the brain, or habit formed so deeply it becomes our essence. The romantic in me wants to believe, like the others, in a miracle, a sign from God, or a sign of God. Or of grace. I do not know if it is science or if it is spirit. But it was clear in that moment that prayer was the path that brought my grandfather peace as he walked in what was left of a mind through his Valley of the Shadow of Death.

It brought a measure of peace to my dad as well, when peace was hard for him to find.

I wish I remember more of Mom and Pop than the Wreck. I yearn for more than the darkness and fear I clung to for years, more than the realization that haunted me. If Mom and Pop could go to a *church camp* and never come back, my parents could just as easily

My paternal grandparents—the Reverend R. L. Archibald Sr.
and Alyce Hillman Archibald—at far left at the baptism of their
oldest grandchild, Murray Archibald

drop me off at school and never find their way home. I could be in
class, studying spelling words, reading biographies of famous figures, and a log truck could spin out of control on the road in front
of them, or a tree could fall on their heads, or they could keel over,
dead, from a disease I could not name. I could be at scouts, learning to tie a half hitch, and they could drive off a Tennessee River
bridge. I worried all the time, then. I worried as a I ran at the final
bell from elementary school to see if my mother was in the parking
lot. If she was five minutes late, my heart began to flutter. If she was
ten minutes late, I began to cry, holding on to a steel support under
an awning by the carpool line. Teachers thought I was afraid to be
alone. I was not. I just thought my mother and father were dead.

That seems selfish now. They are dead, and I worry about my
feelings. Now I simply wish I could have known Mom and Pop
when they made other stories, outside church and service guilds
and Sunday schools.

I wish I'd known the Pop who thought up jokes and one-liners and fine phrases and wrote them down, as they came to him, in his little notebook in handwriting so bad only he could read it. I do that. On my phone. I wish I knew the guy who famously walked the business district of East Lake in eastern Birmingham in the 1950s, joking and smoking with men at barbershops and cafés. I wish I knew the man—so the story goes, though I have always been skeptical—so carefree and sneakily irreverent that he casually tossed a banana peel out the window of his car, only to realize he'd thrown it in the face of a powerful church official in the next lane. I don't doubt Pop did it. I just doubt he did it by accident.

There was a sweetness about Mom and Pop. Back in 1943, with the war still raging and teenagers in the house, Mom's mother grew gravely ill. She lived in Tennessee with the Angels, and Mom boarded the train to visit her. But it wasn't long after she left that her mother died, and Pop got the news. Mom was still on the train, still en route, and could not be told. Pop jumped in the car and drove, as fast as his wheels could carry him, to reach the train station in Chattanooga, where she had to disembark. She stepped off the train to hear his whistle—his loud, unmistakable Archibald whistle, like I could never master—and she knew at once it was him. She knew at once why he was there.

He wanted to tell her, face-to-face, that her mother was gone.

Few of Pop's sermons remain. Those that do—those I can find— were stored in my father's file cabinet, typed single-spaced on the back of old church letterhead, with sermons written in flowing, passionate prose about gospel, and eternal life, and the resurrection:

> Christianity is not a creed to be followed but a life to be lived.
> It is not lived on a mental plane but a spiritual plane. It is open
> to the man who wears a Phi Beta Kappa key and also to the one

who must sign his name with a mark. You don't go to heaven head first: You go heart first.

Or one of my favorite passages, from Christmas 1961:

This business of returning good for evil won't do in a world of "an eye for an eye and a tooth for a tooth." Here we are in the 20th century and doesn't it seem fitting to say, "He came too soon to teach humanity, that the road to humility is the way to spiritual leadership, power and victory? Too soon to convince men that self-renunciation is the way to lasting success and big league living for God? Too soon to advise bragging men, strutting tyrants and belligerent nations that enslavement of others is treason against the sanctity of the human soul and deserves the wrath of God?"

But I don't know him, where he stood on segregation and when he stood for the rights of others. I know his religion, and his legend, and maybe that's all of him to know. The newspapers of his day are full of his sermon announcements, his appearances at churches and graduation ceremonies, of guest speeches at clubs and even synagogues, and of the Wreck. But it is hard to penetrate the veil of the church, the veneer of the jolly and mischievous preacherman.

I learn that he was picked as the "Smile King" by a secret committee of the Optimist Club of Huntsville in 1948, an honor that bestowed upon him a twenty-five-dollar war bond and the right to attend the next meeting as a guest.

But as optimistic as he was, as big as his smile and his faith might have been, he, too, was a product of his time, and for all the talk of the Greatest Generation and the Golden Age, his time sucked for a lot of people.

Pop went to a Civitans Club turkey dinner before Christmas in 1947. As the entertainment. As a minstrel. As *The Huntsville Times* put it—as if it were a good thing—he "rendered three numbers in a black-face impersonation." He sang "Lonesome Road," "Ol' Man River" and "You Must Come in at the Door," accompanied on the piano by a Mrs. Pat Hamm.

Well, hell. Sorry, Mother.

Pop's letters, at times, drift into the kind of Old South reverie that saw Black people as cartoonish entertainment and a source of amusement. As he wrote to Mom in 1928:

> I have not done a lick of singing since I have been home. I started once to bleat forth as I was shaving but on second thought did not do so as Mother told me the other day that they arrested a nigger for disturbing a lady across the street and if I got to singing there might be another nigger in the same fix. My throat has been on the bum all the time.

Double hell.

Sorry. Not sorry.

I'd never known where Pop stood on issues of race in the sixties, or the fifties, much less the twenties. As a child I presumed he stood on the right side of history, because to think otherwise was blasphemy. And besides, that's what I presumed of us all. We were the good ones, the right ones, the *Archibalds*. How can you fall short when you come from all those men of God? As an adult I came to fear the worst, that the church was in the business business more than the God business, and my family, as much as any, were ladder-climbers at Jesus LLC. And that meant go along, get along. "Ol' Man River," baby, with help from poor old Pat Hamm.

Pop performed in blackface into the fifties, and maybe the sixties, my brother Mark tells me. He stopped abruptly after my own father took him aside and told him it was offensive.

The only thing I know about Pop's position on race came from a sermon my dad gave much later in his career, when he recalled the moment in time his pop realized "segregation was a sin." I don't know when that was, or how the epiphany came to him, with a lightning bolt and a flash or a strange, warm feeling. But it changed his life, according to this sermon I had never heard and read only after both of them were dead.

"It was a turning point in his faith."

I guess we all need those points.

Dad talked about Mom and Pop in deferential terms, in vague declarations of admiration. He never talked about the Wreck, or the deaths, or the funerals. Not ever. Not unless asked, and even then it was as satisfying as flossing teeth, clumsy and painful and somehow pointless. It was like asking a thoughtful old soldier to tell you about the war. There's just too much to feel, so little to say. But I never stopped, especially as a child, wondering what was happening inside Dad's head, and how he went on without looking back. It was his way, I know. Be strong, do your duty. Kill the chickens when they must die and make sure, before all else, to take care of those who depend on you. They are more important than yourself.

I see it in the sermons he left behind. They tell me more about the Wreck than he ever did. But they tell me even more about him.

It was August 29, 1965, the week after the Wreck, a week after Dad drove to Chattanooga to find his father in a coma and his mother dead, six days after he had buried her as Bishop Goodson gave the eulogy and preachers like Lawrence Dill and Duncan Hunter served as pallbearers. That told me something. They were, the way I've come to understand it, on the progressive end of the

Methodist spectrum. But the Sunday after that, the Sunday after his world had turned cartwheels, Dad took to the pulpit to preach, as if it were any other Sunday.

The name of his sermon was "Is God Dead?" It was based on the 130th Psalm, and his words read hollow to me, forced, like a column I might write when I can't muster a strong opinion. Perhaps only because I can't hear his voice, and the emotion it must have held. Perhaps because I can't imagine standing up at a time like that in a place like that at a moment like that and saying anything that wasn't forced. Dad did something while writing that sermon that he didn't often do. He didn't write out the story he intended to tell, but made himself a note: "Riding to Chattanooga I felt God's support." I guess he knew it by heart.

I hope he felt God's support. It didn't seem like he felt anything—not that I'd blame him. I wonder if he was not simply preaching faith until he found it, because he felt it his sworn duty. But this is what he had to say on that day:

> For 13 years I have been preaching that "God is our refuge and our strength, a very present help in time of trouble." It has been true all along. But I have discovered it in a new way. I have felt the sustaining strength of God in my life.
>
> I have been saying the words of Jesus in John, "Let not your hearts be troubled . . . I will not leave you comfortless . . . I will pray to the Father and he shall give you another comforter . . . The comforter, which is the Holy Spirit, whom the Father will send in my name shall teach you all things." I have experienced the comforting presence of the Holy Spirit.
>
> I have said that nothing can separate us from the love of God in Christ Jesus. This is so. In the extremity of my soul I have experienced the love and power of the Risen Christ.

I have been preaching that the Church is the Body of Christ—a fellowship of believers, the koinonia. I have experienced the living fellowship of the church. (Seven men visited me in the Hospital on Friday night.) (The calls, letters, cards, and telegrams all came from Christians in the fellowship of the Church.)

I have been preaching that the Gospel of Christ is the power of God unto salvation. I want to say it does have the power to save, to redeem, to support. I have experienced it.

What I am trying to say is that in the hour when my faith has been tested as never before, I have found that the Living Christ has sustained me.

So let me say this. The Bible has said it, the saints of the church have said it, and my own personal experience bears it out—the answer to your problems of aloneness—when your soul is naked—your sin and suffering, your defeat and death, your answer to these problems is found in Jesus Christ. Put your faith in him, your trust, your life.

His soul cried. Even if the rest of him didn't. I feel I should cry as I read it. But I don't. Not now, not a drop, not a sniffle. Because I see him and I read him and I don't hear *him* at all, except in the psalmist's cry. I hear echoes and emptiness, and that makes me *want* to cry. What I hear are just words. Safe, spare, hard words held like a shield, biblical armor that allowed him to show up for work, because that was everything, to say what he could say without revealing the hole in his soul, or how and why the grief cut like a dagger through his heart.

It was later, in April 1967, that Dad preached a sermon that looked deeper into his soul, into his grief, when he explained how difficult it had been to reveal his own weakness, even to himself, after that horrible day.

He had not been able to cry—not that it was something he had a habit of doing. He had not been able to deal with the pain for months, he said. He had simply shut it out. He had simply shut it all down.

Until one day—ages later—for reasons unspoken or unknown, he had broken down and sobbed in front of my mother, Mary, his wife. She had said five words in return.

"Thank you for trusting me."

I still have questions, and I don't expect they will ever be answered completely. I am lost, and searching, like Pop, after the Wreck.

Sue Angel tells a story. It was in the early days of her time in Alabama, after the Wreck but before Pop went to the nursing home. She was in her mid-twenties, just out of college and trying to do all she could to help in a situation that at times seemed impossible. Pop struggled to make words, but on this day he found them.

"Who am I?" he asked.

"You're R. L. Archibald," she said brightly, as one in her twenties can do. "You're a Methodist preacher."

He stopped her. Frustrated, angry.

"No," he said. "I know my name, but who am I?"

I'm asking the same thing.

14

Remember Who You Are

Last Sunday afternoon was a milestone in Archibald family life. On that afternoon we carried our eldest son off to college. I had to restrain myself to keep from giving him a bushel of advice as to dos and don'ts. Then I remembered something that my mother used to say to me, not just as I went to college, but on frequent occasions when I was leaving home. She would quietly say, "Son, remember who you are."

—REV. ROBERT L. ARCHIBALD JR., August 30, 1972

There it is again. *Remember who you are.* I heard it a hundred times, a thousand, for all the good it did. I don't know who I am, and every time I look back to find out, I think it might have been better not to ask. Myths are better. Easier to reconcile.

I knew the luster and the legends, how Great-Great-Great-Great-*really*-Great-Grandfather William Archibald—he spelled it "Archbald" at times and "Archbold" on the seal when he signed his will, and I thought of him as Arch the Bold—arrived in America in the late 1740s or early 1750s, driven by the bastard English from his home in the Scottish Highlands.

The old ways, the family clan systems, were pounded as badly as the Jacobite forces at the Battle of Culloden, the last campaign of the Jacobite Rising of 1745, "the '45," in which the Scots tried to reclaim the British crown for the Stuarts. He and other Scots were cast out by the Brits, by circumstance if not at the point of a halberd. Nobles' lands were seized, along with those of the ignoble. Presbyterians like Arch the Bold—Methodism didn't catch on in the family until later—ran headlong into the Church of England. My wife, Alecia, figures this means all the American Archibalds, from William's grandchildren on down to my kids, have none other than Henry VIII—centuries before—to thank for our very existence. Henry, that is, and his lust for Anne Boleyn.

Who knows what was running through William's head. Get out while the getting's good, perhaps. The common and uncommon folk were up in arms and the economy shot to hell, burned up like a witch on a British stake. The British were a ruthless and unsentimental lot, all right. The last witch went up in flames when William was twenty-seven, though I have no idea how he felt about that.

He came to America about 1750, landed in North Carolina and began helping to found churches—which would become another one of those family traditions. He was elected constable in 1757, the brogue still heavy on his lips, as it was for many of his new neighbors.

William was pious, and he comes off a little pompous, and he held to the ways of the Old Country, speaking Gaelic at services at what was the then-new Fourth Creek Presbyterian Church in Statesville, North Carolina. He's buried there. They call it First Presbyterian, now. On his deathbed he scrawled out his last will and testament. It was not brief. This was the first line:

In the name of God Amen: this seventh day of January, 1764 I, William Archbald of the County of Rowan and Province of North Carolina being weak and sick in Body but of perfect mind and memory, thanks be given unto God: therefore calling to mind the mortality of my body and knowing it is appointed for all men once to die, do make this my last Will and Testament: that is to say principally and first of all I give and recommend my soul unto the hands of Almighty God that gave it, and my Body I recommend to the Earth to be buried in a decent and orderly manner nothing Doubting but at the general Resurection [sic] I shall receive the same again by the Almighty Power of God.

That was just *the first line,* complete with three colons. Amen. Those ancestors of mine were long on righteousness, if short on brevity. William went on to divvy up his plantation, as he called it, giving his wife half the land, and an unmarked grave next to his own marker at the church. She also got the "use of the Negro wench."

God-a-mighty. Sorry, Dad.

It's better not to look back sometimes.

William's son Thomas Archibald got a chunk of land, too, along with a herdlet of cows. He was just a kid when his dad brought him to the New World, about the age I was for that frog-jumping contest in Decatur. It must have been a helluva journey, and I wonder at his first thoughts when he saw the Carolina mountains. He grew up to find success here, the American Dream. He fought in the Revolutionary War, like his son Samuel. A Highlander can cross a whole ocean but still can't get away from the damn Brits.

Thomas built on his estate and bought hundreds of acres. And he owned slaves, too, or so says the 1790 census. There were three of them. When he died ten years later, he left another slave—"the Negro child"—to his daughter Betsey. The little girl didn't even warrant a name. But Thomas warned in his will that his slave Samson might live up to the name he was given.

"In case my executors find it unconvenient [sic] to handle my negro Samson I hereby appoint them to sell him and such price to purchase another negro for the family," he wrote.

Great. Great, great, great. Grandfather.

Thomas left his second wife, Elizabeth, some land and a grave next to his that didn't even merit a headstone. She was forty-eight when he died, locked into loneliness by a man who considered her a piece of property, like Samson, or the nameless girl. Elizabeth remained in his will only with the stipulation that she'd lose it all if she dared to remarry. Everything but her spinning wheel, a couple of sticks of furniture and her saddle and bridle. Not even the horse she could ride out on. If she did stay true, and unattached in the wild new world, she got the reward of lying beside him for eternity, unnoticed, in the graveyard.

Alecia, again, believes this might have been the American origin of the hashtag #whitemen? Nah, I say. It was way before that.

I almost feel bad judging people from other places, other times, other circumstances. Almost. These men and women are in my blood. I can feel them in the mountains and in music and in their words, if I stop to listen. I worry that I'm ungrateful, traitorous. But I don't really worry. For these righteous men preached loudly of loving sinners and hating sin. They spoke of a brotherhood of man, and failed to see humanity in the child who did their washing. They spoke for generations, with certainty and vigor, about the need and the power of repentance, of proclaiming one's wrongs and of renouncing them to the Lord, and to the world. Out loud. If they could not see the beam in their eye, the hypocrisy in their hearts and their time, we can at least recognize it now.

We cannot change the sins of the past. Only ours. But if we don't know the horrors of yesterday, we won't know what we are capable of today. If we don't know the triumphs of long ago, we can't know what we'll be able to do tomorrow. I can almost hear those words attributed to John Wesley again: *all the good you can . . . at all the times you can . . . as long as ever you can.*

People like my ancestors left plenty of lessons to learn. But not just from the pulpit.

I guess evil is hardest to see when it's all you know in your time, whatever time that might be. It's toughest to spot when it's accepted by masses and powerful majorities who use Bibles or billfolds or campaign stops or pulpits to dehumanize whole swaths of people. It's hard, now, to imagine a world in which a pious man could fail to see the sin of buying another human and putting him out back to plow the fields against his will. It's hard, now, to imagine a world in which that pious man's wife labors a lifetime to please him, only to be held hostage to that love by the threat of poverty, to be rewarded with an eternity in a nameless hole. It is sadly easier to imagine a world where people who are different, who look different or love differently or believe differently or speak in languages we do not understand, are dismissed as something less, as something strange. It is true now as then. Those outside our own worldview are difficult to accept.

It's only possible to love and respect people when you bother to try. It's only possible when you step back and remember who *you* are. Not mothers or fathers or sainted grandparents or forebears who fought in the Revolution or fought for nothing. You. Me. Remembering who you are is one thing. Deciding who you will be is something else.

If I could decide now—if I could choose my bloodline and my great-great-great-great-grandfather—it would be Robert Archibald, the brother of Thomas the Douche. I always thought Robert, not Thomas, was my great-great-great-great-grandfather. He was the first, I was led to believe, in a long line of Roberts, eight generations that include my grandfather and father and brother and son—Robert Andrew Archibald. But I was sadly wrong. Confused. He was my great-great-great-great-great-uncle. And it crushed me to find that out. Because I feel a kinship with Robert. I feel him pumping in my blood and relate to him in ways I can't to his father or brother, to the imperious preachers through the generations, with their pomp and certitude.

Robert went to Princeton—the College of New Jersey—in the class of 1772, which included another complicated character: Aaron Burr. Apparently they got along okay, because Aaron did not shoot him dead.

Uncle Robert was brilliant in ways I cannot fathom. He spoke seven languages, and spoke English in a way that could captivate all who would stop to listen. He studied medicine, but went into the ministry instead. He was licensed as a Presbyterian minister in 1775, and went back to North Carolina to serve the Rocky River Presbyterian Church, where he ran into trouble and, for lack of a better term, was branded a heretic. He was brought up on charges of "preaching erroneous doctrines," spouting off about humanity, love and grace, and universal salvation—not to mention a belief in purgatory. He was kicked out, and was unapologetic about it. As a nineteenth-century writer put it, Uncle Robert "was wrecked on the shoals of false doctrine and ungoverned appetites."

An Archibald family history, written by distant relatives in 1969, cuts him a little more slack. Robert, they said, was:

> a very learned man whose intellect and ways of thinking could easily excel that of some of his colleagues, and especially that of the general run of the people then. He is not readily forgotten. No doubt, he was ahead of the times in his doctrines and beliefs, the feasible cause of his conceptions and religious presentations seeming so ridiculous and preposterous to his unlearned congre-

gation and to some of his fellow religious leaders. Their reaction was that of rejection of him and his doctrines, after many, many years devoted to the ministry.

But a history of Princeton in the eighteenth century is less . . . familial:

Mr. Archibald was a man of talent, of an amiable disposition and considered a good classical scholar, but was careless in his manners and extremely negligent in his dress and general appearance. Some domestic afflictions, fancied or real, preyed upon his spirits, and were the occasion of indulgence, to an unwarrantable degree, in intoxicating drinks. Mr. Archibald never returned to the communion of his church nor retracted the errors for which he was deposed.

He was a drunk. And he bucked the church for the sake of humanity without so much as a "sorry."

He was revered and pitied and admired and admonished, all at the same time. He got no land at all in his father's will—as if he were a daughter or something—and that was before he crashed unceremoniously onto the shoals.

He still went on to be listed in the book *Lost Tribes of North Carolina* as one of the "Leading Men of Wealth and Influence" in the state. But the more I look back, the more wreckage there is. Uncle Robert may have preached the heresy of universalism and grace for all humanity, but he owned humans, too, four of them, with no sign of a second thought. God-a-mighty.

At least when he died he left his possessions to his wife, Mary, with no strings attached. His nephew Thomas Archibald II was my great-great-great-grandfather.

Thomas, oh Thomas. He was trouble in the church, too. But he's also the reason I live in Alabama. I suppose we can thank him, along with Henry VIII, for our very births.

Thomas II was a man of some wealth, who named a son Robert. I like to believe he named the boy after his notorious uncle. But in 1836—Thomas II would have been forty-five—he followed in Uncle Robert's footsteps and ran afoul of the church, which suspended him for unspeakable crimes against all that was holy. Well, maybe not unspeakable, but they were not spoken so we don't know exactly what they were. After the suspension he sold a large chunk of land and moved to Pickens County, Alabama.

Thomas II bought about eight hundred acres there, near the Sipsey River, and depended on fifteen slaves to work them. He was a planter, one of the elite, so it wasn't surprising when the white men of the Mt. Olivet Presbyterian Church met in 1838 and decided he should be allowed back in the good graces of the church. What's a little sin between friends? What with the previous charge, they revealed, "being singular and involving apparently extreme difficulty."

So they offered forgiveness. It would be less than a year until he found himself again careening toward the church's rocky shoals. Just like his uncle.

Thomas II—maybe I should just call him Singing Tom—was caught teaching a "singing school on the Sabbath Day," which was considered a serious ecclesiastical transgression, a sin far worse than, say, owning fifteen human beings. So they told him to stop. But the same thing happened again the next year, and Singing Tom was called back in:

Mr. Thomas Archibald appeared before the Session and after conversation with reference to the overture against teaching

Singing School on the Sabbath day promised to discontinue as soon as he closed his present school.

He survived again, though he would later be stricken from the rolls because he "removed out of the bounds of the church." The authors of the Archibald book say that is merely a reference to his geography. I tend to think he was out of bounds in other ways.

On it goes. Singing Tom's son Robert Washington Archibald was my great-great-grandfather, a fire-breathing Presbyterian—the last of its kind in my family—who was also a planter and slave owner in Pickens County. The courthouse burned, so a lot of records were lost. But the writers of that Archibald book, Jessie Lynn Bell, J. Herman Massengill and Marvin L. Harper, wrote, "It is said that no man, white or black, who sought his advice or assistance was ever turned away without obtaining satisfaction."

By the time the Civil War rolled around, Robert Washington was too old to fight in it. But two of his kids did. He had eight children, five of them boys, two of whom he named Robert. There was Robert Bruce because Scotland and . . . *Freedom!* And Robert Murray, who was born after the war, in 1869.

Here we come to the point of family memory, outside the probate courts and the history books and into lore passed down from people who actually knew a thing or two.

Robert Murray Archibald—the first one, because that's also my brother's name—was my great-grandfather, the one Dad called T-Daddy, the one who looked like my cousin Chad. Dad used T-Daddy's desk chair for a time in his office, and I have it in my basement still, in desperate need of restoration, like my soul.

T-Daddy's parents died young, and he was raised by family. But he was the one who brought the Archibalds to Methodism. And boy, did he.

He joined the church when he was twelve, in 1881, and got a license to preach after he turned nineteen.

He was a student at the old Southern University in Greensboro, Alabama. He found himself too penniless to make his way home for the Christmas holidays, even if it was only a few counties away. So, as he later told his son, he went to the Methodist church in Greensboro and found himself deeply moved by a force he took to be God calling him to the ministry. But he fought it, T-Daddy did. He wrestled with this feeling, and tried to write it off as indigestion, or loneliness. He went to his room and vowed not to come out or eat or drink until, as he put it, "the question was settled." He fasted, and prayed, and read scripture, and whether that spoke to him or whether the answer came in a wash of boredom and malnutrition, he made his choice. He would devote his life to ordained ministry in the Methodist Church.

T-Daddy died in 1929, like the stock market. The same year Dad was born. But he was larger than life in the family, larger than death. T-Daddy did not, it was said, mince words. If you believe the Archibald book—it may be overly optimistic, but it is precise and speaks with authority—T-Daddy "was a man of strong convictions, and he never hesitated or counted the cost to himself in declaring his convictions. Respect and honor were gained everywhere he went, but his convictions and opinions were always worth more to him than words of praise or places of honor."

That's an epitaph I could get behind. And it brings us down the family tree—or is it up—to Pop, Robert Lambuth Sr., and my dad, Robert Lambuth Jr.

All those Roberts. All those Archibalds. All those preachers, and that doesn't even count the Hillmans or the Hollands along those other branches. All those people, with warts and wisdom and failings and flaws and sins and successes and humanity. All those people you never stop to think about when you listen only to the legends, with pain and pleasure and heartache and wonder and questions that sometimes bring the wrong answers. All those people with dreams and regrets and sins and sorrows and sadness. And hope for something better, even if they didn't know what it was. Like everybody else.

Remember who you are. Remember who you want to be.

15

Sounds of Silence

The vision must never be allowed to remain silent. It must come alive in our own creative action. Without the fanfare of political parties, without the hue and cry of vested interest, but quietly we must affirm it to the world.

—REV. ROBERT L. ARCHIBALD JR., September 15, 1968

I thought 1968 was the turning point. It had to be, right? It was bloody and shocking, shattering the do-nothing stillness like a phone call when you've slept too late. Martin? Dead? Bobby, too? Riots across America? Vietnam? A police beatdown at the Democratic Convention in Chicago, and that damned George Wallace running for president again with a "Stand Up for America" campaign that drove and was driven by fear and anger, presaging the rhetoric of Donald Trump a half century later? It had to be a wake-up call for this country, or else the God to which so many of those good folks offered their 10 percent every month really was dead.

It had to be the turning point for those with conscience, those who wanted to see America be what it claimed it always had been. It had to shake them, even if all those Southern bombs and lynchings had failed to rouse them. I thought '68 was the turning point for Dad, too. I thought that was when he would find his voice.

But he was a little early, as it turned out. A little. Of course he was. It was his way. He was early to church, to weddings and funerals and meetings and luncheons and those potlucks they used to call "dinner on the grounds." If he had an 8:00 appointment he was there at 7:50. Punctuality said a lot about character. It was one of those lessons that stick with you, always, like the image of chickens running around the yard with their heads cut off. Be on time.

Not that Dad was early, by any means, in discussing race, or reasons to change. He was late to that party. How many bombs must a white man see before he calls it a sin?

But he beat my prediction. He tried to find his voice in 1965 and he found a little rhythm in '66 and '67. Perhaps not loud, but he found a groove. Not in-your-face, but subtle, so you'd hardly notice unless you were sitting in a pew paying close attention. He found ways to talk of racism without ever saying the word. He used parable and allegory to sneak it into sermons before they could see it coming, to leave them wondering what hit them, if anything struck home.

He didn't use the words *Black,* or *white,* or *segregation.* Not often. If he talked of race outright he did it like the newspapers, condemning obvious wrongs but fretting about procedure and protocol. He hid behind phrases like the church-approved "brotherhood of man," and developed a euphemism for racial injustice. He preached several times on the dangers of "snobbery." It was less loaded, less explosive. If it's hard to look out over a pulpit and condemn white people sitting in the pews for generations of deeply ingrained sin, it's easier to decry the snob. Nobody liked a snob, even when they were fine with a racist.

In 1967 at Monte Sano, Dad preached a sermon called "Snob-

Dad, in the early 1960s, thought to be in the office at
Alabaster Central Methodist Church

bery and the Christian Faith Don't Homogenize." He began talking
about things that go together, "like cornbread and buttermilk and
hog jowl and black-eyed peas." He spoke—I'm sure he sang a few
bars, if I know him at all—of Frank Sinatra's "Love and Marriage,"
and how they go together like a horse and carriage.

"Since snobbery and the Christian faith do not go together, we
must not be snobs if we are serious about being Christian," he said.
"Snobbery destroys faith."

He apologized for the crude use of a word like *snobbery*—no
kidding—and talked of how Mahatma Gandhi went to South
Africa to study at a Christian school, how he admired the New
Testament but found the Christians there unwelcoming. In truth
Gandhi once wrote that he found Methodist services in South
Africa uninspiring and dull, but Dad told his congregation Gan-
dhi was driven away when "snobbery destroyed his budding young
faith." Dad asked his congregation to imagine a world with a Chris-
tian Gandhi. Which—I would add—might look a lot like Martin
Luther King Jr.

Then he told a story from the 1940s, when his dad was a district superintendent in Florence, in that region of northwest Alabama now known for the rhythms of the river, and the music of Muscle Shoals. District superintendents are administrators who often travel from church to church on Sundays, so Dad and his sister, my aunt May, who would have been teenagers then, joined Florence First Methodist with their mom. This is the rest of his story.

> I shall never forget an incident which occurred while we were there. It made an indelible impression on my young mind. Some of the ladies of the church became interested in the welfare of a very poor woman who lived out on the edge of town in a mill village section. Her husband was dead and she had three small children with no skills to earn a living for them. The WSCS [Women's Society of Christian Service] bought her some clothes, they took her groceries, they bought shoes and toys for the children. The next Sunday morning this lady and her three children showed up at church and Sunday school. Consternation reigned throughout the morning. One mother took her child out of the nursery because that other baby was there. During church, the poor lady sat down on the second seat with no one near her. After the service, only a few people really took time to speak to her and tell her that they were glad to have her. Later in the week some of the ladies went back to see her and suggested that she would be happier in the little Monument Park Church which had recently been organized in the mill village. I never saw that woman in church again. The snobbery of a few people destroyed a budding young faith.

Was this a parable for race? Or was it just about putting on airs, about bringing the lowly and the less fortunate to Jesus? I'd gone back and forth, because he had spoken of snobbery before, and I could never be sure. But on this day he moved forward. He declared that snobbery was a sin, and described how even Saint Peter had trouble figuring this out at first, when he hesitated to take the gospel to the unclean Gentiles. It took a dream, a vision from heaven, as the faithful would say, to make him see that God did not pick favorites. Then Dad spoke directly to race. Late, but directly.

He spoke of an incident in Jackson, Mississippi, from 1963, when five Black students from Tougaloo College tried to attend the nearby Galloway Memorial Methodist Church, and were turned away at the door. The pastor, the Reverend Dr. W. B. Selah, drew a line in the shifting sands of Mississippi that day. It would be his last at the church. My dad spoke of it this way:

> I think all of you are aware that Dr. W. B. Selah was pastor of Gallaway [sic] Memorial Methodist Church for some 18 years. Gallaway is the largest Methodist Church in Mississippi—located in Jackson. You are also aware that when his official board refused to allow some Negroes to come into the church for worship, he immediately asked his Bishop for a change in appointment. He said "For 18 years I have been preaching a Gospel of love, and that there must not be a color bar in the church. If my preaching means no more than this, I had better resign." And he did. I do not know if that was the right way to deal with the matter, but I am sure that he is correct when he says that we must not put up any artificial barriers at the door of the church.

In my heart I long to hear him say it forcefully, indignant and damning. But "I do not know if that was the right way to deal with the matter" was his way. At least it was direct.

I did ask my mom, much later, if Dad had ever been in such a situation, and she said he had made his feelings known. Ushers in at least one church came to him and asked what they should do if Black people tried to come into the sanctuary.

"What did he say?" I asked.

"He said the same thing as my daddy."

"What was that?"

"Seat them."

Churches across the South faced the same question, as Black activists pushed to test the boundaries of the sanctuary, to integrate what King called the "most segregated hour" of the week. Dad's answer was better than most.

My wife recalls a time, one of her early memories, when a Black woman sought to sit down at a service in Montgomery's Forest Park Baptist Church—the church where we would ultimately be married. Alecia was scarred, she says, to see the commotion it caused, to see the ushers force the nice lady to leave.

"Here's the thing," Alecia told me once. "You are an usher. You've got one job. To ush."

I don't doubt that Dad did exactly as Mother said. He was the captain of his ship, when push came to shove off. But it was clear he struggled through those years, after the Wreck and the loss of his parents. The church he loved was locked in its own upheaval, splitting and splintering over race and direction as it moved toward integration.

The world was changing and his children were growing and my mother was beginning to suffer from debilitating migraines that knocked her out for days at a time. There were people to visit and prayers to say and some days it seemed Dad was just going through the motions from the pulpit. He was human, as it turned out. It took me a long time to understand that.

There were other times his frustration came through in words from the pulpit, when he did the thing he never had before, when he challenged the church out loud:

"The church moves haltingly and feebly because we don't believe anything strongly enough to act decisively upon it," he lamented in the fall of 1967.

He told a story about one of us kids, on a vacation on a hot and sunny day. One of us looked out the window of the Rambler and saw heat waves dancing off the pavement. One of us pointed, surprised, and said, "Look, Daddy, it's been raining down there. It's wet." Because we didn't know what we were seeing.

"You know, we are so often blind," he said. "Our insight is hazy, out of focus, illusory."

It is. Even in hindsight, especially in hindsight, it shimmers off streets and turns scorching sand into cool water. But there are moments of clarity.

They come like a wake-up call. Like 1968. Rev. Dr. Martin Luther King Jr., standing on the balcony of the Lorraine Motel in Memphis, there to plan a Poor People's March, of all things, a clear cry for help for *the least of these*. Dr. King, the man with the Dream of peace and the balls to stand up to a Bull, shot dead by the asshole James Earl Ray, at a cowardly distance, with a high-powered rifle. It was April 4, the eve of my birthday.

Bobby Kennedy heard of King's assassination that evening at a campaign stop in Indianapolis. He announced the news to the crowd, and called, famously, for America to decide what it was going to become:

For those of you who are black and are tempted to be filled with hatred and distrust at the injustice of such an act, against all white people, I can only say that I feel in my own heart the same kind of feeling. I had a member of my family killed, but he was killed by a white man. But we have to make an effort in the United States, we have to make an effort to understand, to go beyond these rather difficult times. . . .

What we need in the United States is not division; what we need in the United States is not hatred; what we need in the United States is not violence or lawlessness; but love and wisdom, and compassion toward one another, and a feeling of justice toward those who still suffer within our country, whether they be white or they be black.

So I shall ask you tonight to return home, to say a prayer for the family of Martin Luther King, that's true, but more importantly to say a prayer for our own country. . . .

Let us dedicate ourselves to what the Greeks wrote so many years ago: to tame the savageness of man and make gentle the life of this world.

Tame the savageness of man. And make gentle the life of this world. Remember who you are. And who you want to be.

But it would be only two months later, on June 5, that Bobby would be shot at San Francisco's Ambassador Hotel, having just won the California primary. Sirhan Sirhan was his killer. Another Kennedy gone. Another voice for change silenced. In his own campaign for president that year, Wallace aired ads with homemade videos of imaginary firebombs thrown through windows of anonymous small towns, warning white America of the menace of the Black mob.

I was five years old. The memories are hazy, when they are there at all, but one is vivid. I lie on the linoleum floor of the parsonage on Panorama Drive on Huntsville's Monte Sano Mountain, on my stomach, with my elbows on the floor, palms holding my head up by the cheekbones. Mother is on the couch, crying, and on TV there is sadness, and sobbing. It is a funeral. There is a procession. The house is still, but for the sobs. A darkness has come.

I don't know if that funeral was King's or Kennedy's. I assume it was Kennedy's, because it was full of the pomp and circumstance I now associate with a state funeral, the kind that would bury a Kennedy. I presume it was Bobby, because Mother was swept away by the Kennedys, by John and Jackie and Bobby and Camelot and hope and a dream of something better, in pearls and a pillbox hat, in a way she could understand.

Something changed that summer, with finality. The Methodist Church would decide, in 1968, to dissolve its Central Jurisdiction— that part of the denomination reserved, like a separate drinking fountain, for Black preachers and worshippers. It would come together with the Evangelical United Brethren Church to form the United Methodist Church, with what was supposed to be a more enlightened sense of direction. Perhaps it gave Methodist preachers like Dad a jump start, or just permission to speak freely. He preached it in church after the unification. "If we cannot stand up for what we truly believe in a time of crisis, then it's not necessary to do much standing at any time," Dad said.

Yeah, but Jesus Christ, Dad. Oh. Sorry, Dad.

By fall, Dad's files are full of lyrics from the likes of Bob Dylan and Simon and Garfunkel. He—the great-great-grandson of the exiled Singing Tom—decided to begin a series of sermons based on secular songs. "Blowin' in the Wind." "The Times They Are a-Changin.'" "The Sounds of Silence." I know it was the influence of Murray and Mary Beth. And of my mother.

In his sermon on Dylan's "Blowin' in the Wind"—he knew it from Peter, Paul and Mary, no doubt because he assumed they'd popped out of the Bible—he read the words to the song, and spoke of their meaning.

"There is the problem of race," he said, asking his congregation how many times they could pretend not to see.

Which is of course what Dylan asked, and King asked, and Rutland asked, and I'm trying to answer now. Except I get stuck on his "problem of race"—again—because race wasn't the problem. The problem was and is and will be one of rights and wrongs and power and privilege and humanity.

But it is good to see him take it on. Besides, that sermon also had one of my favorite things: a Bankheadism. He was speaking then of the youth revolution and the generation gap.

"I am told Tallulah Bankhead was visiting an aristocratic Englishwoman who had a badly spoiled teenage son," he said. "The lady said, 'We don't know what to make of him.' Tallulah said, 'How about a nice rug?'"

Rim shot.

But it is his sermon on "The Sounds of Silence" that draws me, for surely it must be about timidity and reluctant courage and finding a voice. Dad played the old fogy from the pulpit, speaking of those two young musicians Paul Simon and Art Garfunkel, and confessed that it was hard for him to understand all the words in a song of that style. "But after a deliberate attempt, and with help from my family, the words began to reveal themselves." Listen to them, he said, and he played them, or sang them, or more likely played them and sang along to them, in their entirety. He spoke of the way silence really does grow in the church, and in all of us.

"Silence does make sounds," Dad wrote in his sermon. "And when you and I and the Church remain silent, we are speaking loud and clear to this secular society. We are saying to them, "We

Rev. Frederick Outlaw reads a transcript of the Emancipation Proclamation at Metropolitan AME Church in downtown Mobile, Alabama, in 2015. Outlaw said that Dad was on the right side of history, even if his role was a quiet one.

don't want to become involved with you, for we have lost our sense of purpose and direction of the people of God."

Yes. Yes, you are. Yes, we are. He spoke of voice. Even when it sometimes might be . . . hushed:

> We must have a ministry of quietness. Not the quietness of confusion or of failure to communicate, but the quietness that comes from certainty of purpose, peace of spirit, and confidence in love.

I thought of Frederick Outlaw, one of the Black ministers from Decatur who knew Dad, who argued there was never a secret to where Dad stood, that every movement had two fronts and that all the great battles, from Alexander the Great on down, were fought with two armies: the soldiers who won with bloodshed and the researchers and philosophers and humanitarians who won the people.

"Your dad was on the right side," Outlaw said.

I thought, too, of a term paper Dad wrote in seminary, describing the work of a minister as an educator, in which he argued that the pulpit was only part of the way to reach a reluctant congregation:

Although the pulpit is usually considered to be the minister's greatest opportunity for teaching adults, there are hundreds of daily contacts in which he also has excellent opportunities. It is in these situations that people are caught off their guard, and can be reached.

Is this what he meant by "the quietness that comes from certainty of purpose, peace of spirit, and confidence in love"?

Dad went on, in his sermon, to quote the song again, and to call for a louder voice.

"The vision must never be allowed to remain silent," Dad finished. "It must come alive in our own creative action. Without the fanfare of political parties, without the hue and cry of vested interest, but quietly we must affirm it to the world."

This I believe. I know Dad did, too.

II

THE PRODIGAL'S RING

16

Moral Law

There has been talk about new morality. Well, there really is no such thing as new morality. There is still God's moral law.

—REV. ROBERT L. ARCHIBALD JR., July 17, 1966

It's good being last in a brood of kids. Mom and Dad are tired by the time they get to you, so they overlook the small wrongs. They realize the errors of their early days, their early ways, and strive not to repeat them. Or they simply lack the will. They pick their skirmishes and understand you will start your wars. It's good being the last of four kids. If you survive.

I was three, outside on Monte Sano Mountain with my big brothers and sister, crawling across the stretched canvas of a neighbor's trampoline. It felt good to be with the big kids, good to be outside, laughing and playing, a center of attention that made them smile. Not left out, like when they sledded down the mountainside, when Dad towed them back up the slope behind the station wagon. It made me feel older, like I was five. What could be better than to be part of a pack, to be one of the gang, to be . . .

Oh, shiiiit!

Sorry, Mother.

I didn't know that word then, of course. I didn't know quite a lot of words. In the photos I just sat and smiled and peered about, wide-eyed, nose always running, for the camera. Of course I didn't know that word. But the translation is accurate.

Some bigger kid—Murray or Mary Beth, or maybe some other member of my momentary neighborhood tribe—sailed through the air and landed heavily on the trampoline, and I learned Newton's lesser-known fourth law of motion: For every active sibling there is an equal and opposite trip to the hospital. I'm sure it was an accident. We were all too young to have taken physics classes—though many of those Monte Sano neighbors were children of rocket scientists working at NASA in Huntsville to put a man on the moon. I flew through the air, flipping and flailing like a test launch gone awry, and landed, scalp first—I have a head like a winter melon, so the trajectory steadied and I flew straight as a lawn dart—on the steel frame of the trampoline.

Whack.

This was about the same time Ralph Nader started to warn people about safety, but the notion hadn't penetrated America's skulls like the trampoline penetrated mine. It never occurred to anyone that a trampoline might be improved with pads or netting. That would take the daring out of it. It was a world of station-wagon ski lifts and childhood wandering, of mercury from a broken thermometer rolled across the palm of your hand. It was a time when my favorite family pastime was to make lead soldiers, melting blocks of the toxic metal and casting it in molds of Revolutionary War troops and armaments. I don't suppose I was actually allowed to pour the molten lead until I was older, but I loved playing with the soldiers, biting their heads off to chew like petrified gum. It's no wonder I don't recall who made that fateful jump onto the trampoline.

What was it we were talking about?

I don't recall hitting the frame, either. I don't recall pain or blood or fear or the reaction of any kid in that yard. All I recall—one of those snapshots again, this time a grainy Polaroid in my brain—is riding to the hospital in what must have been that old Rambler ski lift. Mother drove, with purpose, and Murray—if I was three he would have been twelve—held me in his arms in the front seat, pressing a clean washcloth to my head, telling stories of the Lost Boys, and how I flew through the air on the wings of pixie dust and fell to earth. But only after saving Peter from that dastardly Captain Hook. That's what I remember.

I was five when Mark and I played a game in the brand-new second story of the brand-new parsonage in Jacksonville. It was so new and untamed that scorpions crawled in through the fireplace, that spiders and bees and skunks and flying squirrels made our fort in the backwoods—built mostly of imagination among wild huckleberry bushes—feel like real survival. But on this day we were inside, playing a game of Mark's design. In my memory Mark's rules were: "Hit the window as hard as you can without breaking it. You go first." Simple.

It is only fair to say that Mark disputes this version, while offering no clear or believable alternative. But I must give him the benefit of the doubt. The fuzzy photographic memory of this one might have been Photoshopped by time. I was five, after all, with a lead-soldier-chewing habit. In either case it is not in dispute that I went first, that I hit the window and it broke and I lost the game. I stood at the top of the stairs crying as my mother peered up from below to see what the commotion was about. I was scared, shattered, not by the pain but the pane, oblivious to the fact that a shard protruded from my wrist. So I blurted, "Mama, I-I-I broke the window."

I did not at first understand why she looked at me and gaped, horrified, and began to take the stairs two at a time. I looked down, and saw red. Lots of it. I screamed. As everything went dark.

That's all I recall until the hospital. Or the doctor's office, or wherever it was. It was sterile and white and Mother held my right hand across the table and Dad leaned against her until, watching me bleed, he sagged unconscious to the floor, dragging Mother with him. I sat on Murray's lap as they slipped out of sight. He held my left arm steady, so the nurse could clean it and the doctor could stitch it up at the wrist. He whispered jokes and distractions in my ear—much of it about Dad's sudden disappearance, I am sure—as the numbing shot came and then the sutures. He spoke of sword fights and bravery. That's what I remember.

Murray is nine years older than me, so when I was nine he was twice my age, grown, ready to leave for college, to go away for life. We shared the upstairs in the Decatur parsonage then, his room on the front end of the house and mine toward the backyard, by the bathroom, which overlooked the carport roof and a triangular antenna tower beside it. At night, he would sneak past my room in the dark, into the bathroom, out the window and down the antenna. I watched him go, and sometimes I woke up to hear him come in, early in the morning, when Mark was getting up. I never told. But I remember.

Of Murray's childhood, I know mostly what I hear in old stories my siblings metastasize into adventures or faux horrors, or from what I extrapolate from the family slides and the narration that goes with them. He's the one in costumes of pirates and sailors and Gypsies and cowboys, with his plays and productions and drama of all kinds, on- and offstage. I read of Murray—like I do all of us—in Mother's old letters, and newspaper clippings, and in Dad's old sermons.

In 1957, two months before Sputnik pierced space, as television began to catch on and drive-ins and soda fountains stole the time of American youth, Dad preached a sermon called "Our Leisure Hours." He spoke of how, in the age of space and scientific magic and automation that gave people more free time than humans had ever known, Christians needed guidance for their down time. He spoke of Murray then. Murray would have been three years old:

> Recreation has a definitive service to perform in this machine age. Creative living has almost become a lost art. Every man needs to have the experience of creating things. Creative recreation can take the place of much of the prosaic work of life. My son, Murray, after building a house with his blocks, called: "Mommy, look what I made." There is something significant in being able to say that.

There *is* something significant in being able to say that. And to see it, in Murray, at the age of three. For that is Murray, now and forevermore, amen. *Look what I made.*

He's the one who built a Globe Theatre the size of a riding lawn mower and to meticulous, precise scale. I remember. It lived in the garage for years. He built a flawless Scottish castle—Edinburgh Castle, perhaps—out of cork, on a hillside of papier-mâché and inside a moat of azure acrylic. He and Mary Beth painted beautiful pictures, and Easter eggs that looked more Fabergé than family. He built sets for school plays and props for church musicals and designed costumes for every day. He put on lavish productions, like the doomed *Year Without a New Year,* and he starred onstage in all those pieces. I remember.

Mommy. Look what I made.

That was Murray. It was more than that, I know. It was the family, because of Mother, mostly, who believed we were put on earth to create and to be kind, in the image of her God. And because of Grandmother Holland, who taught china painting and created beautiful floral place settings, and Mom, who wrote poetry, and Dad, who whittled wild animals from scrap and built precise furniture in the garage. But Murray made a life of art, as a child and an adult. He lived for creation.

Murray would have been twelve—in the Boy Scouts, on the honor roll, holding me in the car on a wild ride down Monte Sano Mountain to have my melon patched—when Dad in 1966 preached on the sins of a so-called new morality:

Some things are not subject to opinion or to majority vote. There are some things which are not to be manipulated or amended or interfered with or changed by human beings. Some things don't depend on anybody's vote. Some things are wrong even if everybody is doing them. And some things are right even if nobody is doing them.

Let me mention two things which cannot be manipulated.

The first one is moral law. I believe that God has established moral law just as surely as he has established physical law. We do not vote on whether we will have moral law. This is not our choice. Our only choice is to discover it and live, or ignore it and die.

There has been talk about new morality. Well, there really is no such thing as new morality. There is still God's moral law. In 1948 the sociologist Alfred Charles Kinsey published his work *Sexual Behavior in the Human Male,* and in 1953 his book on the Human female. Many people jumped to the conclusion that a new morality was in vogue. Victorian attitudes were laughed at. Mr. Kinsey interviewed over 18,000 [*sic*] people, but his interviews don't change moral law as it applies to sex.

Sex is a wonderful gift from God. But rules still operate. If we follow them, sex becomes fulfillment and joy. If we ignore these laws, sex turns to lust and degradation. As Gerald Kennedy said, "no man can use a woman as a means to an end, nor can a woman use a man as a pawn to fulfill her ambitions." God meant for the relationship between man and woman to be something holy and wonderful and unchangeable. When we forget this, our sophistication becomes only a sorry veneer for failure and defeat and death.

He didn't mention homosexuality specifically. I'm not sure it would have crossed Dad's mind in the 1960s. If such a thing existed, it existed in other people, and to talk about it would be to gossip, and gossip, too, held a special place of dishonor under his heading of moral law. I can't say with certainty that Dad even knew what it meant when Murray came out as gay in the 1970s. His first response, I am told, was to tell Murray he was not surprised. So he knew a little. But I don't believe Mother knew exactly what homosexuality was, despite graduating from a notable Southern women's college two decades earlier with a degree in psychology.

I know what she did, though, because she told me. She hugged him, and said she loved him, and determined to understand. Mother wondered, at first, if she had done something wrong, if she had breastfed too long or too little, if she had listened to that Dr. Spock more than she should. She decided, without much lost sleep, that she had done nothing wrong because there *was* nothing wrong. It simply was. It simply was Murray.

So Mother, being Mother, set off to find out everything she could about this *homosexuality*. It was a lesson that would take years, through Murray's college days and disco fan dancing and the Village People and AIDS. Her education started in the den, as most assignments did, in that battered old set of the Encyclopaedia Britannica that held the answers for decades of school projects and debates. But Britannica was no help.

There were books about sex and puberty strewn around the house, unobtrusive but available for curious children to learn the facts of life, no questions asked. But they were no good, either, unless you wanted to know how women liked to lie at their husband's sides, cuddling for a good fifteen minutes after intercourse.

So when all her resources inside the home were exhausted, Mother went, covertly, to the Decatur Public Library.

Not that she was ashamed. If you wanted shame you'd get Mama Bear instead. But she was circumspect, aware of prying eyes. She wanted to be a good wife, a good preacher's wife, with all that entailed. Good preachers' spouses, she thought, smiled in the face of judgment and innuendo. They looked the part and acted it and practiced the fine art of discretion. They accepted vacations cut short for funerals, and put up with the long hours of the Calling.

Sorry, honey. Jesus on Line One.

Being the wife of the pastor at a First Church in any mainline Protestant denomination in any Southern town is like opening a bay window to your life. People whisper about your clothes if you're there, and they whisper of where you are if you're not. Preachers' lives and their homes, especially then and especially among Methodists, whose parsonages are owned by the churches, were as open as any of the books at the library.

Mother fumed once after a visitor criticized a chair she kept in the parlor. The lady harrumphed, in that bless-your-heart way old Southern church ladies are prone to do. She told Mother the wife of the previous minister—she went there, yes she did—kept a comfortable sofa in that spot, where she could sit and talk all day to members of the congregation.

Mother was too polite—or too dumbstruck—to tell her she never really liked the chair in question, but it was starting to grow on her.

"That's the best reason I ever heard to keep it right where it is," she said later.

"Sweeeeet," was all Dad said. It was not a comment on her mood. Just his name for her, when he dared say nothing else.

Churches are a lot like people. They all have a personality, and a sense of self. They are snooty or welcoming, progressive or . . . traditional. They are haughty or understated, growing wildly or dying a certain death. First United Methodist Church of Decatur was circumspect and cultured, steady and sophisticated, enlightened enough, by Alabama standards, to overlook a little eccentricity. Mother had been thrilled when Dad was sent there in 1969. It was a good appointment, a financial and social promotion. On Sundays Mother was practically Decatur's first lady, if you didn't count the Baptists. And my family never counted the Baptists.

All in all, Decatur was a good place to be, and a good place to conduct her research. She was going to the library, after all. Not the bootlegger.

I can only imagine how she looked when she set out. Surely she tied her plastic rain bonnet tight over her bouffant and slipped on her Jackie O sunglasses. If she met any of the First Methodist flock at the library she launched into flustered explanations that succeeded only in raising suspicion. Maybe she met no one, though, for she found Decatur's few volumes on the latest theories of human sexuality and brought them home. She consumed all she could find and, as always, returned the books on time.

She wanted to know everything.

It was sometime later, years later, after Murray graduated college with honors and we'd moved on to Birmingham, that she digested it enough to share it with me. I was in middle school.

"Sit down, John," she said. "I have something to tell you."

Which is something an adolescent boy never wants to hear. But it didn't get better.

"Do you know what a homosexual is?" she asked. "Sometimes they call it gay. I don't know why."

Oh, my God—sorry, Dad—I did not want to be there. I didn't want to talk to Mother about homosexuals, or gay, or sex of any kind, or the birds and bees, or whatever. It had taken me two weeks to tell her I had to have a jockstrap to stay on the football team. I just stared.

"Well, Murray has told your father and me he believes he is . . . no that he is, homo . . . er, well, you know . . . gay."

I'm not sure I'd ever really thought about whether Murray was gay. I'd been nine when he went off to college and didn't know what gay was. I didn't know or care about anything that had to do with love, or romance, or relationships. I knew that every time my classmate and neighbor Ann Szczepanski walked by, I felt the bottom drop out of my stomach, and I hated it. If that was love, you could keep it.

Even by the time Mother sat me down, I'd never really known anyone who was gay, or admitted it. It was just a word kids threw

Mother and Murray in Decatur, Alabama,
about 2010. He was "different," and she didn't
care who knew.

around when they wanted to hurt somebody's feelings, or they
wanted to fight. Did I know Murray was gay? In hindsight a better
question is whether it was a question at all. It's not like he was ever
in the closet, unless you mean the costume closet, and he was there
a lot. It's not like he was subtle, like many of the LGBTQ people
I know today, who defy stereotypes in a thousand ways. Murray—
though strong and spiritual and unique—embraced the stereotypes, almost like a challenge. He was who he was for any who
dared to see. There were the flower arrangements and the musicals.
He was a drama major in college—at Dad's alma mater, the Methodist school Birmingham-Southern, and was caught on camera, in
the school newspaper, streaking buck naked across campus to the
cheers of classmates and the amusement, we are told beneath the
picture of his bare bum, of the dean. But it was the seventies. All
that could mean . . . anything.

It occurred to me that I *had* seen a magazine in Murray's closet once—when I snuck into his room like a little shit—that was filled with penises of unusual size. POUS. In retrospect, that should have been a clue.

"He's still Murray," Mother said when she sat me down to tell me something that seemed so very important to her.

Of course he was. Of course he is. Like I am me and Mark is Mark and Mary Beth is Mary Beth.

"He's just your brother," she said. "We love him."

We do, Mother. I know. I remember.

17

Pantless Pete

For the Christian there is also the temptation to run ahead of God, to think we are God's anointed and that we can run God's business without consulting him.

—REV. ROBERT L. ARCHIBALD JR., July 15, 1970

The Tennessee River, like Dad's mom, is a child of the Holston hills. It is birthed there, in northeastern Tennessee, at the confluence of the Holston and French Broad rivers. It snakes through Chattanooga, into my state at the corner where Georgia and Tennessee and Alabama meet, near that spot where Mom died in the crash.

It flows southward through Scottsboro, with all its ghosts, and Guntersville, with all its beauty, before bending west.

The river slides through Decatur, between Florence and Muscle Shoals, and Tuscumbia, home to Ivy Green, the birthplace of Helen Keller, which still shows off the pump where young Helen felt cool liquid on her skin as her teacher, Anne Sullivan, outlined the letters W-A-T-E-R in her palm. Helen Keller had an epiphany at that pump, an epiphany of language. Perhaps there is something in the water.

The Tennessee flows northwest again from there, crossing the Natchez Trace, the old Native American interstate trail, and briefly plays the role of the Alabama/Mississippi border. Then it rolls north again, off to Kentucky to meet and marry the Ohio River.

It is dammed now, this mighty river. Muted. But in the old days, Native Americans—before they were marched from Alabama by Andrew Jackson, a man distantly related to my Hillman forebears—believed the river was magic. Some tribes called her Nun-Nuh-Sae, the "Singing River," because she was filled with the music of the soul and the earth and the universe, with a truth that flowed as silent and strong as the current itself. The Yuchi people— pronounced *Ee-you-chee,* as the old native folklorist Tom Hendrix told me before he died—believed a woman lived in that river, and sang her songs for any who would stop and listen.

Hendrix grieved for the music, the way the great dams "softened her song." But he mourned more for those who will not listen, who do not have time, nor interest, nor the reverence to simply stop and hear.

"If you go to quiet places, you can still hear her sing," Hendrix said. And you can.

Dad spent his life on that river, as a child in Decatur and a teen in Florence, fishing for bass and bream at the TVA's "Fighting Joe" Wheeler Dam when it was still new, muffling the music of the river but offering in return a lake, and a measure of economic and recreational prosperity. He learned to gig frogs along the banks of the river and its tributaries, something he would not do later in life, when the croaking moan of a dying animal became a sound he did not wish to hear. Long after he came back to Decatur as an adult, as a preacher, and later a district superintendent—a member of the bishop's cabinet—he and Mother decided to retire there, when the time came, in their own house. It was their first that didn't belong to a church—ranch-style, with a big yard, out by the river and the Wheeler National Wildlife Refuge, where Dad volunteered at the visitors' center.

Dad heard the songs. He always did. He listened for them, and I believe he sang along. He heard the glorious anthems that burst forth in places like the refuge, alive with beating wings, and he heard the mournful laments, the elegies in places like Triana, where chemicals killed the fish and sickened the river itself, along with those who lived on it and loved it.

Dad canoed the backwaters and sloughs his whole life, paddling silently along Flint Creek with his head cocked, as if lost in thought, until a flash of an egret or a sandhill crane or a red-tailed hawk snapped him to attention. He thrilled to see them, no matter how many thousands of times he'd seen them before. So he smiled and pointed and almost burst with joy when you saw them, too. He laughed at otters, diving and darting like children playing tag beneath the surface, and he smiled at beavers, too, though he felt guilty about that. Beavers do all sorts of damage to the old forests and *blah blah blah,* he would begin. But his heart wasn't in it. He was amazed by them, in awe of them, as he was all of nature. They were builders, after all. The engineers of the animal kingdom, doing far less to damage the earth than, say, we were.

Dad heard the songs on the main river, too. He paddled along her banks, out of the channel, away from the wakes of barges that turned Nun-Nuh-Sae into a clattering rock-'n'-roll highway.

As a young man he dreamed of canoeing the Mississippi River through Memphis and all the way up to Paducah, Kentucky, moving on to the Ohio River and maybe even east to Pittsburgh. Mark would have gone with him. I might have made it as far as the state line.

In his older years Dad dreamed of traveling the river on a steamboat, like Mark Twain on the Mississippi. He researched and called and wrote for information about riverboat tours, with all the purpose and detail he had used to plan our childhood vacations. But he could never convince Mother to spend two weeks on a river that ran a few blocks from their home. He never made that trip. But he took his children to that river, and taught them her ways. He took his grandchildren, too, and implored them to hear her song.

And on one of his final days, he stood in the sun on the bow of a paddlewheel riverboat called the *Pickwick Belle,* a geriatric Leo DiCaprio, gripping the rail and laughing to himself, just laughing into the wind and Decatur's "Steamboat Bill" Hudson Memorial Bridge, until he could no longer stand. We had to carry him off that boat when the day trip ended after only a few hours. He was spent. But happy.

Dad was always happy on the river, or talking about it to tourists at the wildlife refuge who maybe didn't want to hear quite so much about the migratory patterns of mallards or snow geese, or the plight of the bats, or the osprey that nest each year on towers that hold up power lines, or the chorus frogs and Fowler's toads or that time when 125,000 ducks came to the refuge all at the same time.

The river is part of me, too, I see now. It is part of all of us, and moments that stand out in my life, like Dad's, took place on its banks, or on its current. Homemade peach ice cream on an island in the Tennessee, at a cabin owned by Dad's friend Eddie Self. I taste it, and ice cream will never again be so sweet. Mayflies swarming on the river, clinging to docks and porch screens by the thousands, the millions. They are not a horror, Dad said. They are beautiful, for they will fall into the water and make the fish fat, and trusting, and easy to catch. I hear the river and smell it, like summer. I feel the chill of swinging over the surface on a rope and falling, free, into the cold water. For me it is a brave act.

The river is beautiful, but it is hard, and powerful, and unyielding, too. It is dangerous and frightening and in moments wears the perfume of oil and sulfur.

Mark and I played as children on that grittier side of the river, where that hog plant bled into the water and petroleum tanks stood like lighthouses. I shot at those tanks with my BB gun, just to hear the reverberating *piiiiiing*. Nobody seemed to care.

The river was only a few blocks from the parsonage in Decatur, and I delivered newspapers along its banks and backwaters. I delivered to a senior-living home at the river's edge, a high-rise built in a square, so that every floor had a balcony overlooking the open center. I ran the corridors, from apartment to apartment, dropping *The Decatur Daily* to the floor and kicking it gently through the crack under the door. I absorbed the news in those seconds, apartment by apartment, line by line, as the papers lay on the ground before final delivery. I can still see front-page reports from Vietnam—ANOTHER B-52 LOST—and Watergate.

When Mom and Dad were older, and no longer able to care for themselves, they moved into an assisted living facility next door to that one. It was called Riverside. Of course.

Only now do I see that we are all of the river, by the river and for the river, that we speak its language and tell its stories and sing its songs without even realizing it.

When I talk of the miraculous path of my life, I see myself as a piece of driftwood, floating along aimlessly on a river, somehow avoiding the biggest of the barges. I see myself on the Tennessee.

When Alecia and I were with Murray once in Norfolk, Virginia, and he was harassed on the street, I bowed up, ready to fight for him. But he brushed it aside, in the language of the water.

"Be a river rock," he said. "Let everything else wash over you."

When he tells of the moments in his own life that made their splash, that mark his path like radiating rings on the surface, he does it in the words, in the music of the river.

"If I skip a stone across my life . . ." he begins. Where do they land?

The river is a constant. It tells our stories as much as we tell them ourselves. It is life and death and beauty and grime and truth. Ugly, dirty, beautiful, persistent truth. It was constant in Dad's life even more than mine, as abiding as camp was to me. It let him feel like Huck Finn, like a kid again, forever. So Dad lived it and he loved it and he told stories about it. He told of the time he rescued a hawk and carried it to the raptor center in Birmingham, and the time he used netting to build a trap that funneled vipers into a cage.

Some of the stories were tedious—I won't lie. There are only so many times a guy like me can listen to a tale about a yellow-rumped warbler in which nothing faces death, no one is injured and there is no villain. Some of the stories were beautiful, too. But not all of them. Not all of them.

Back in the 1940s, when Dad was sixteen or seventeen, as the war came to an end and all of America breathed with relief and release, Dad and a few friends from Florence went to spend an afternoon on the river, to swim and to fish and to enjoy being outside in a world that no longer held a Hitler.

A fellow named Pete tagged along, unwelcome and apparently uninvited. Or at least not invited with vigor. He was not a friend of Dad's, particularly. Not a scout or an outdoorsman. He was not, more important, someone who respected nature or heard the river or stopped long enough to even listen.

Perhaps, though, he was just shy. For when the others stripped bare and jumped in the river, Pete followed in his trousers. It wasn't long before the weight and the chafing took their toll, so he left the water and the others, and went to high ground in search of a rock on which he could dry. Dad found him there later, sprawled naked and basking in the sun, chewing leaves to pass the time.

Dad told the story so often it had a name: "Pantless Pete's Painful Predicament."

"Pete was one of those sissy boys," he'd begin. And by the time he got to this part, he'd start to laugh, sometimes so hard he could not breathe.

Because Pete was lying naked and oblivious on a bed of poison ivy, which covers Alabama more completely than kudzu, and is easy to identify by its three jagged leaves, easy to spot by any kid who has ever been outside and touched it. If that wasn't bad enough, Pete was propped up on an elbow chewing a sprig of it, cool and smug and without so much as an inkling.

It was a dad story, a bad story, the kind a kid hears and rolls his eyes and pleads: *Daaaaad!* To no avail. He told it, I think, because it took him to a place in his youth when he didn't carry the weight of a church and a family and a world. He laughed because it starred a poor schlub who failed to understand or respect nature, or the order of the universe, and in literary form reaped his just reward. He laughed because that fellow thought he knew all he needed to know, and it came back to itch him in the ass.

But it always bothered me because it wasn't like Dad to laugh at a poor sap's pain. It didn't seem like him, and maybe that's why he laughed too hard, to cover the guilt. I wanted to know what happened to Pete. Did his insides itch? Did his bottom burn?

I was deathly sensitive to poison ivy as a child. I could walk by the stuff and come home with the telltale lines of itchy red bumps and blisters. When I was about fourteen, I climbed an oak tree at Christmastime—no idea what kind of oak—to pick mistletoe from its branches. It was a warm December, as it sometimes is in Alabama, and I wore shorts. I took off my shirt to shimmy up the tree. But it was December, warm or not, and the poison ivy vines around those trees had no leaves. I had no idea they were there, or that they could still cause pain. By dinner time I was coated with layer after layer of rash, from head to foot. It was agony—though I was never again so sensitive to the plant. But it made me feel for Pete.

"Was he all right?" I asked.

"Well, yeah," Dad said. "He was fine. I think."

I was grown, I guess, when I noticed how Murray walked out of the room when Dad told the story. I thought he had the same issues I did, that it lacked a good ending and, well, simply wasn't as funny as Dad thought it was. But that wasn't it. Or at least it wasn't all of it.

"You know he always calls that Pantless Pete a sissy boy," Murray said. "What do you think he means by that?"

"I don't know," I lied. But I knew. We both knew.

18

Camp, Part II

A father's kiss will set you free. All those years of struggling and failing, of fear and anxiety, of trying to be good enough and never succeeding will be wiped away when your father's lips press against your forehead. You are forgiven, accepted, loved, brought back into the family. And your presence is the occasion for celebration and joy.

—REV. ROBERT L. ARCHIBALD JR., June 16, 1991

It was 1978 when Murray brought a man home for Christmas, to the parsonage of East Lake United Methodist Church in Birmingham. His name was Steve Elkins. He worked for President Jimmy Carter, and Murray had met him—I don't believe it was quite by accident—while delivering a painting to his office in the White House.

I was fifteen, playing offensive guard and defensive end at a school that won two state titles that decade, that had produced Johnny Musso and Jimmy Sidle and Jeff Rutledge. I played on a freshman team that lost every game, but that went on to win varsity regional titles when David Cutcliffe, who would later find greatness coaching the Duke Blue Devils, took over. I was fifteen, the preacher's kid. I was fifteen, trying every day to prove I was something else. I was fifteen, caught between two worlds, so I kept them apart.

Steve was buttoned up and Brooks Brothers, with Atlanta in his heart if not his tongue. Unless he needed it there. He was an Eagle Scout who said "Yes, sir" and "No, ma'am" and knew our ways. He could debate the finer points of sweet tea or pimiento cheese, or international financial policy, like any Southern son. He was a frat boy, a Georgia Bulldog, and talked to me of SEC football. He sang hymns out loud in church and talked to Mother—I guess this is ironic, now—about Chick-fil-A founder Truett Cathy, and his brilliance and philanthropy in their beloved Peach State. Steve joked when the room needed a laugh and nodded sympathetically when it didn't. So it didn't take a lot of time or an epiphany, no change in philosophy or calculated decision, to give him the benefit of the doubt. There was no determination to walk around in his shoes or to think more of it. It just was. Steve just was. And in that moment, in that snap of a finger, Murray became Murray and Steve.

I don't know what Steve said when he met Dad, or what Dad said when he met Steve. Murray doesn't know or doesn't recall. But I have a good idea. I think Dad treated him the same way he treated all the Outlaws. He asked Steve what church he belonged to, and invited him to ours.

Steve was family, from then on, though I didn't talk about him to my friends at school or anywhere else. It makes me feel like Saint Peter in the garden again, denying a brother with my silence. I did not think of it that way then. I did not think of it much at all. I just did not cross the streams.

Dad must have been that way, too. But in ways he was more upfront than I. He invited Steve to church—which was, let's face it, his workplace—and bragged on his successes, in the White House and afterward, when he took a job as an executive in a big computer company.

Mother was different, though. Always. She would come to introduce us all to anyone in the pews.

"You know Alecia and John," she'd say later, "and this is Mary Beth and her Bob, and this is Mark and Sally, and this is Steve. Steve belongs to Murray, you know."

Dad did not talk much about it. Not in so many words. I suppose he thought he must be careful. For after the United Methodist Church was formed in 1968 in the merger to end religious racial segregation, it turned around and fired a shot at gay people. Can't have open hearts and minds for everybody, after all. In 1972, in the first General Conference after the merger, it approved language condemning homosexuality as incompatible with Christian teaching—language that stands today.

Dad did not say otherwise, from the pulpit. He preached as he always did, on gospel and grace and the words of Jesus, who was all about the love. He didn't preach the moral-law sermon again, but he preached the parables of Jesus a lot. One of his favorites was that of the prodigal son, in which the younger of a rich man's two boys took his inheritance early and went off to travel and party until he frittered it all away. I always figured, when Dad preached about it, that there was a hidden message meant for me. But I guess that's the point of parables. There's a message—spiritual or otherwise—for everybody. The son, broke and hung over and jonesin' for home, wanted desperately to return to his family, even if he had to beg to live in the house as a servant. So he came, but his dad saw him coming and threw one helluva welcome-home party. He even killed a fat calf for the barbecue. He celebrated, even as the good brother, the one who had stayed home the whole time, couldn't believe his eyes. That didn't seem fair to me. But Dad knew all along it wasn't really a story about the problem son, or the well-behaved one. It was about love that is not predicated on behavior. He preached it in 1973, the year after the General Conference voted to include that language vilifying the gay community. He preached it again in 1991, the year before the same body voted to ignore a recommendation to take that language out:

> What does the father do? The father welcomes him back into the home. This is the grace of God in its finest expression. The father never gave him the chance to ask to be a hired servant. The father gave him a robe, and a ring, and shoes.

Dad preached it more often than that, in other words and other ways. But he was always subtle, like he had been with the "race problem." He preached of how "we must remember that our judgments must be rooted in love," but did not say the word *homosexual,* or define the issue out loud. If he had questions, he answered them like the father in the prodigal son parable.

He begged Murray and Steve to come home for Christmas as early as they could, and to stay as long as they could, as he did us all. He welcomed them with a bear hug so big it cracked their backs and convinced them it might be wise to take a dose of Beano a few minutes before their next arrival.

But the 1980s came soon. Murray cut his hair and moved with Steve to New York City, in a decade adorned in pastel Polos and Swatches, marked by excess and indulgence, and obsessive fitness— the unlikely third wheel. The decade was wild and free and seemingly without consequence. Until it ran headlong into AIDS.

It started as a thing you heard on the news, a mysterious disease that targeted gay people, and the stigma grew from there. Nobody understood it and the press got it all wrong at first. Even *The New York Times* ran a front-page story in 1984 on a study that seemed to show AIDS could be transmitted by saliva. Middle America responded with fear and revulsion, afraid it would rub off. Black and Hispanic people were dying at a higher rate than whites, and it took a kid like Ryan White, a Caucasian hemophiliac in Indiana who'd contracted HIV in a blood transfusion as a child, to make America see the humanity behind the disease.

Murray saw it. Steve saw it. They watched close friends and acquaintances die one by one, couple by couple; they got sick and melted away, in a world that thought the sick should feel shame. I was far away, in Alabama, where news of a boy with AIDS triggered a school to kick him out of class, where reporters lined up to ask his parents how they *felt*. Where the straight, white churchgoing majority clucked a rueful *Told ya so*.

I spent the last half of the eighties in fear, like I did as a child after Mom and Pop's wreck. I knew it in my heart, felt it in my bones, if I did not say it out loud. I believed the day would come, as it would for Murray's friends Tom Poston and John Van Meter, that the news would arrive by phone. Mother would hear it first, or Mary Beth, and it would trickle down to me along with the tears. Murray, or Steve, or both would have that awful disease. I dreaded the call. I prepared myself for the conversation that had to happen.

But it didn't. Instead there would be another conversation. In 1988 Murray had an awakening while dancing at The Saint, a huge gay club in the East Village, that sent him on a sober search for meaning and meaningful religion. He and Steve mapped out a future they had never anticipated, and a couple of years later, he sat the rest of us down to explain it.

Murray would have been a good preacher, if his religion would have had him. He talks and paints and writes in the language of the church, of light and flame and bells and affirmation and the spirit. But he saw a need elsewhere.

He and Steve, like a lot of gay men and women on the East

Coast, had vacationed for years at Rehoboth Beach, Delaware, a tourist town on the Atlantic that began on 414 acres, after the Civil War, as a Methodist camp meeting ground.

It had to be a camp.

Camp was what Murray wanted to talk about. He and Steve had already figured it out and it gushed out of him all at once, like it couldn't stay inside. They would leave New York, and go to Rehoboth, and start a nonprofit that would work to build bridges between the gay and straight communities, which had mixed, some summers, like suntan oil and water. The local homeowners' association had launched a campaign to "Keep Rehoboth a Family Town," and the message was clear. They needed some camp. Murray and Steve would raise money and awareness and put out a newsletter and offer health screenings and HIV tests and a hundred other things. Steve could run it, in time, and lobby the legislature for change.

It sounded like a lot, to me. It sounded crazy, from a guy living in New York City, an artist who sold colorful paintings at fancy galleries for sums that seemed to me like riches. It was nuts, from this man who had dreamed of Broadway lights for as long as I'd known him.

He tried to explain it to me, and to Dad.

"We're going to call it CAMP," he said. "CAMP Rehoboth."

It was everything all at once, all those memories of childhood and Boy Scout trips and Camp Sumatanga and Nina Reeves's songs sung in dining halls. It was Camp Glisson, and its precious illusion of permanence. It was the big blue tent and trips across the country and near-death risks and real-life experiences. And it was *camp*, as he tried to explain to Dad and me as we tried to keep up. *Camp*, the art and humor of the ironic and the absurd that thrived in the gay culture, especially when being gay required a coded language all its

In 1991, Steve and Murray moved from New York to start CAMP Rehoboth, a nonprofit in Rehoboth Beach, Delaware, a city built on a Methodist campground.

own. Camp was the calling card of the drag queen, the humor that comes when someone takes himself too seriously, so seriously that it would make a Baptist deacon laugh. Maybe.

It would come to be CAMP Rehoboth. It stood for Creating a More Positive Rehoboth. It stands for a whole lot more than that.

Murray skipped the stone across the surface of his life and it caromed from Rainbow City to the White House, from The Saint in New York City to a tiny little Atlantic tourist town. It splashed down there, in Rehoboth Beach.

That's where he and Steve found their pulpits.

It would take a little longer before they found their church. Murray tried other religions, other denominations. He explored and searched far and wide, and found the door open right down the street. It was there in Rehoboth, where it was said Francis Asbury himself rode as a circuit rider after the Revolutionary War. It was there in Rehoboth Beach, a town that had grown—like our whole family had—from a Methodist campground.

19

Technicolor Yous

You set in the clouds a rainbow of promise. We are thanking you, oh God, for the Technicolor hues of life as seen through your rainbow.

—REV. ROBERT L. ARCHIBALD JR., April 9, 1989

I met Alecia at *The Crimson White,* the student newspaper at the University of Alabama. I was editorial-page editor, writing pious columns about Alabama's outlandish sodomy laws—you could go to jail for consensual oral sex back then—about Interior Secretary James Watt's aversion to trees, and other weighty issues I knew next to nothing about. Alecia covered the Student Government Association and wrote stories about The Machine, a ghostly secret society on the UA campus that was modeled after Yale's Skull and Bones and would come to haunt her.

I'd seen her across the room. She was tiny—four feet ten—with brown hair and eyes, like a woodland pixie. She smiled a lot and talked even more, in sentences that ran for miles without stopping for breath. There was an innocence there, I thought, that put her at odds with the rest of us cynics who gathered in the newsroom at all hours of the day, who skipped class to put out the paper, who worked hard, at twenty-two, to pull off the role of ink-stained old cranks. I was wrong about that. The innocence, I mean.

Our first real conversation took place when she swished across the newsroom in a turquoise denim mini skirt and plopped down on my desk. Well, she didn't plop. She climbed up, as if mounting a small pony, and sat on my desk, her feet dangling down by the drawers.

"I'm Alecia," she said. "You know, from over there." She pointed to the news desk.

"I'm John," I began, but she said, "I know," and didn't stop. "So what'cha writing about? Are your classes good? My classes are good. Except for my Shakespeare class—that's kind of hard. But you know I'm double-majoring, in journalism and English, so I have to take it. I like the literature—it's not that—it's just a lot."

She smiled, and I guess I did, too.

"Ugh," she went on. "My professor is making us go see a play tonight. We have to watch *Richard III*. I bet that's worse than what you're doing. What are you doing?"

I told her I had to work a half shift at the car wash that afternoon, but would be off by six-thirty.

"But that's a great play," I said, having never read it or seen it or thought of it at all. "That'll be fun."

And her eyes lit up, like she'd found a Shakespeare enthusiast, a fellow traveler on the road to literary wisdom.

"Oh, do you think so?" she said. "The play doesn't start until seven. You should go with me!"

And so begins a life.

I got off work and flew home to shower and asked Mother for sage words about *Richard III,* but all she had were soliloquies from

Hamlet, and *Macbeth,* and *Romeo & Juliet,* which she began to spout with enthusiasm, as if she had waited a lifetime for me to ask. I ran out of the house with my hair still wet as Mother found her words:

A horse! a horse! my kingdom for a horse!

That's the one.

In retrospect, the venue for this production of *Richard III* should have given me pause. It should have been a dead giveaway that something was rotten in the state of Alabama. It was not to be held at the performing arts center, or the drama department, or any of the Tuscaloosa theaters. The directions Alecia gave brought me, some ten minutes late, to a large classroom in UA's ten Hoor Hall. When I opened the door, it dawned on me that I didn't really know her very well. She had just climbed onto my desk and, with a two-letter word like "Hi," I was rushing from work to open a strange classroom door in an after-hours English building to watch a play I pretended to know and certainly would not enjoy or understand. I didn't know this girl at all. When I walked through the door, the place seemed like nothing more than an English class.

Because it was.

There was no stage or set, no actors or ticket takers or ushers. There were a hundred students, sitting in those little school chairs with the desks attached, and when the door opened they all looked at me instead of the play. If that was a play.

Who could blame them for being distracted, I guess, for Act I was under way not on a stage, but on a tiny black-and-white TV set on a cart in the front of the room. It was a BBC production, I think, played for three different classes who gathered together to watch it. They looked none too pleased.

I beseech your grace to pardon me . . .

But there was Alecia. Smiling and pointing to an empty desk she had saved. On and on, the actors droned from their little box.

Stay, you that bear the corse, and set it down.

So I sat. And smiled, with appropriate regret over my tardiness, and feigned excitement about the ongoing entertainment. I whispered knowingly how I'd heard this was a splendid performance, and could not wait to settle in.

At some point the children would be put in the Tower of London and Richard's conspirators would be double-crossed in an English language that seemed as familiar as Sanskrit to me. But by then the room had grown dark and heavy. I drifted away, thinking that all the world's really just a tiny television, and the men and women merely channels I would very much like to change.

I awoke with a nudge. Alecia was shaking my arm and students I didn't know were looking at me, smirking.

"You're snoring," Alecia said, not for the last time. But she was smiling.

Great, I thought, wiping drool from my cheek as the play kept talking to me in a language that was getting clearer.

Was ever woman in this humour wooed? Was ever woman in this humour won?

No. I was thinking no.

Thou elvish-marked, abortive, rooting hog.

Yeah. Got it.

But we went to a restaurant on the Tuscaloosa strip afterward and laughed about it. We talked until closing, though we could not avoid the shocked looks of our *Crimson White* coworkers who saw us together, but could not *see us together*. I walked her to her sorority house and we sat on the porch, talking until dawn. That was it. The future was decided, and we both saw it and knew it and were good with it. If it wasn't a done deal by then, it would be a little later, after Alecia wrote an exposé on The Machine and was told by her sorority adviser—a real estate agent in Tuscaloosa—she'd have to ditch me and quit *The Crimson White* if she wanted to stay in the good graces of Phi Mu. She picked me. And the paper.

So by the next year we were engaged and the year after that we were married, in the Southern Baptist church in Montgomery, where Alecia had been raised. A Baptist church. The temperature in hell must have dropped a few degrees.

My brother-in-law Bob Ramsey was best man and Mary Beth the matron of honor, and Dad performed the ceremony. Alecia did not want a Baptist service, with a sermon and maybe an altar call and vows that would have foolishly demanded she obey. She would agree to none of that, and Dad was fine with it, if her Baptist preacher was not.

The wedding is a blur for me, a montage of colliding worlds and blue satin bridesmaids' dresses and cheese cookies and nonalcoholic punch and moments that block out all the words and promises said that day. I remember sitting alone in the Sunday-school room where they kept me in isolation until my time came, pecking out the first notes of "Lean on Me" on an upright piano. I remember leaving the church with Alecia as her young cousin hit me in the face with a bag of birdseed—a stand-in for rice—thrown as hard as the little shit could hurl it. I remember Alecia holding me back in the limo so I didn't throttle him. I remember feeling everything. Scared, shy, happy, angry, worried, excited and in love. I felt everything but grown. It would take a long time before I felt that.

It would not be easy. It never is. We were young, twenty-four and twenty-two, and all we brought to the marriage was a few sticks of furniture and a couple of Emily Post etiquette books given by my mother—and given again for emphasis. I had a job at *The*

Birmingham News and was just beginning to figure out what I was doing, and Alecia took a marketing gig with the Alabama Symphony Orchestra. There was one other thing we had. It was Stella, my salamander, a water dog I'd raised from a pollywog that Alecia insisted on calling a newt. She was jealous of Stella, for some reason, and Stella was not all that fond of her.

I had noticed during our engagement that Stella refused to eat when Alecia came to visit. No crickets, no mealworms, no nothing. I thought it coincidence at first, but grew concerned as time passed. I felt sure it wouldn't last, confident that the two would come to mutual understanding when we all lived together in one happy home. But it was not to be. Stella initiated a hunger strike as soon as we arrived back from our honeymoon. She looked at her worms with disdain, the same way she looked at Alecia. There was a sadness there, a fatalistic understanding that the house was only big enough for so many of them, that a choice had been made.

It was a matter of time, then. Only a small time. Stella grew thinner by the day, it seemed. She became sad and withdrawn, and drawn up. Just weeks later, she was gone. I got the word before work, as I got out of the shower. I got it from Alecia, with her typical gentility.

"Hey, John. I think your damn newt's dead."

"She's not a newt!"

Marriage can be hard.

It was only a few months after Stella's death that we learned the side effects of failing to follow the instructions on prescription drugs. If you don't take your birth control pills every day, as prescribed, and as written in large and small print across the prescription itself, the side effects can be life-changing. They can result, for instance, in a brand-new person.

I was scared to death when I heard the news that we were going to have a child. I blamed Alecia and Big Pharma and the whole wide world. We had talked about it—out loud, even—and had come to the mutual decision to wait to have children until we were thirty, until we were financially stable, until we were established in our jobs, until we knew what the hell we were doing, which could take a long, long time. All I could think of was Stella.

"How are we gonna do this?" I finally shouted. "We can't even keep a newt alive."

Drew arrived by C-Section in December 1988. He came with a shock of hair so blond it looked white, with lungs like a locomotive and a will to match. The nurse took his vital signs, washed him and handed him to me quick, like a hot potato, and I forgot all about that effing newt. The world changed in that moment, along with every hope and dream and expectation in it. The world was bigger than me, and bigger than me and Alecia, and for the first time in life I began looking out, and not just in. Looking out, for Drew. Looking out, a little later, for Ramsey and for Mamie. Looking out, and learning more about myself than I ever thought I could know. And about family.

Dad baptized Drew—as he did all the children—when Drew was old enough to travel to First United Methodist Church of Huntsville, where Dad served at the time. We wrapped him in white—a white suit and white shoes and socks and a white newsboy cap that Alecia described only as "adorable"—and drove from Birmingham to Huntsville, where the sign outside the church told the title of Dad's sermon that morning: A CONVERSATION WITH DREW.

Drew wailed as we took him to the chancel rail, as he did for most of his first months on earth. He cried louder and louder until his grandfather picked him up and placed him gently on his shoulder, walking back and forth, as he had done after we brought Drew home from the hospital. Dad sprinkled holy water over Drew's

head and made Alecia and me promise to raise him right, and the
congregation oohed and ahhed and agreed to help us do it. Then
Dad prayed: "You set in the clouds a rainbow of promise. We are
thanking you, oh God, for the Technicolor hues of life as seen
through your rainbow."

Then he gave his sermon, his first real conversation with his first
grandson, though Drew slept through that sermon, like I had as a
teenager:

Drew, we were so happy when you were born. Daddy brought
you to the hall in the hospital with his strong arms. He was so
proud of you. And I'm so proud of both of you.

You were in the room cradled in your mother's arms, and with
indescribable joy she held you close. And so on this baptismal
day there are some things I would like to say to you and to all
babies.

When you lie there in bed and play with your toes, you may
not have learned the words as yet, but you are exploring your
own little world and asking who am I, and that's a basic theological question.

I'd like to work with you on an answer to that question. I
would like you to know first of all that you are loved.

He quoted scripture from Paul's letter to the Ephesians, and
talked of the love of God and family and how, as someone who
is loved, Drew would be a person equipped and capable of loving
others in return:

I'm well aware that a lot of children come into this world and
they feel they are not loved. Feeling that they are not loved, they
don't really know how to give love in return. Thus they are suspi-

Dad preached a sermon to his first grandson from the pulpit of First United Methodist Church in Huntsville, Alabama, in early 1989.

cious. They are fearful. They're distrustful of people and of life and as such, they have difficulty growing to spiritual and emotional maturity.

You may have moments when you don't feel loved yourself. But know that you are.

He talked about family, and belonging, and what it meant inside and outside the church. He talked of the privileges, and the expectations:

I would also remind you, son, that you have the responsibility to protect the good name of the family. You have a responsibility to live your life above reproach, to live your life above question, to live your life to honor your heavenly Father.

He told Drew that life itself was sacramental, and quoted the theologian Frederick Buechner to explain what that meant. A sacrament, Buechner said, was when something holy happened. "It is transparent time. Time you see through to something deep inside time. When you were born something holy happened." Dad went on:

> And here today your parents bring you to the altar of the church and they renew their own faith and promise to teach you the faith. There is something holy about that as well.
>
> And when you go to school you'll find yourself gazing in wonder at some brand-new found truth bursting upon your mind and you may pause in that moment of wonder and recognize something sacramental about discovery. . . .
>
> And when you select your life's vocation, and you give of your energy and your ability and your training for the betterment of humanity, know that your work is holy.
>
> And when you stand at the altar of the church and say your marriage vows and pledge your love and your faith to your life's mate until death do you part, be aware of the sacredness of that vow.
>
> And when maybe in a moment of anger in your life, you say something or do something that hurts another person and then you recognize that hurt and in true penitence go to that person and say, "I'm sorry," know that that is a holy moment as well.
>
> When you reach old age and learn the serenity of maturity, that's a sacrament.
>
> And when you contemplate your own mortality and stand on the threshold of death, that too is a sacrament.

All that is holy. It is. Truth and penitence and forgiveness and the betterment of humanity and stopping, if only for a moment, to recognize the wonder and the purity of all those things. They are sacramental. In the moment they brought tears to my eyes, but now I would wish for more.

I would wish for an addendum to "A Conversation with Drew" (or with Ramsey, or Mamie). Because there is more to say, and more than is typically said by those with the loudest pulpits. This is what I want them to hear:

Drew, do not ever use the glory of a God as an excuse to ignore the needs of humanity or justify the marginalization of others. It is evil.

Ramsey, when you lack the strength or the words to speak for yourself, speak for someone who has no voice. That's where you find strength.

Mamie, don't look sorrowfully at yourself when you lack the courage to stand or speak out or fight. Look at those who have been oppressed, and they will give you will.

All of you, it is not enough to remember who you are. Because who you are has nothing to do with who your parents might have been, or where you were born, or how much money you have, or what has been passed down to you. You decide who you are every single day, with everything you choose to do and say, and everything you don't. Only you. You are the Technicolor hues of life. You are the Technicolor yous, and your job is to shine. That's sacramental.

20

Stand, Please

There are lonely persons who stand on the outside, or across the tracks, or somewhere in the shadows of life. They are not like us. They are different. They perhaps are not hated. Just ignored, and left alone. . . . Many of our people are crying for equal rights and opportunities. And many others are continuing to deny them. This breeds hatred and ill will and distrust.

—REV. ROBERT L. ARCHIBALD JR., February 9, 1969

By 1988 the United Methodist Church was taking on gay and lesbian issues the same way the Methodist Church had taken on race in the decades before its overdue integration: badly, with one glance at the Bible and another—a long, worried gaze—at falling attendance rolls and church budgets.

The issue was argued passionately behind the scenes, and in manifestos put together by factions as sure of their spiritual superiority as they were in their faith. Conservative elements argued that things should stay as they always were, and defaulted to the words of Saint Paul, or the damning verses of Leviticus, to justify their contempt for those crazy gays.

More liberal Methodists defaulted to the words of Jesus: *Love your neighbor.*

Back home nobody said much of anything from the pulpit, and in the same way you could read Dad's sermons from 1960s Alabama and fail to find evidence of a civil rights movement, you can hear his sermons from the 1980s and miss many of the steps toward gay and lesbian rights. Perhaps it's in there, in places, in allegory and sweeping language about compassion. Perhaps it is there in a sermon from September 1988 called "God's Love Story," in which Dad told of serving on a district committee responsible for granting prospective ministers their license to preach.

Dad told how a man came before the committee and was asked, as all candidates are, why he wanted to become a Methodist minister. The guy said he had struggled with the question, with the Calling, for years, but had finally settled it the old-fashioned way, by opening the Holy Bible and reading the first verses he found, like tea leaves. He closed his eyes and the book fell open and he circled his finger over the page and . . . *there.*

It was smack dab on an Old Testament list of the kings of Israel, and he could not figure out what God was telling him to do. So he closed his eyes one more time, tightly, turned his Bible around in his hands and let it fall open on its own. Around and around his finger whirled again, and down to a verse about rebuilding Jerusalem. The man couldn't find his answer there, either, he told the committee.

So with some desperation he said a little prayer and let the pages fall open one more time to the book of Matthew. Eyes still closed, he pointed, his future in the balance, to a verse that read: "But go rather to the lost sheep of the house of Israel. And as ye go, preach, saying, The kingdom of heaven is at hand."

That was all the message he needed. His prayers had been answered and his future decided. Ask and He shall answer, and all that. The Lord spoke to him and was decisive. God himself called, and told this fellow to preach.

But that was not Dad's message. The message from his pulpit was this:

> I don't think this is the way to read the Bible. This young man must have had God to un-call him because in less than two years he had surrendered his license to preach. The Bible is not a magic book to give instant answers.

It's not a crystal ball any more than it's a book of Mad Libs to pick and choose ways to ostracize people. It's a love story, Dad said, that tells how it should be, how it could be, if people choose to listen. He told of the prodigal son—again. And the Good Samaritan—again. He pointed out how Jesus told that story after a lawyer questioned just who this neighbor was that he was supposed to love as himself. Dad defaulted to love, and expected people to interpret that in their hearts. So change came slowly, if at all.

He wasn't just a spiritual guide, of course. He was an employee, with a house and a salary and a wife and family and pension and a company line. No matter what he thought or learned or how he had evolved, he worked for the church. And the Methodists had been on a seesaw since 1972, when a progressive committee recommended to the General Conference that the church add language to its "Social Principles" that recognized the worth of gay people. But that went horribly awry.

The proposed language in 1972 said:

> Homosexuals no less than heterosexuals are persons of sacred worth, who need the ministry and guidance of the church in

their struggles for human fulfillment, as well as the spiritual and emotional care of a fellowship which enables reconciling relationships with God, with others and with self.

An accompanying statement insisted "that all persons are entitled to have their human and civil rights ensured."

But of course some delegate from the heartland got up to ask what in the Sam Hill they meant by ensuring the civil rights of homosexuals, and it went downhill from there. That question led to debate, which led to changes, and before you know it, a disclaimer was stuck into the well-meaning phrase to change everything from the church's intent to the meaning of the clause and the consequences, for decades to come:

Although we do not condone the practice of homosexuality and consider this practice incompatible with Christian teaching, we affirm that God's grace is available to all. We commit ourselves to be in ministry for and with all persons.

So the final version read like this, and rather than express the view that all people were loved, it wound up saying, *Fuck You.* This was the message that went out like Paul's letters to Methodist churches across the world:

Homosexuals no less than heterosexuals are persons of sacred worth, who need the ministry and guidance of the church in their struggles for human fulfillment, as well as the spiritual and emotional care of a fellowship which enables reconciling relationships with God, with others, and with self. Further we insist that all persons are entitled to have their human and civil rights ensured, although we do not condone the practice of homosexuality and consider this practice incompatible with Christian teaching.

Love your neighbors. But know they don't belong.

And that was all it took for the silence, outside the vocal few, to remain. For those in the church looking for a reason to condemn, it was as handy as an embroidered scarlet letter. For those who believed all that guff about loving and leaving it to the heavens to judge, it was a reminder of how the Bible had been used in the South to condone slavery, and segregation.

There was nothing remotely new about it. Racists for centuries had pointed to some convoluted story about how Noah got drunk and cursed his kid Ham and all his descendants to lifetimes of servitude (and here I thought Great-Great-Great-Grandfather Thomas was a douche), and how, over centuries, white people dyed Ham's progeny Black to manufacture biblical authority to buy and sell and own dark-skinned slaves. It was a reminder of how the Methodist Church cloaked itself in caution and passed by on the other side of the street, that it took the secular world to step in as the unlikely Samaritan.

It was a reminder of how preachers—even those like Dad, who believed the vision of his God would one day be realized in love—could not find words to shake the status quo of segregation, to shake the gates of hell.

The world was moving forward. And the church was pulling back. In the Orwellian year of 1984, the United Methodist Church made it even clearer, with a statement of "fidelity in marriage and celibacy in singleness." It said:

Since the practice of homosexuality is incompatible with Christian teaching, self-avowed practicing homosexuals are not to be accepted as candidates, ordained as ministers, or appointed to serve in The United Methodist Church.

As the debate played out, Dad preached his parables about neighbors and love, and in a sermon in late 1983 called "Prayer for Christian Unity," he spoke of the need to take risks:

> We must have such a warm, open, loving, caring spirit about us that people will be drawn to us and to Christ. This means that we must be willing to risk something for the sake of this caring, loving sense of oneness in Christ. Actually, a fundamental necessity for the success of most anything is the willingness to risk. Marriage is an example of this. For real love always knows that sacrifice and risk are demanded.
>
> When was the last time you really risked something for the sake of Christ and His Church? Looking back over my own life, I find that I've had it pretty good. I haven't really risked very much. I've played it pretty safe. Most of us are that way. We go along as long as it doesn't cost too much or as long as the risk is not very high.

I never heard him speak that way, about risk, or safety. Or the consequences of it. That kind of reflection, public or not, was rare. But as the church was involved in questions of right and wrong, Dad wrestled with himself, too. He loved his family and he loved Methodism, so he stuck to the things he knew.

In 1988, the United Methodist Church set up a four-year committee to study the issue of homosexuality "for theological and ethical analysis," and to "seek the best biological, psychological and sociological information and opinion on the nature of homosexuality."

Not that the church would knowingly let any actual gay people on the committee. Only heterosexuals were allowed. One of them was Kevin Higgs, a young preacher from Alabama. He was appointed to the committee, and when it voted on a proposed course of action to present to the General Conference in 1992, Higgs voted with the majority: for full inclusion of gay and lesbian members.

The committee largely agreed that the seven biblical references to homosexuality reflected the ancient world more than God, and the scientists assured its members that homosexuality is a "normal sexual variant." Psychologists and sociologists told them committed gay relationships could be healthy, and theologians told them you could see God's grace—the magic word in Methodism—in the lives of gay and lesbian church members.

So the majority of the committee recommended moving toward a more open and inclusive future. It came to this conclusion:

> The present state of knowledge and insight in the biblical, theological, ethical, biological, psychological, and sociological fields does not provide a satisfactory basis upon which the church can responsibly maintain the condemnation of all homosexual practice.

The committee also urged the denomination to express support for gay and lesbian members, and called for acts of simple justice to protect the rights of same-sex relationships.

But after four years of work, the committee was ignored by the larger church, which needed little prodding to do nothing at all. The General Conference took action only to receive the report, to acknowledge it existed. It did not approve it. So by virtue of the church's inertia, the minority view remained the social law for all United Methodists. Again.

In the early 1990s, the Reverend Kevin Higgs served on a United Methodist Church committee and voted for full inclusion of gay and lesbian people in the church. After that, he came home to retaliation from a senior pastor he said wanted him fired.

That was that. Except it wasn't. For back home in Alabama, Higgs served as associate pastor at Athens First United Methodist Church, near Decatur. Higgs paid a price for the risk he didn't even realize he had taken. He wrote of it later in a public internet posting.

I voted with the majority (21–6) of the Committee for full inclusion of Gay and Lesbian People into the United Methodist Church. After this, I was attacked by the Senior Pastor at Athens 1st UMC, who wanted to remove me from my employment at Athens 1st UMC because of my vote on the Committee. John's father, Rev. Bob Archibald was my District Superintendent. I called him and let him know what was happening to me. Bob immediately called the Senior Pastor and instructed him to immediately stop his spiritual violence against me. Bob called me to his office, congratulated me on faithfully serving the church, and instructed me to let him know if anyone harassed me related to my service on this committee.

Higgs practically begged me to see. "John, your father was one of the best men I ever knew," he said.

I know. I know. But is it enough to be a good man? A good person? Are there not times when you must say more and do more? Are there not moments in history when you must take your fist or your head and pound on your podium, on your pulpit?

Dad did begin to speak and preach about AIDS by the late eighties and early nineties, to urge his congregation to have empathy and compassion. It was clear I was not the only one who feared a call from Murray, who mourned with every friend he lost and funeral he was bound to attend.

When young AIDS activist Ryan White died in 1990, after years of pushing for respect and humanity and the simple right to go back to school, Dad preached of him on Easter Sunday morning.

> Last Sunday our nation was saddened by the announcement that Ryan White had died. Ryan White in 1984 at the age 13 got AIDS from a blood transfusion. He fought a valiant battle, not only against the disease, but also against the ignorance and fear of students and their families. In so doing, he attracted the admiration of the nation and won a new understanding of this disease.

Ryan White did for Dad what he did for the rest of America. It is why we remember him, why he was important not only to changing perceptions but to building momentum for research, and funding, and decency. Ryan White took the risk out of being compassionate to AIDS patients. Ryan White opened America's eyes to something it did not want to acknowledge.

Perhaps Dad's eyes were open more than I was able to see. It would be years before my mother told me the story of the moment Dad confronted his own discomfort and faced his own fear of risk.

It was at that 1992 General Conference in Louisville, Kentucky, she thought. She knew how he loathed mixing politics with religion, how he preferred to let Jesus speak for Christendom. But the way she told it, Dad stood up at conference, in front of all the Methodist preachers and laypeople who were quoting the Bible to condemn gays and lesbians and his own son, and he found words to argue for their inclusion.

"It is not a choice," he said. "And it is not a choice for us, either. Jesus said to love. And love is unconditional."

I don't know the rest. Truth is I don't even know if those are the exact words he said. I don't know that it matters. What really matters to me is that Dad stood, in the place he was the most uncomfortable, and challenged the church to which he had so long deferred. He took a public stand, a political stand, a controversial stand. He practiced what he preached and what he dared not voice from his pulpit.

He took a risk, and in the family, anyway, it is remembered more than anything he said in decades of sermons.

Not the words, perhaps. The words themselves are secondary. What was important was the fact that he said them.

He and his contingent, those who would offer love instead of judgment, were voted down, or ignored, or dismissed, and his words had no impact on a vote, and made no difference in the broader world. In fact, the slide toward Methodist exclusion continued, and at the next General Conference, in 1996, the body would poke its finger in the eye of progressives again, making it clear that Methodist preachers could not officiate at same-sex unions, and those ceremonies—they wouldn't deign to call them "marriages"—could not be held in Methodist churches.

Dad would never talk about such things, but he too felt some blowback when he got back to Alabama in 1992, the way Mother

Dad was never happier than when joining a couple in holy matrimony, as long as they completed his required premarital counseling.

told it. Oh, he got some quiet support. In time, he would get calls from members all over north Alabama, wondering if Dad might counsel them on how to deal with the sexuality of their sons, their daughters and sometimes even themselves. And he did. He told them to love.

But he got letters and calls of another kind, too, ugly threats and uglier promises. One preacher told him to his face he was disappointed, that he'd known the Archibald family for generations and had respect for all of them.

"Not anymore," the man said. "Not anymore."

Dad learned something else when he alienated people like that: He found that it didn't bother him. It didn't bother him at all.

21

The Great Moccasin Massacre of 1998

Our society is filled with violence. You've heard the expression "Don't get mad, get even." Revenge is sweet. If someone hits you with a stick, you hit back with a bigger stick. An eye for an eye and a tooth for a tooth. Abuse for abuse. That's the way of the world . . . and violence does not make for better people.

—REV. ROBERT L. ARCHIBALD JR., April 25, 1999

I wanted to be a responsible man. So on the rare occasion it snowed enough to cover the streets of Birmingham, I did not do as my father had done. I did not tie sleds to the back of my Subaru and pull my children, screaming and praying for life, up the steep foot-hills of Ruffner Mountain.

I stood at the top of a daunting hill above a five-way stop sign and put a helmet on six-year-old Drew's head. I set him atop a sled he had never seen and prepared to push. He looked down at the bottom of the hill, like the Grinch staring down at Whoville beneath, and shook his head silently.

"Do it!" I said, and gave him a little shove.

I wanted to be a responsible man. So I told three-year-old Ramsey he would have to wait what turned out to be years for the next snow. When Drew gathered speed and crashed headlong into a boulder on the side of the road about two-thirds of the way down Lance Road, I did not drag Ramsey with me as I ran, falling and slipping and sliding, to see if my oldest was okay. I left Ramsey at the top of the hill. In the snow. I was, after all, coming right back.

I finally reached Drew. He'd hit the rock headfirst but was thrown over the top into a bush a few yards away. He was dazed but mostly unhurt, except for a few scrapes and welts and a look of shocked betrayal.

"I think you'll live," I said. "Better walk it off. Go ahead, do it."

When Mamie got to be a little older, I wanted her to know the thrill of sliding, too. But I thought myself a responsible man, so I did not let the Slip 'N Slide lead down our steep front lawn and into the street, where cars passed from time to time. Instead I pulled the Subaru to the curb. Like a backstop.

I didn't have to say, "Do it!" She did it on her own, pushing off with glee in her eyes and a grin on her face. It was worth it in that moment. She had the most fun she'd ever known in her life, for approximately 1.2 seconds, until it all ended as suddenly as it had begun, in the side front-quarter panel of a Subaru Impreza.

I tumbled down the hill to see if she was okay. She'd smashed a dent right into it, and vice versa. Her forehead was red and already swelling.

"Looks like I'm gonna, um, have to cut it off," I began. And when she just looked at me, "Shake it off, now. Shake it off. Before Mother sees us!"

I always wanted to be a responsible man, for Pete's sake. It just didn't always work out.

We went as a family to Camp Glisson in 1998, when Drew was nine, Ramsey six and Mamie four. Even then it was a place as constant for them as it had been for me, a wonderland where the roar of the waterfall tucks you in bed at night and the creek beside the cabin glitters with flecks of mica. It clings to your body when you wade into the creek, or swim—now illegally—under the Cane Creek Falls. When wet and sandy children ran into the cabin, they left tiny footprints that sparkled when they dried.

I always thought the camp was named for that glisten. It was not. It was named for the Reverend Fred Glisson, a contemporary of Grandfather Holland who found the falls—they were generating power at the time—and thought them a fine place for a camp. The name is as perfect as the place.

Drew ran freely through the camp with an abandon he rarely felt elsewhere, and Ramsey marveled at the birds and the fish and the snakes—we counted fifty one year, all harmless little northern water snakes that sunned on the rocks in the creek and at first glance gave the heart a little jolt. Mamie always loved the cabin, perhaps more than any of the others. She fished for trout stubbornly below the falls, fishing longer, catching more and bigger fish than her brothers, who soon abandoned their rods and ran to find crawfish beneath the glimmering rocks. Even as a child, she fished her fill, carefully letting all the rainbow trout and little bass go before she leapt into the water below the NO SWIMMING sign. They thought the place was theirs, like I thought it was mine, and she'd beg me to follow.

Come on, Daddy! Do it! Don't be a baby.

I wanted to be a responsible man. But I followed. Easing into the cold water that made the last step a doozie.

The first time I saw the snake, he was coiled on the creek bank under the walking bridge below the falls, where the children turned over rocks to find crawfish, where campers waded on creek hikes every summer day. He was as big around as my wrist, I was certain. He was almost Black, far bigger and far darker than the harmless snakes we'd counted on seeing. He disappeared quickly, so I could not be sure, but he seemed to have the pointed head of a viper. I was sure he was a water moccasin, a cottonmouth, as we call them in the South. Almost sure.

I'd seen enough snakes to know. I'd seen Dad catch the good ones and kill the scary ones, and I had done the same. I knew when to be alarmed, and when to simply be interested. On this day I was bothered. I waited nearby as quietly as I could, but the snake never resurfaced. The silence was broken by the sound of my three children wading up the creek toward that spot where the snake had been. They'd come to play beneath the falls, to maybe even sneak a forbidden swim to the hidden ledge you could find behind the falling water—if you knew the secret.

"C'mon, Daddy, we have to swim," Mamie said. "Don't be a baby."

She thought I was just being me, that I needed prodding and cajoling and berating before finally stepping waist deep into the icy water. I didn't want to tell her I'd seen a venomous snake the size of my bicep coiled in the waters she'd just walked through. They were waters that, to her, until that point, were the safest on earth.

"I—I just don't feel good," I said. "We can wade a little, but no swimming today."

I lay awake that night, haunted by the snake. He must have been the size of my calf. I do not often dream vividly, but with the sound of the creek rushing in my ears, snakes slithered through my dreams, hissing and tormenting me and threatening my children.

So the next morning I grabbed a hickory staff and raced with the sun back to the falls. I looked on the creek bank where I had seen him, but found nothing but a few egg-size rocks that had not been there before. Nothing.

This went on for most of a week, nights tormented by dream

snakes, followed by frustrating days and excuses to swim as little as possible. We could go into town and mine for gold, or to lunch at the Wagon Wheel, the nearby meat and three—as we also say in the South—for fried chicken and collards and corn and maybe some fried green tomatoes like I'd once tried to pass off as meat to Ramsey, who did not as a child enjoy his vegetables. Ramsey was outraged at that deception. He will tell you that was one of my worst moments in parenting. Until the week of the snake.

Mamie, more than anyone, wanted to go to the falls. It was Camp Glisson, after all. Why would you do anything else?

So I looked for the snake almost every morning that week, armed with my Swiss Army knife and the walking stick Dad had carved into the shape of a snake. All I found were more rocks. Apple-sized. I was almost ready to give up. What did it matter, anyway? We would leave for home in a couple of days. I was beginning to wonder if I'd blown the whole thing out of proportion, if I had misidentified the creature and exaggerated his size in some kind of protective hysteria.

Until, on the day before we were to leave, I saw him again, under the bridge by the opposite bank on the water's edge. Surely he really was as big around as my knee, and he stood upright, if a snake can stand, like a mesmerized cobra or a rattlesnake ready to strike. His head was cocked at an odd angle, and his tongue flicked relentlessly. I thought he was sensing me, challenging me, toying with me. I held the staff firm, scooted across the bridge and crept down the grassy bank. He was definitely a water moccasin, with wide jaws and white gums and a look in the eye that would shake a saint. There really was something odd about the head, though, the way it poked up but tilted at a strange angle.

I had no plan. Just a stick and a tenuous foothold and a few days without sleep. I never really expected the snake to stay and fight, anyway. I figured he would disappear like—like a snake, and I'd be lucky to get a swing of the staff. But he did stay to fight. He turned to face me, his black eyes blank and cold and that tongue going a hundred flicks a minute. He was prepared to defend himself. And I finally saw why.

It was clear that I was not the only one tormented by the sight of the snake. Now I got it. Now all those mysterious rocks made sense. Sherlock Holmes would have figured it out on the spot, for a gash was visible across the back of the snake's head. He'd been hit with a stone. I was, alas, no Sherlock Holmes, but I finally put it together, and took it to be a mortal wound. He was alive, and fighting, but with little choice but to take a defensive posture. Circumstances, it seemed, had made my decision for me.

After all those sleepless nights, after all that fear and rage and obsession, I stood before that wild animal and told myself I must do the humane thing. I must put him out of his misery. I held the hickory stick like a baseball bat, and swung it like Hank Aaron. I felt the impact, but only as the follow-through pitched me out of balance and I tumbled off the bank and into the water. I scrambled upright, sure the serpent would pounce, but he was already in the throes of death. I hit him once, or twice, or three times more, to be safe. And he was gone.

I stared down, wet and proud and pumping with adrenaline. I was the hunter and he was the vanquished. He had tormented me in my dreams, and I had returned the favor in the light of day. I forgot all about that "putting him out of his misery" thing. I picked him up, on the end of my hickory stick, only to notice for the first time that there, on the other side of the creek, stood my three children, dead still and gaping.

"He's a water moccasin," I said. It was clear, now. "I got him."

He really was as big around as my wrist, in places, and as I held him, I got the greatest of dad ideas, the greatest of all ideas. Like I said: I wanted to be a responsible man.

So I yelled, "Come on!" and took off down the path along the far side of the creek, with the surprisingly heavy snake dangling from the walking stick. The children ran behind, unsure what to expect.

"Alecia!" I yelled along the way. "Alecia!"

When we arrived at the cabin—a couple hundred yards downstream from the falls—Alecia stood on the screened front porch with her hands on her hips.

"Are the children okay? Where are they? What did you do?"

"They're there."

"Oh—what the hell is that?"

"It's a water moccasin!" I said proudly. "I killed him."

I did not say—yet—that my victim was mortally wounded when I found him. Just "I killed him."

The children had caught up by now. They stood at a distance, staring.

"Why?" Ramsey asked.

"Why what?"

"Why did you kill him?"

The answer, of course, was that I had to. I had no choice. I had to protect my family, to do the difficult things, to—oh, who am I kidding? I had to sleep nights.

"Well, he was poisonous," I said. But they already knew enough to know that.

"He was already wounded," I began again. "I really just put him out of his misery."

This was true, to a point, and sounded far more reasonable. It was tough, since I had led with the whole hunter/bravery thing, but I had begun to warm to the mercy idea by the time Alecia spoke up again.

"But why did you bring him here?"

I knew the answer. It was because I wanted her to think me a great hunter and protector, able to shield my family from great venomous serpents the circumference of my thigh.

But instead I said something that seemed like a good, reasonable, responsible thing. I said:

"We're going to skin him."

"What?"

"We're going to skin him."

"Why?" Drew asked. "And who is we?"

I ignored the second question.

"Look how fat he is in the belly," I said. "I bet there's a rat or something in there. A fish, maybe. I bet we can get it out!"

This time it was Mamie's turn.

"Why?" And then there was Drew again.

"You keep saying we—"

I cut him off.

"It will be a learning experience," I said. And it turns out I was right.

I had skinned snakes before, like most Southern boys of my generation. A couple of copperheads when I was young, gutted, skinned and nailed to dry on a wooden plank. I grabbed my kill and my Swiss Army knife and stuck the blade in, hoping a rat or a chipmunk would tumble, partially digested, out onto the ground.

That would make a memory, all right.

But instead of the snake's breakfast, something else tumbled out. He was not all that well fed, my snake. In fact, he was not a he at all. He was a she, pregnant and ready to pop. A small snake, fully formed and already breaking through a clear reptilian placenta, squirted out. It was maybe four inches long, and it squirmed on the ground.

Alecia, believe it or not, was actually impressed.

"How did you know where to cut it?" she asked.

I glanced up.

"I know a lot of things you don't think I know," I said.

But it wouldn't have mattered where I stuck the knife, because the baby snakes just kept coming. Another came, and another. I didn't know what to do with them, but I didn't seem to have a choice. Something inside me took over. It was like the snakes twisting and slithering through my nightmares. I took my little knife and sliced their heads clean off.

"Oh, my God," Drew said. "Do you have to kill them all?"

But still the snakes came, in clear casing connected like squirming sausages. There were ten, eleven, twelve of them, now. I was in a fever, squeezing out snakes and executing them, one by one with the tiny guillotine of my pocketknife.

Drew had joined Alecia on the porch, where they peered through the screen windows while describing for me in painful detail why this was a *terrible* idea. But Ramsey and Mamie were next to me, staring from a few yards away. Baby water moccasins, I had been told all my life, were filled with venom like their parents, but were unable to control it and could be far more deadly.

"Stay back," I said, using that old wives' tale to justify the cold bloodshed. But it wasn't necessary for Drew or Alecia. They turned away from the carnage. Ramsey stood rooted to his spot, and Mamie stared in fascination and horror, unable to look away as she inched forward. She was, if I have failed to mention it, just four years old.

And still the snakes came. Fifteen, sixteen, seventeen. I held the mother above my head with my right hand, wrapping the fingers of my left around her like a clamp. I squeezed and pulled, as if milking a cow, as if wringing the remains from a giant, still-wriggling toothpaste tube, and snake fetuses piled in a heap on the ground. These were slightly less developed than the first ones, less active and encased more completely in film. They formed a moving, writhing pile at my feet. I was completely lost to bloodlust, rending, slashing, chopping, in a preternatural desire to kill the serpent.

I don't know. Blame Eve. She gets blamed for everything else. But I chopped and chopped. If I saw movement, I jabbed with my blade. I counted thirty-two before I looked up from the slaughter, and saw Alecia's back. She was out by the bushes now, bent over and heaving. Ramsey stood still, stunned. But Mamie had come closer. She knelt, just out of spatter range, and poked at the squirming mass with a stick. She was hypnotized by the carnage.

"Oh, my God," Drew said again, and he, too, began to gag. He ran to join his mother, and there they bent, vomiting together, as a family.

Snake blood was everywhere. And placenta. And unidentifiable ooze. I needed to dispose of the bodies, of the evidence, so I picked each one up with the tip of my knife, just as I had held its mother with the stick, and dropped it in a plastic grocery bag. I scooped up the heads and dropped them in, too. I triple-wrapped the bags, tied the tops tight and dug a grave deep in the Dumpster.

I walked back to the cabin more afraid than I had been when I had approached the snake originally. What had I done? What if the kids were scarred for life, afraid of snakes or creeks or, or camp, of all places? What if they refused to leave the house, or go off to school? What if I had stunted their development so severely that we'd be forced to grow old together, a family of fearful old cat people locked away in the safety of our home? Or worse, yet. What if they had liked it? What if I had created three little monsters?

What had I done?

I had no words as I walked into the cabin. I didn't really need them, for Alecia met me at the door. She is soft, you know. Soft and sweet like the summer rain. She reached up and whispered softly in my ear, so only I could hear:

"What the fuck was that?"

But Ramsey was there, too. I wondered what to say to him. I wondered how to ask him if he was all right.

"Wow," he said, seemingly pausing to contemplate the Great Moccasin Massacre of 1998. "Can we go eat dinner at the Wagon Wheel?"

"Sure, son. Sure."

Like I said, I always wanted to be a responsible man.

"You know what this means?" Alecia said on the way home. "There's a daddy snake still out there. And he's really pissed off."

22

Cry Amen

Let us be content and happy with what we have. And thank God. But we must never be content with what we are.

—REV. ROBERT L. ARCHIBALD JR., September 14, 1997

Dad could never be still. Not fully, not totally. There was always something left undone, unseen, undiscovered. He was like his river, placid on the surface, until it stormed, but ever-moving at its depths. There was always something to do, a person to visit or a service to attend, even when he was on vacation. There was a garden that required tending or a job that wouldn't be done unless he did it. It was in retirement that he tried to do it all. So it was in his retirement, I think, that he was as close as he'd ever get to contentment.

He and Mother bought their dream home on a large lot in Decatur that butted up next to a farmer's field, which made the front yard seem like the suburbs and the back a pastoral retreat. He volunteered at the wildlife refuge and offered himself up to serve part-time at a tiny little church just down the highway in Falkville. He updated old sermons and delivered them with an ease and joy he hadn't found in years, without the pressure of a large, expectant congregation or the managerial stress that came with being a district boss. He loved those people at Falkville, and they made him feel loved, too. He told them stories of his children and grandchildren and talked comfortably of kindness, and fulfillment, and the perils of prejudice and judgment. At least in a generic way. He preached of love a lot, and grace to the third power. And damnation not at all. He told stories of fishing with Drew, and found sermon illustrations in the chaos of the entire Archibald clan. In February 2000, Dad told this story about Mark and Sally's son Samuel:

> Back during the Christmas holidays, our children and grand-children were with us. One afternoon Murray and Mark put the children in the van and carried them on an outing to Adventure Land at Wilson Morgan Park. As they rode, the children were playing a game. One would announce, "I'm invisible," and others would play like they couldn't see, and would ignore him. He would say, "I'm visible," and the others would speak to him. Samuel is 3 years old. And he was playing too. He had said, "I'm invisible," and the others began to ignore him. Then he said, "I'm visible." But by that time the others were talking with each other. Twice more Samuel said, "I'm visible," but was still ignored. Then he shouted, "I'm visible." A lot of people travel on the Beltline [the highway around town], and we are unaware of the invisible people who are hurting for attention.

Dad visited church members when they were ill, and prayed with them, sick or well, but there were not so many of them that it took all his time. He married them when the few young people found true love—but only after extensive counseling, as was his way—and he buried them when their end came. But that was blessedly intermittent, and rarely premature. He was joyful, for he could finally do all the things that had been brushed aside by a life more full of responsibility than time.

Until the morning he felt a strange knot in his chest, between his nipple and his armpit. Until that moment when hours and days took on a brand-new definition. It all changed when Dad learned he had breast cancer. At the time, he didn't know men could get breast cancer. It was hard, for a guy who had rarely been sick a day in his life, who knew people at every hospital in north Alabama but hadn't been a patient since he was twelve, since his mom and dad told him he was going in to have his tonsils out, but woke him up circumcised.

"I think you missed," he claimed he said, but at least he didn't have a sore throat.

Dad endured his surgery for the cancer, and his treatment, and learned what it was like to wait on the inside of a doctor's office. He knew he ought to retire for real, then. It was time. Mother was not well—she suffered from polymyositis, an autoimmune disease that caused pain and weakness, and was prone to frequent migraines. So he left Falkville in the spring of 2000, with a sadness that comes from leaving a job that forms the identity of your whole life. The congregation poured love on him as he retired.

Church member Polly Holmes gave him this advice: "Truly take time to pick daisies and enjoy being with Mary and doing things you haven't had a chance to do."

He tried to do it all. He continued to volunteer at the Wheeler National Wildlife Refuge, and he considered that a ministry, too. He took an ecology class at the local community college. He wrote papers on the threat of climate change and spoke for what seemed like days about humanity's duty to be good stewards of the Earth. He grew tomatoes and peppers and okra out back behind the mulch pile and the peach trees, next to the farmer's field, where the grandchildren sought their own refuge on family visits. He learned to make stockpiles of cranberry-strawberry jam for Christmas, and fig preserves from the trees that thrived in his own private Eden.

Dad identified a wide range of trees at Camp Glisson, then came home to make little placards with their common and scientific names:

COMMON NAME: CAROLINA SILVERBELL
SCIENTIFIC NAME: *HALESIA CAROLINA*

He mounted them on two-by-four posts and planted them next to their matches at camp, so children and adults alike would know from whence they drew their shade. He traveled to watch his grandchildren swim or play soccer, and went so far as to learn the rules. Almost.

Dad had once preached that contentment is not some kind of societal status quo that leaves half the world hungry and the other half on a diet. Contentment comes from purpose and the effort to do all you can to understand, and empathize, and help. If that is contentment, Dad had reached a new level.

He had always loved Christmas, but never more than in these years. At the first sign of autumn, Dad began to make lists of Christmas gifts for his children and grandchildren, for neighbors and preachers and the paperboy—as he still called the middle-aged woman who delivered his news in a pickup truck. There were board games for the Drews—both Mark and I have children named Drew, though only one is an Andrew, and neither is Andy Archibald— and soccer balls for Mamie and the others. There was perfume for

Alecia—Tuscany Per Donna every year—and jewelry for Mother and Mary Beth. He thought about a fruitcake for the "paperboy" but I encouraged him to just write her a check, and there was always mail-order fruit for his sister and cards for the neighbors. He listed whatever popped into his head or was suggested for the rest of us, and spent the next months looking for it all, marking gifts off his notepad at the local hobby store or his favorite jeweler downtown.

Dad loved Christmas, theologically and otherwise. He loved it most because he knew his family would come to him, that he could say, "Come as early as you can and stay as long as you can," and they would appear, like ballplayers amid the corn in his field of Christmas dreams. He didn't even have to say that, though he liked to, because all of his children made plans to come long before he even started his list. We arrived, every year, one by one or five by five, people and dogs and presents and stories and surprises. Always surprises. He'd run to the airport or the driveway to meet them, with a big bear hug and long, loud laugh, like he could never really believe they'd all come home again.

He loved Christmas. But mostly he loved that we were all there, the children and the Outlaws and the grandkids and the dogs, all those dogs. He loved it on Sunday mornings when we'd all get dressed up and go to church, and take up more than a pew. He loved it when we stood on command in that sanctuary and sang the hymns of Charles Wesley and Fanny Crosby from childhood memory. He even loved it when Mary Beth and I merely moved our lips and pretended to sing, as long as we smiled doing it.

It was a wonder to me, always, that he was so proud of this bunch. We'd caused so much trouble, at times forgot who we were, and went down dark and embarrassing paths. I used to think he looked at us and saw the progress, the process, that no matter what alleys we entered, we came out in the light in the next block. But that wasn't it. That was never it. He was proud of us because he loved us, in the good times and the bad. That's what love was to Dad, from the pulpit or in a courtroom beside a shameful son. It was permanent, and constant, and without condition.

Dad loved having us together. He especially liked it when his baby girl, Mary Beth, arrived. She was on her way, that day in December 2002, when Dad ran out of the house to check his list one more time. He was going to be gone only a few minutes, to wrap up details he'd never get to after all twenty people set up camp in the house.

He went out the door smiling, whistling "Red River Valley," the song he used to sing to Mother and taught me on the ukulele when I was six.

He left the house laughing, and came home forever changed.

Mother began to fret almost the moment he drove away, which was odd, because Dad left the house every day, to visit or volunteer or wander. But those of us in the family knew enough of Mother's fretting to take it with more than a shake of salt. She'd known when I proposed to Alecia, before we told her, and when I'd been hauled off to jail, before I told anybody but the saint who bailed me out. She'd always known when a child was in trouble, when the world had been especially hard on him or her, or vice versa. When we were children, she left notes under our pillows if she sensed those days. When we were adults, she called, uncannily, when things seemed most dire, to ask what was wrong. She told us she would send "pink clouds" of love and good wishes and positive vibes. Like thoughts and prayers, I suppose. But she worked hard to send those pink clouds, and when she did, her children could invariably look into the morning or evening sky and find them, and believe everything for which they stood.

She was in the kitchen, making a Jell-O mold, as she had done with regularity since the 1950s, since *Southern Living* and *Better Homes & Gardens* had taught her life was better with just about any combination of Jell-O and fruit and nuts. She'd made them all over the years, with cream cheese or fruit cocktail or sour cream and Coca-Cola, if she was feeling adventurous. But she couldn't get it straight this day. The teakettle screamed and there was fussing and banging and . . .

"Oh, heavens!"

"What, Mother? What?"

I ran in to see her standing over a steaming dog bowl she'd just filled up with cherry gelatin—or maybe it was strawberry.

"I just—can't right now," she said, and put the dog bowl in the refrigerator to set. "I'm worried about your father."

I didn't say a word. Perhaps I knew better. Perhaps I knew it was the wrong time.

It was only a little later, I suppose—though it seemed longer—that the garage door opened, and I breathed relief.

"There he is," I told Mother, glad she had overreacted. But she brushed past me to meet him.

In he came, fast, like he had to go to the bathroom. He held his arm down straight with his hand by his crotch, again like he had to go, listing as he walked until he bumped into the hall walls. He said nothing and shot for his bedroom. But instead of going on through to the master bathroom, he lay down on the bed, right leg on top of the covers while the left dangled off the edge.

We should have called an ambulance as soon as his bottom hit the bed, because that simply didn't happen in his afternoons. We should have called as soon as Mother said, "He's having a stroke," and shoved aspirin down his throat.

Dad tried to say, "I'm okay," but it came out in pig Latin, or something like it. He protested all the way as we helped him to the car, as I drove and Mother fretted and Murray patted Dad on the back, and spoke to him of the geese he saw out the window as we passed the refuge, and the doves that puffed up fat on the outside feeders, and the joy of seeing Mary Beth that very afternoon.

Mother was right, of course. Dad had a stroke, a serious one that could have been a whole lot worse without that aspirin, the doctor told Mother. Dad was in intensive care for days, begging for coffee to clear his head, though he'd stopped drinking the stuff around the time Carter was president. He struggled for his words and asked for more coffee when he couldn't find the right ones, and drank it down through a straw without waiting for it to cool.

He asked for Mary Beth almost exactly as she arrived from the airport. She wiped away her tears and hugged him in his bed.

"I love you, Daddy," she said.

He answered in pig Latin again, but we knew what he meant: "I love you, too."

Dad spent days in the hospital and ages in therapy to get his strength and speech back. He was rigorous, as he was with everything, and worked his arms with weights, his legs with elastic bands, and his brain with reams of worksheets, like standardized tests for elementary-school students. He asked his children, all of us, to go with him to church one more time before we returned to our homes across America.

So there we sat, on a Sunday morning after Christmas in the year of our Lord 2002, taking up a whole pew or more at First United Methodist Church in Decatur, where Dad had preached when I was a child, where Mark had hit Skipper Stewart over the head with that hymnal on the front row, where Mother had worshiped in retirement as Dad took over at Falkville, where Dad was always welcomed as a sort of unofficial pastor emeritus who helped serve communion when asked. I sat quietly, between Mary Beth and Alecia, feeling a little more grateful than usual.

Dad was with Mark's family and the children, and they arrived at the rear of the church with an Archibald clatter. He was slow coming down the aisle, with Mark on his arm for support, and made a point of speaking to everyone he recognized, and to some he didn't. The old church ladies—grandladies, as Ramsey has called them since he was a toddler—crowded around to touch him, to hug him, to tell him he was in their prayers.

Dad nodded, and smiled like he was singing a Wesley song, and tried to say what was on his mind. But it wouldn't come out. So he grinned and shrugged and hugged so much that when he finally got to the pew, he smelled of lavender and mothballs, the unmistakable scent Bob Ramsey refers to as Oil of Ol' Lady.

Dad could not stop smiling.

Mother always felt strongly that the few moments before church should be used to still the soul, and should be spent in silent meditation, in contemplation or prayer or in the dissemination of pink clouds. None of this, however, was possible that Sunday. They kept coming, men and women, old and not quite old, to touch him and hug him and see him as if he were Lazarus, risen from the dead. Dad got up each time to grab a hand, to nod and sputter his thanks, and to laugh at himself, if just a little too loudly.

Until the bell tolled, signifying the start of worship, and the congregation—and the grandchildren—settled into their seats. Of course it was Methodist calisthenics from there.

Up for a hymn, down for announcements.

Up for the scripture, down for the choir to sing.

Up for the Apostle's Creed, down for the offering, when they passed the plate.

Up for the doxology—the song Methodists sing in praise of their

God, especially after giving Him or Her their money—and down for the sermon.

It was during the doxology that it happened. Not so that anybody would notice, but it happened.

Praise God, from Whom all blessings flow . . .

Dad began to look around, to the pulpit where he had so often preached, to the chancel rail, where he had welcomed me and Mark, as children, into the church. He saw the Christ candle burning in the Advent wreath that meant so much to him, and he listened to the sound that was so familiar.

Praise Him, all creatures here below . . .

What was that on his face? A tear? I hadn't seen him cry outright more than twice my whole life, and once was just a little sniffle when Mary Beth stood before him and said her wedding vows. But on this day a tear began to well up in the corner of his eye and trickled down his cheek. And he did not reach up to brush it away.

Praise Him above, ye Heavenly Host . . .

It rolled down his face, beside his smile, and fell onto the shoulder of his suit.

Praise Father, Son, and Holy Ghost.

I punched Mary Beth in the shoulder and told her to look, as another tear formed in Dad's eye—and tears rolled down our cheeks, too. Dad just smiled and sang "Ahhhhhhhhhhhhhh-mennnnnn."

"Amen," he said out loud after the song was over, as he always did. It didn't sound at all like pig Latin.

Years later, on a day the family buried Mother's only brother, my uncle Harvey, Dad talked of that Sunday again. He'd beaten back a couple more cancers by then, trudged through a few smaller strokes and a diagnosis of Parkinson's and of diabetes, too. Into his eighties, he had found a way to smile, and laugh loudly and long enough to hurt himself.

Dad mentioned, that day of Uncle Harvey's funeral, that he had, ever since the first stroke, felt "weepy" from time to time. He felt somewhere inside that he should be embarrassed about it, but he simply wasn't.

"I find it endearing," Mary Beth told him.

He didn't need the excuse to hug her, but he hugged her again, his only daughter. And he talked about that day in church. He remembered the entry and the greetings and the crowd of people. He remembered rising for the doxology, looking around the church he'd served in the prime of his career, where he'd begun to find his voice and learn what a ministry meant. He remembered singing, but also the feelings that had flooded over him.

"I heard those words," he said, but instead of finishing the sentence, he began to sing the doxology, softly.

Praise God, from Whom all blessings flow . . .

He finished the song and was silent for a moment. Then he spoke again, as eloquent as he had been before the stroke had taken the ease of language away.

"I looked around and I saw the church," he said. "I looked around and I saw my family—my children and grandchildren—my *family*. I cried," he added, with a smile that looked almost like pride. "I was so happy to be there that I cried."

Amen.

23

Homesick

There are all sorts of flagpoles—some tall, some short, some wooden, some metal, some polished, some rusty; but the important thing about a flagpole is not its size or condition, but the colors which it flies. What do you stand for today?

—REV. ROBERT L. ARCHIBALD JR., May 12, 1974

I sat with Dad in the summer of 2013, in a single room in a little rehab center in Decatur, not far from the hospital where I'd waited as a child for him to finish his visiting rounds, where I'd burned concentric circles on my pointer finger, where I'd hit the jackpot on Ma Bell's coin return.

He'd lit up when he saw me come in—the same look he got when his children appeared in the driveway every Christmas, when he ran to see them and grabbed them around the middle and hugged them until something cracked. Or escaped. His eyes had said all those things, and his big crooked smile, even if his body could not. So he'd grabbed my hand, and had not let go.

I asked how he was doing, as if holding his hand in a place that seemed a whole lot more like hospice than rehab did not say it all. It was difficult for him to talk by then. The words took effort, like hard labor, and frustration showed in his clear eyes when he could not find the ones he wanted. But he smiled, and repeated the phrase he had said often in the last of his years, after strokes and cancers and Parkinson's and a weakness he despised. He quoted his grandfather T-Daddy.

"Heaven's my home," he said. "But I ain't homesick."

And he laughed, like he always did when he said that. Not as loudly, this time. Not as strongly. But the twinkle was still in his eye, because he believed it, and he meant it. His faith was as strong as his belief in all those kinds of grace, and he was not afraid of death. But he loved this earth, and the people on it. He loved his wife, Mary, and he knew, if others did not see it, that her mind was beginning to slip, that people failed to notice only because they were too busy fussing over him. He had been diligent with his money and his investments, preparing a will that would leave her comfortable. He was a scout until the end, and prepared for the world whether he would be in it or not.

Heaven was his home, but he was certainly not homesick. He still found joy in this world, in nurses that came to the room and told of their home churches and how their grandchildren were beginning to walk and talk. He found joy in them, and in news of his own children and grandchildren. He found it in family and the church and the sunrise he could almost see through the window, and the birds that sang along with it. Sometimes I think he loved the birds most of all, and for reasons I can't explain, the thought always makes me smile. Perhaps because it reminds me of Atticus Finch. Again.

Mockingbirds don't do one thing but make music for us to enjoy . . . but sing their hearts out for us.

Dad could not carry on a long conversation by this time. It was too frustrating, too tiring. But he could still listen to one, most of the time. His eyes were bright, and his expression spoke his feelings for him. He made a motion with his hands—as if writing with a pen on his outstretched palm—and pointed at me with a questioning look:

What have you been writing about?

I didn't know where to begin. I write three columns a week about politics and everything else across Alabama and the South, and can barely remember what I say from week to week. That's why I write them down, I guess.

I'd written a lot about the environment then, and the way the head of the Alabama Public Service Commission used the language and style of George Wallace to stand in the greenhouse door and rebuke efforts to clean up the planet, all for immediate political gain. I knew Dad would be interested in that.

I'd written about segregation, too, how fifty years after Wallace's stand in the schoolhouse door, Alabama schools had been resegregated faster than they were initially integrated. I'd written about the way churches had failed to live up to the Dream of Dr. King, and quoted a Baptist historian named Chriss Doss, who said, "You hear the pious statement that Sunday morning is the most segregated time of the week. My observation is that many of the clergy on both sides of the racial line would rather leave that dog asleep."

I'd even written a fictional obituary for the fictional Atticus Finch, dead of a broken heart in an age when compassion and decency seemed as doomed as his old client Tom Robinson.

But I didn't say any of that. It was hard to explain, off the cuff. I always feel self-conscious describing my columns anyway. So I just sat for a moment and thought how none of it really mattered. Just words thrown at a world that did not always care to listen, that insulated itself from opposing views. What did any of it matter as

Dad lay in a bed in a place he didn't know, unable to carry on a conversation, or to walk to the bathroom on his own?

This was the man who had carried me for a full stretch on the Appalachian Trail, who could mount a canoe on a car without help into his seventies, who could always open the stickiest jelly jars with his bare hands. He was the one who had pushed us hard, and had pushed himself harder.

He was almost gone.

I thought to myself that much of him was already gone, the strength in his arms and his hands, and the independence that sometimes made him carry too large a load on his shoulders, with a stoicism he felt he owed us all. But the sparkle reminded me that much of him was still there, too, trapped in a body that had failed him, that was frail and pale and wracked with disease he did not earn from hard living or late nights or drugs or alcohol or anger. And before I could say a word about what I'd been writing about or working on, he reached out again and grabbed my wrist, with a surprising grip, and a purpose.

Out of the blue he said, clearly, "I'm proud of you, son, for taking on the race question."

Just like that.

I did not, I must admit, think all that much about it in the moment. I was stunned into a brief silence, but then just thanked him, and hugged him, and made the comforting small talk that comes when the end is near. I thought little about it because I am paid, in my job, to say what I think three times a week, or more, in a city that is itself a race question. I could not do that work without discussion of race and right and wrong, and my bigger concern always is and always will be whether the words I choose are the right ones, in the right moment. I'm sure there are moments they are not.

I did not think much about it then because I didn't know—
I did not realize until I began to read his sermons—how he had
struggled to take on that thing he called the "race question," how
he labored, particularly as a young man in the time of fire, to say
without equivocation that racism and bigotry were devils, and the
church had too long protected them like armor.

I hugged Dad as I left that evening. I kissed him on the head,
on the bald spot where I'd stuck that chartreuse popping bug, and
drove home to Birmingham. It was the last time I would see him
alive.

Dad died a few days later. Quietly. It was time.

So I did what I always do when a loved one dies. I wrote the
obituary. I have always loved obituaries, for they tell the world
the stories of the men and women who walked this earth, of the
accomplishments they would never tell you about, of the honors
they tucked away and never revealed in polite conversation. I have
often thought that the problems of newspapers began when they
decided to charge customers for obituaries, by the line. If a death is
not news in your community, then what is? I feel strongly, then and
now and always, that everyone has a story that deserves to be heard.
I enjoy writing obituaries because they are cathartic, because they
allow me to pour myself into a life instead of a death, to grieve and
celebrate and, on a good day, leave loved ones the only gift I know
how to give. This is the obituary I wrote for Dad:

Robert Lambuth Archibald Jr., better known to United Methodist congregations across North Alabama as "Brother Bob,"
died early Saturday in Decatur after a long illness. He was 83.

Brother Bob was an ordained Methodist minister for almost
six decades, serving as senior pastor of First United Methodist

Church of Decatur, First United Methodist Church of Huntsville, East Lake United Methodist in Birmingham, and other congregations in Alabaster, Huntsville, Jacksonville and elsewhere.

He started Birmingham's Grace United Methodist when the congregation met in tents. Each Sunday—little did the congregation know—he rose early to clear black widow spiders from beneath the seats.

He served two stints on the cabinet of the North Alabama conference, as district superintendent of the Decatur and Tuscaloosa districts.

While he achieved success and recognition as a preacher, he was best known as a pastor who cared about the people in his congregations. He brought joy with his big crooked smile, bouncing on his toes during the singing of hymns—especially those of Charles Wesley.

He smiled bigger, and sang louder than anyone else in church. Especially during the Methodist staple "Oh, for a Thousand Tongues to Sing."

Brother Bob didn't just love being a preacher. He loved the Church. He followed in his father's footsteps, in his grandfather's path before him, to become a Methodist minister. He graduated from Birmingham-Southern College and received his divinity degree from Emory University. He later received an honorary doctorate from Huntingdon College, where he served on the board of trustees.

It was while at Emory that he met Mary Holland, a student at Agnes Scott College. The two were married and lived a lifetime together, raising four children and loving them no matter what.

Brother Bob was an Eagle Scout and a longtime scoutmaster

who loved nature. He was an avid birdwatcher and camper who showed his children the country—identifying plants and birds along the way—in a big blue canvas tent.

His advice in life, to his children, his scouts, his campers, his congregation and the children who flocked to him for post-sermon candy, was much the same: Leave your campsite cleaner than you found it; leave your neighborhood, your community, your city, more joyful than you found it; let the world be better because you were there.

He practiced what he preached. And he will be missed.

Of course all the children came home to Decatur for the funeral, falling into the roles and duties we had become used to. Mark handled the business arrangements while I held Mother's hand and bit my lip as she and Alecia picked out a casket, and Murray chose the flowers for the service. Mary Beth printed a beautiful program for the funeral, with an architectural angel she had drawn on front, and gathered photos for a poster and slideshow that showed her daddy in a life that could never, to her, be eclipsed by death.

The siblings and their families stayed in my house in Birmingham the night before the funeral, as if it were Christmas. I woke early, and walked my dogs, Benny and Betsy, to the nearby dog park like every other morning. We've done that so early and so often the dogs have come to believe their park is their private club. But on this morning, while it was still dark, another dog ran to meet them inside the fence.

He had no owner, no tags, just oversize ears that stood up and spoke like Dad's eyes had on that last visit. He was emaciated and covered in bug bites, with thin hair that looked more like a hog's than a dog's. He had been abandoned there, just a puppy, left in some last-ditch hope that someone, anyone, would find reason to give him a life better than he had known before. But the little guy—he looked part pit and part friendly visitor, as Dad would say—bounded over, without fear or malice or hesitation, and made instant friends with Benny and The Bets.

I brought him water and he drank long and loudly—Lord, how loudly. He nuzzled my calf and licked my hand with a tongue like a flank steak. He looked up and cocked his head and I swear he smiled.

Of all days. It was the day of my dad's funeral, and my house was full and the day would be long and trying and emotional. We had to drive to Decatur—75 minutes away—for the funeral and drive back for the burial. I had no time for strays.

So I was quick with the gate as we left. I figured, like whoever had put him there in the first place, the park was still his best chance for survival. I was quick with the gate, but not quick enough. The dog shot like a dart through the crack and danced, euphorically, just out of reach. I tried to lure him back but he wouldn't go, for Pete's sake. I tried to catch him, but the more I chased, the more those ears laughed at me. I was running out of time, so I began the walk home. I expected him to turn back at any moment, but he did not. He ran, just out of reach—once under a city bus as it stopped at a stop sign—and I cringed, hoping this day would not become more traumatic.

But as Benny and Betsy and I arrived home, this dog was with us. I sighed and walked around back and he followed me into the gate. I gave him a quick bath and went to get him some food, and nervously told the others how this dog had followed me home. I knew they would be worried, or upset to have an emaciated little pup out back, with God knows what ailments. But I was wrong.

"It's a sign," Mary Beth said. "It's a sign from Daddy. You have to keep him."

Nobody argued. Not even Alecia or Ramsey or Drew. Not even me.

We named him Barney, and he became a bullheaded, hedonistic, exuberant, troublesome, gassy, extremely loyal member of the family. I don't know if Barney really was a sign from heaven or from Daddy, but I'd like to think he was. If he was a sign from Dad, it was a good joke, and a little payback, with a twinkle in the eye.

It would be that kind of day. Dad's funeral happened to coincide with the week of Vacation Bible School at First United Methodist Church of Decatur. VBS is like a themed day camp, a week or two each summer, in which children and youth come to church and learn of the Bible through songs and skits and stories. They play games and eat lunchroom pizza and make crafts to take home. I went to Vacation Bible School at that same church as a kid. We built stilts out of two-by-fours, attaching triangular footholds with heavy bolts and wing nuts. I got hit in the head with a stilt that week, wing nut first. Murray took me to the hospital. I remember little about that trip. Perhaps because I'd just been hit in the head with a stilt.

The week of Dad's funeral, the theme of Vacation Bible School was "Kingdom Rock—Where Kids Stand Strong for God," and an elaborate set had been built in the sanctuary, wrapping around the pulpit and obscuring the choir loft. It was built of cardboard and foam core and wood, painted as the interior of a gray stone castle. A giant, bejeweled throne overlooked the chancel rail, which had been turned into a green hedge. The preacher was apologetic about the castle. He was unsure whether it could be moved for the funeral.

"Leave it," we all said. Dad would have loved it.

They rolled Dad's casket down to the castle gates, and his children paid tribute. I stood, and said something I do not recall. Steve sang, a solo, the hymn "Shepherd Me, O God."

Murray spoke, too, from the pulpit of the church where he had reluctantly gone as a teenager. He spoke with the voice of a preacher, and began to describe the man he'd known in life. He spoke of sitting down to tell Dad, in the 1970s, that he was gay, and he told of finding acceptance and love. He told of bringing Steve home, and how Dad had found more room in his heart.

It was why the family was there today, and every Christmas, and always. It was what held the family together and made it stronger, and fiercer and more lasting. But as he stood beside that cardboard throne he told a congregation packed with churchgoers and preachers, both active and retired, that it was more than that. It was only because he was accepted and loved by his father that he could return to a church, to a Methodist church, and feel love for and loved by God.

"During a period in my life when I felt that the church had turned its back on me, I never felt that from my dad," Murray said. "And the strong faith and deep relationship I have with God today is built on his example."

We drove together to Birmingham for the burial at Elmwood Cemetery, a graveyard that served as the eternal home not only of my father's parents, but of Denise McNair, one of those four little girls killed in Sixteenth Street Baptist Church, and of Milton Grafman, a rabbi who was one of the eight Birmingham clergymen whom Dr. King had addressed in his "Letter from a Birmingham Jail."

The skies opened up as they put Dad in the ground. It rained hard, like the whole world was sobbing. It dried up as quickly as it had begun.

Decatur First United Methodist Church decorated for Vacation Bible School at the time of Dad's funeral in 2013

I think of that day, now, as perfect. It was family and home and children and church and voices and dogs and the sudden surprises of nature. And Dad went on, homesick or not. From a castle.

I've thought more often lately about that other day, that earlier day, when he reached out and grabbed my wrist, when he told me he was proud of me for taking on the issues, in my time, that he had been uncomfortable taking on in his. I tell myself it is his permission to question. I tell myself it is his blessing to say the things he was never quite comfortable enough to say.

"I'm proud of you," he said.

I am proud of you, too.

24

The Ring

What does the father do? The father forgives and welcomes
him back into the home. This is the grace of God in its finest
expression. The father never gave him the chance to ask to be a
hired servant. The father gave him a robe, and a ring, and shoes.

—REV. ROBERT L. ARCHIBALD JR., August 26, 1973

They put Dad in the Alabama ground, in a burst of rain he'd have
called a gullywasher, on the afternoon of June 18, 2013. Thirteen
days later in Dover, in that capitol building where Steve had worked
to change so many hearts and minds, the Delaware legislature legal-
ized same-sex marriage.

It was historic. It was a long time coming, but it came, with a
certainty and an assurance Murray and Steve could and did predict.
Once people start to talk about issues of justice, progress becomes
inevitable, Murray once told me, with a confidence I did not and
do not share. But he was right that time, and he was a part of it.

There was celebration in Rehoboth Beach then, a sense of freedom to love and to live like everyone else, to have the same rights
in the eyes of the courts and communities and insurance compa-

nies and justices of the peace as any other couples. Nothing more. Nothing less. There was joy and dancing like the world had really changed. It had.

It had been illegal in Delaware for two people of the same gender to have sex at all back in 1972. That changed the following year, but equal rights took far longer. As the twenty-first century began, Steve and others at CAMP Rehoboth—and elsewhere across the state— worked with legislators to enter a new century of rights and respect for gay and lesbian people, too. After more than a decade of failure, the political tide turned, and the legislature by a large majority voted to give LGBTQ people the same protections from discrimination it gave others. When it passed, Governor Jack Markell came to the beach to sign it into law. It was Steve's birthday.

Delaware continued to move forward. Other protections were granted, and in 2012—with urging from Steve and Murray and Equality Delaware and coalitions of many more—the state okayed same-sex civil unions.

But Murray and Steve were church people. They wanted a wedding, at Epworth United Methodist Church in Rehoboth Beach, where Steve sang in the choir and rang in the bell choir and where Murray dressed the sanctuary in the colors of the liturgical seasons. Civil unions had been a step, a tick forward, but they wanted a wedding.

Now, after thirty-five years of life together, they were engaged to be married.

The Methodist Church, as a whole, was far less progressive than the State of Delaware. It was in 1972, after all, that Methodists legislated the view that gay people were incompatible with the teachings of the church. And while in years to follow, Delaware and other states and the U.S. Supreme Court would begin to take a fairer and more progressive view, the Methodist Church—with the heavy support of delegates from the African continent and the American South—thought the good ol' days looked just fine.

Oh, there were places like Epworth, in Delaware, "reconciling" congregations that as early as 1990 seized on the original language in that 1972 church legislation that acknowledged a church should offer all people "fellowship which enables reconciling relationships with God."

Reconciling congregations were popping up across America— even in Alabama—but they were the exception rather than the rule.

So even though the State of Delaware said Murray and Steve could be legally married, and even though their own church welcomed them fully and completely, they had to make concessions. They had to tread lightly, if only to protect those who would perform the ceremony, those who might be disciplined if it became known they allowed a gay marriage to take place inside the sacred walls of a Methodist church. So Murray and Steve called it a "covenant blessing" instead of a wedding, and they found a retired minister who was eager to take a stand for love. They set the date: October 26, 2013. It was four months after Dad died. The family needed a little celebration. And Rehoboth Beach was ready to throw down.

Back home in Alabama, though, other elements were at work. A congressional candidate named Dean Young, backed by the Bible-thumper-in-chief himself, Supreme Court Justice Roy Moore, railed against "homosexuals pretending like they're married." Moore and preachers in more conservative churches spouted their moral law, picking and choosing their scripture to damn those who did not see the world or whatever lies beyond in the same way they did. Moore and Young and their allies decried equal rights for gay people as an abomination against God, using the same rationalizations Bull Connor had used to confront John Rutland in that Woodlawn sanctuary five decades before. There was familiar pushback in Methodist churches, too, as leaders urged caution, and moderation, and deliberation.

It was only by chance that two Alabama men—Joe Openshaw and Bobby Prince—decided to have their own Methodist wedding on October 26, the same day Murray and Steve planned to say their vows. The Alabama men could not have the ceremony at their church outside Birmingham, and they could not ask their own pastor to officiate. It would be too risky, especially because Bishop Debra Wallace-Padgett, the spiritual and administrative leader of the North Alabama Conference of the United Methodist Church, made it clear, in repeated statements, that such an event would be too divisive, and would detract from the true mission of the church.

Open hearts. Open minds. Open doors. Perhaps it was a directive to her. Especially the doors. It was not a description of her position.

Openshaw and Prince found a bishop from outside Alabama, Bishop Melvin G. Talbert, who had marched for racial civil rights a half century before, who was willing to come to the state to officiate over the marriage. The men had been together a dozen years and, Talbert said, "fulfilled all the requirements for marriage by our church, with the exception that they happen to be two gay men in love."

So he committed to do the job.

Bishop Padgett-Wallace responded just as the Waitful Eight had all those years ago, with excuses, and fear that the time was not right, with concern of how it would look to the outside world. And with words that did more harm than good:

I have urged the bishop [Talbert] to not officiate at the event which centers on a complex issue that is polarizing our society

United Methodist Bishop Debra Wallace-Padgett—
the bishop over Alabama United Methodists—made
it clear in 2013 that gay weddings and similar services
in Alabama Methodist churches were too divisive, the
same argument Methodists made in the 1950s and
1960s to avoid desegregation.

and church. The anticipated media coverage of this event will
test our capacity to remain focused on our vision, mission and
priorities that have emerged over the past year.

Better to wait. Better to wait.

And of course I hear the words of Dr. King, talking about a
different kind of discrimination, a different era of wait. His words
ring out, as his words do, and stain that bishop like those who came
before:

> We know through painful experience that freedom is never vol-
> untarily given by the oppressor; it must be demanded by the
> oppressed. Frankly, I have yet to engage in a direct action cam-
> paign that was "well timed" in the view of those who have not
> suffered unduly from the disease of segregation. For years now
> I have heard the word "Wait!" It rings in the ear of every Negro

with piercing familiarity. This "Wait" has almost always meant·
"Never." We must come to see, with one of our distinguished
jurists, that "justice too long delayed is justice denied."

Talbert came, as promised, and performed the ceremony. He
was brought up on charges because of it, though he didn't stop
marrying people who loved each other. Openshaw and Prince said,
I do. They were married, over the objections of Alabama's bishop,
who continued to say *Do not*.

Things were different for Murray and Steve in Delaware, even if
the church had to take part in the covenant blessing with a wink
and a nod. There was no resistance from the state, or the church.
So Murray and Steve prepared for the ceremony, and the reception,
with style and dignity and reverence.

They loved their families and valued the blessings and love that
came from them, so they decided to ask their mothers—Steve's
father had died years before—if they could have their fathers' wedding rings as their symbol of unending, eternal love. They asked if
they could be married in those wedding rings.

It was a long way from 1966, when I was three and Dad preached
his sermon on moral law, the one in which he spoke of how God
meant for the relationship between man and woman to be something holy, and how our sophistication about the sexual revolution
becomes only "a sorry veneer for failure and defeat and death." But
it was a long time, a long journey, a long evolution. And the more
I read the sermon, the more I realize there is no inconsistency. He
was talking first of commitment. That is what's holy, and wonderful, and unchangeable, as he said.

So Mother said yes. Of course Mother said yes. She had grown
more vocal in the time Dad had grown ill, and especially since
he had died. In the days after the controversy over Chick-fil-A's

financial support of groups seen as anti-gay, and after CEO Dan T. Cathy spoke against same-sex marriage, Mother couldn't see a Chick-fil-A commercial or billboard without harrumphing like Dad had when he had to watch a Miller High Life ad.

"Those idiot cows can't even spell," Mother fumed. And it's true. They can't.

So of course Mother gave Murray Dad's ring. It would go around Murray's finger just as it had his father's. We knew he'd be okay with that, he'd be fine. He was Home, after all, and he wouldn't be needing it.

Of course it is hard for me to think of that ring now without thinking of all those sermons, all those parables of the prodigal son and his father. The father never gave the kid a chance to beg for welcome or forgiveness or to ask for that job as a hired servant. The father just ran to meet him, where he was, and offered him a robe and a pair of shoes. And a ring. Of course a ring.

So on October 26, 2013, Murray and Steve were married in their Methodist church in a covenant blessing in front of their mothers, and siblings, and nieces and nephews and friends who crowded into the sanctuary to witness something that had happened in Murray's and Steve's hearts thirty-five years before, but was allowed by the law only then, in that place.

They said, *I do,* and the whole town cried: *Oh, yes you did.*

In Alabama, that same day, church and state officials wrung their hands and clicked their tongues and fretted about what people might think as Openshaw and Prince were married in their outlaw service. In Delaware the Speaker of the House of Representatives, Pete Schwartzkopf, showed up at the wedding, and at the reception he presented Murray and Steve with the highest honor for service that the State of Delaware gives, the Order of the First State, which had been bestowed on them by Governor Markell.

The official Methodist Church stance was condemning of Murray and Steve. Many in that body did not bother to know them. But their governor found a commendation necessary, and appropriate, as the order itself says, "to bear witness to their outstanding Efforts, Knowledge, Integrity, Prudence and Ability as displayed by the Evidence of their Accomplishments. Their consistent dedication to Excellence in serving their Community and their State is to be lauded."

The family laughed, and smiled, and sang that day. Happy to be together, after so much sadness, after all that grief. Dad had always been like a glue that held us as one, the hero who showed up when we needed help, the man who begged us to come home for Christmas or otherwise, the one who drew us together in our concern for him. So the family ate, and told stories, and sighed in the relief of knowing not that Dad was gone, but that he had prepared a way forward for the rest of us. We were still us. Different, but together. Different, but a family. Different, in a way that made us stronger.

It was good to see Dad's ring shine on Murray's finger. It belonged there.

Steve, though, had to make other arrangements for his ring. He had come to his Southern Baptist mother outside Atlanta and asked her if he, too, might use his late father's ring for his own wedding.

His mother, the dear, sweet Lucile Elkins, had regarded him, a funny look on her face.

"Silly," she had said. "You're the one who stood there by his casket and told me to put it on his finger."

25

Holes in the Dark

A few days ago, tired from a busy day, a busy week, and a busy Lenten season, I prepared to go to bed. Pulling the covers back, and lifting the pillow off the bed—I seldom use a pillow—I found an envelope. Opening it, I found a card from the one person I love more than any other human being in all this world. This card from my wife said, "Who can doubt that we exist only to love? . . . We live not a moment exempt from its influence." This is a quotation from Pascal. Inside the card were the words "I live to love you."

—REV. ROBERT L. ARCHIBALD JR., April 5, 1964

Heaven, my mother told me as a child, is a place where everything is fair. She spent her youth trying to make that heaven for us in our household, trying to prove it was possible.

I don't believe that heaven exists, and neither did she. Heaven is here on earth, in the constant if futile attempt to make it something better, something fairer, to turn it into that place she imagined.

It cannot be done, of course. There's too much randomness in the world, too much sickness and disease and natural catastrophe that can fall, like a tornado or a tree branch or a meteorite, on a house, in the night, in your sleep, on your head. Cancer and worse take the best among us, ravaging our bodies and causing us pain we do not deserve. Dementia can steal our souls and ourselves, leaving us to die without our memories and our stories, the things that make us who we are.

It's not fair.

We can be born in a family that loves us, in a proper and respectable pack that sees itself as blessed and believes it so much it can't help but come true. Or we can be born to those who struggle, who have no expectation but failure, and punishment, and a dream of something better on the other side. Some of us can sleep through high school and flunk language classes and spend the night in jail for shoplifting and fall back on family until we find ourselves, and success. That's what they call privilege. Some try harder, and make fewer mistakes, and still find themselves locked up or locked out, without so much as a second chance. I don't believe in heaven.

Mother hated unfairness, whether it had to do with race or gender or religion or sexuality or any of the differences her big, kind, welcoming God cherished. She hated inequity on the playground, if one grandchild was left out or bullied. She dreamed of a heaven not with streets of gold, or harps, or angels singing the protest songs of the sixties that always made her cry, but of a place that was fair.

As children, we found that heaven in her arms and her words. We found it in the books she read out loud and the poems she recited by memory, and in the pink clouds she sent us our whole lives. I don't know if she ever found her heaven at all.

Mother's dementia came slowly, so only those who spent the most time with her could see. She was not diagnosed with Alzheimer's, or Lewy body dementia, or any of the frightening diseases that steal the stories of so many. It began with repeated conversations, and with an anger that was unlike her, toward Dad and family and the church and the world and things left undone. She lost her hearing as she lost her mind, and frequently misheard conversations that sent her to dark places.

I was angry at the way Mother changed, until I finally came to realize it was not her at all. Not anymore. So I was angry at that disease. It stole more than my mother's memories. It stole and twisted my memory of her.

If heaven is a place where everything is fair, dementia is hell. Or is it just life?

Life comes as it does, in peaks and valleys and highs and lows. I've covered life as a reporter long enough to see that it comes as bombs in Birmingham and stray bullets in nurseries and not-so-stray bullets in schools and churches and it comes in trucks on a Tennessee road. It comes as evil and it comes as accident and it comes as storms that fall on the innocent in the echo of thunder.

I walked the rubble after a tornado hit Goshen United Methodist Church in north Alabama in 1994, on Palm Sunday, of all mornings, during an Easter cantata, a performance about the crucifixion of Jesus. The storm came without warning and killed twenty people, including six children. Toddlers Jessica Watson and Zackery Mode died—along with Zackery's mother and father. So did five-year-old Jonathan Abbott, ten-year-old Amy Woods and twelve-year-old Eric Thacker. Just like that.

Hannah Clem, the four-year-old daughter of the pastor, the Reverend Kelly Clem, was among the dead. A preacher's kid, like me. Like Mary Beth. It was so familiar, walking through the place that had been called a sanctuary, but did not live up to its name. The Methodist hymnals scattered across the wet ground, the blue and pink shoes of little girls, dressed in preparation for the holiest week of Christendom. Bibles and baubles and notes written on the back of the registration pad where members and visitors sign their names in what Methodists call the "ritual of friendship." Everything was familiar in that place, in that moment. Everything but death. It did not belong.

The world asked why. The world asked how. How did you worship a God who allowed this, who would descend upon a church in the middle of celebrating God's very name and wipe it away, children and all? I had no answers, but the preacher, Kelly Clem, did.

She came outside a few days later to address those questions to reporters and to the world. She explained that we all lived in a natural world, and in a natural world bad things and good things and random things happened. She said it was our job, as people, to try to use those bad things to bring about good. *Why* was not the question. The question that mattered was *What next?*

"We do not know why," she said. "We just have to help each other through it."

What I remember most is what happened next. There was an Easter egg tree in the parsonage yard, a branch that had been planted in a flowerpot and adorned with Easter eggs, like a Christmas tree is hung with ornaments. It had been erected before Palm Sunday, surely to the delight of Hannah and her little sister, Sarah. Kelly Clem walked to it, with purpose. She bent down—her face so bruised it was purple—and replanted it. Then she walked away, to mourn her tragedy, and use it to make the world around her a better place.

Not fair. Hell. But there's a little bit of heaven there, too.

I've tried to remember Kelly Clem—and those who were killed in that church—when things go bad in life, because things inevitably do.

Such was the case in 2017. I'd been immersed in my work all year. Alabama's governor, Robert Bentley, would be shamed and charged after a relationship with a much younger staffer, and would leave office in disgrace. Doug Jones would take on Roy Moore in a senatorial race that would draw global attention. He would win and shock the world. Work, for me, was a refuge.

For as Mother's mind and body declined, Steve was diagnosed with lymphoma. It was aggressive, and quick. He spent months in treatment in Philadelphia, but it was no good. He died the next spring, in March 2018. Of course I wrote the obit. It is all I know to do:

Elkins, Stephen Wade

Stephen Wade Elkins, who spent a quarter century working to make Rehoboth a more open and positive place, died Thursday night, March 15, from lymphoma.

He was 67.

Steve approached his illness as he did his life: with a sense of humor and resolve. But it was cancer. And it was determined.

Steve was a Southern boy by birth, and he never lost a taste for barbecue and sweet tea. He grew up in Atlanta—an Eagle Scout—with a drive to succeed. He graduated from the University of Georgia and soon went to work in the White House of President Jimmy Carter.

It was in that White House in 1978 that Steve met Murray Archibald, the man who would become his life partner and finally, after people like him and Murray opened the eyes of the world and the courts, his husband.

On leaving the White House Steve excelled in business. He worked in computers before they were household tools, climbing the ladder in cities like Syracuse and Norfolk. He was at the top of his game in New York City, enjoying his success and his partner and his friends and family when all the sparkle of the Big Apple began to dim.

AIDS came to America, and he watched friends die. Far too many, with far too much promise. He saw people who needed a hand and a hug and a place to feel safe, and to learn how to be safe. Rehoboth was that place.

Steve and Murray founded the non-profit CAMP—Create a More Positive Rehoboth—in 1991 to open doors and hearts to all people in the community, whether gay or straight. They were, in the early days, met with resistance.

Steve, with a mind for politics and business and the humor to cut through the coldest heart, took on city hall and zoning laws that would discriminate. He took on closed minds in the city who warned this CAMP would bring the wrong element to Delaware. He began to preach his gospel of "room for all."

That was 25 years ago, before CAMP Rehoboth became one of the most respected and successful non-profits of its kind. This week, as Steve lay in his deathbed surrounded by family and friends, the governor called to give his respects. So did a U.S. senator and a congresswoman, and people of goodwill from across the Eastern Seaboard.

Because Steve did what Steve always did. He shattered stereotypes and opened hearts with his example, his humor, his attention to detail and his sheer will.

And of course his singing voice. Which he found later in life.

He was a showman—a "bossy showman," as his sister, Judy, would put it. He was never happier than when belting out an old Methodist hymn, and was as likely to burst into song in an Alabama Walmart as he was in church. But he never sang more sweetly or beamed more brightly than he did from the choir loft at Epworth United Methodist Church in Rehoboth.

Steve loved his family back home in Georgia, and he visited his mother and sister every Christmas of his life. He loved Murray's family, too. He was brother, uncle, backbone, shoulder to lean on and friend.

He could cite law or scripture, and follow it up with a bawdy joke and tittering laugh.

He could do to any room what he did in his professional life. He could surprise, and change minds, and comfort, and fill the space with laughter and love. He could make it better because he had been there.

· He loved. And he was loved.

Steve leaves his husband, Murray, who carries on his work and his light. He leaves his mother, Lucile Elkins, and sister, Judy Buchanan. He leaves nieces and nephews who remember him both as clown and voice of clarity. He leaves too many friends to count.

A Celebration of Life will be held at Epworth United Methodist Church. Flowers are welcome, and he would also ask that donations be made to CAMP Rehoboth. And that you treat each other well. And to remember there is "room for all."

His funeral was a celebration, in their Methodist church, packed with family and friends, with gay people and straight people and politicians and media and Murray, who looked frail, and Steve's mom and his sister, who loved Steve's world for loving Steve.

Back home, I was used to seeing stones thrown in judgment. On this day, I almost believed in Mother's heaven.

Murray was broken. But he marveled at the crowd, and the way he and Steve had been treated by hospitals and insurance companies simply because they could say they were married. The word was like a magic button that opened doors they'd never walked through, that made them know, before Steve was gone, that all the years and the fight had been worthwhile.

The two of them had started CAMP Rehoboth to bridge the gap in a city that feared gay people. When Steve died, the city flew its flag at half staff. It named a street after him: Steve Elkins Way.

Like Murray said at its dedication, Steve would have been thrilled to finally get his way.

What I remember most, though, are the words of the Reverend Jonathan Baker, the then-retired pastor who had drawn Murray and Steve to Epworth, who had seen their spirit and welcomed them, even when others did not.

Jonathan quoted Robert Louis Stevenson, who, as a child, saw a stranger with a candle and cried, "Look, there's a man coming down the street punching holes in the darkness."

That's what Steve did, the preacher said. Steve used his voice to speak for those who did not have one, who did not feel comfortable or confident or competent to use their own words. He spoke not of "us" and "them" or "them" and "us" but of "room for all."

Murray and Steve had gone to Jonathan years before to ask him about attending the church. They wondered if they would be welcome there, in a church that did not have "out" gay members at that time, in a community that had looked askance at the sometimes flamboyant tourists. They wanted to know if it would be a distraction, or a problem, or a concern to call themselves Methodists.

Jonathan had opened his arms wide, and said two words: "Welcome home."

He gave us candles to burn that day of Steve's funeral, and sang "This Little Light of Mine" as we lit them all for Steve, who was still punching holes in the darkness.

Punching holes in stereotypes.

Punching holes in expectations of differences.

Punching holes in the silence.

I went home from the funeral to learn I'd been given the one thing I'd always wanted, the Pulitzer Prize, for commentary about all those Alabama politicians and the darkness that seemed to follow them. I thought of Steve, who would be pleased his obit was written by a Pulitzer winner. I thought of my mother, who would hear this news—news that once would have made her ecstatic—but would not understand.

Life is arbitrary, and random, and requires a sense of purpose just to take the good with the bad, and the bad with the good. It's not fair. It is not heaven. But I'm convinced one often follows the other, and for some reason that gives me hope.

Mother died six months later. It was October. And as with Dad, it was time.

I sat down that day, and with tears falling unchecked, I did the only thing I know to do:

Archibald, Mary Holland

Mary Holland Archibald, mother and wife and an unceasing voice for kindness and hope for a better world, died Oct. 11. She was 86.

Mary—Mom to her children and grandchildren—devoted most of her life to being a United Methodist preacher's wife in North Alabama. But that role did not define her. Nor was it her greatest achievement. If you asked her what gave her strength or joy or made her tick, she would talk of her children. She put all her faith and trust and effort into the four of them, and nothing made her prouder than seeing them rise from their own errors of immaturity to share her vision of a more equitable world.

She read to those children—Murray, Mary Beth, Mark and

John—from the time they were born. Poetry and adventure and the classics.

She wanted them to understand a wider world, so in the 1960s, when finding global cuisines was rare in the South, she created "international day" each week to honor the food and culture of other countries.

She taught her children to be unafraid of the unfamiliar, to know all people have lessons to teach, and lessons to learn. She came to understand her children with a near sixth sense. She knew when to speak aloud of their worries or when to leave notes or snippets of poetry on their pillows at night to give them comfort. She could pinpoint their deepest concerns with an eerie accuracy and always found the right words—her own or those of her favorite poets—to bring a smile or a precious tear.

In later years she would call or send letters out of the blue when she felt something was bothering her children. She sent "pink clouds," as she called them, positive wishes she felt would make a difference. And remarkably, they did. She knew when her children were to be engaged. She knew, somehow, when they were expecting children. She knew when they were in trouble or in grief or simply in need of love.

Once, when a son was having a particularly difficult time after leaving home, she sent him a passage from a Robert Frost poem that he quietly carried for years. "Home is the place where, when you have to go there, they have to take you in."

He went home. They took him in, and he wondered for a lifetime how she knew.

Mary Archibald loved dogs and never met a canine that did not steal her heart. She revered the act of creation, of art and literature and showing love with food—roast and rice and gravy was a specialty—or elaborate birthday cakes and hand-sewn Halloween costumes for grandchildren.

She deplored unfairness almost as much as poor manners—for which there was never an adequate excuse.

To her the American Dream had nothing to do with buying a house or acquiring wealth. It was in believing your generation could be better than the last, and that maybe, with effort, the next generation could come to represent the dream of freedom and equality voiced, but never fully achieved, by the founders.

She was, perhaps, naïve in that regard, because her own father, a prominent Methodist minister in North Georgia, nurtured those ideals. But at times it caused problems. She did not understand, in the South in 1950, that others would look askance when she welcomed African American friends to her father's church in suburban Atlanta. Her dad—Harvey Holland—supported her and was soon transferred from the church because of it.

For years Mary felt guilt about that, but later came to see it differently. In the end the simple welcoming of all became the constant refrain of her life and the primary lesson passed to her children.

The world should be a gracious place, and it is up to you—to us—to make it so. Even in the face—especially in the face—of those who would build barriers.

Though her health caused her pain through much of her life, she greeted the world with a smile and a kind word of welcome. Even when she did not feel like it. Even, for the most part, when her body and mind failed her.

A graduate of Agnes Scott College in Decatur, Ga., she lived most of her life in Alabama with her devoted husband, the Rev. Robert L. Archibald Jr. Together they served Methodist churches in Jacksonville, Alabaster, Huntsville, Birmingham and Decatur—a place she forever loved.

A memorial service will be held for her later in the fall at Camp Glisson in Dahlonega, Ga., a place precious to her.

We held that memorial service at Camp Glisson, that constant in our lives, like our mother and father, that place we had always thought our own. We did what we do. Mary Beth made a slide-show, and a lovely program. Mark and Sally sang "Hymn of Promise," a hymn Mother always loved.

Mark read a poem he'd prepared. I don't remember what it said, but it sounded a lot like Mark. Murray spoke words he'd prepared, too, that sounded like Murray. I did not prepare. I said something. I have no idea what, but I know it sounded like me. I'm pretty sure we all said the same thing, in our own distinct ways. Even the funeral spoke of our differences, and why they do not matter.

We woke before dawn the next morning, punching a hole in the Georgia darkness to make our way up to the high ground, to a special place Mother always loved. We scattered her ashes in that place as the sun rose. When they had settled, we looked up to the sky.

It was filled with pink clouds.

26

What a Way to Live

Have you ever been in a position where you knew that to stand on principle could mean hurt in your life or business, while to compromise that principle would mean you couldn't respect yourself?

—REV. ROBERT L. ARCHIBALD JR., August 9, 1998

I come back to the Letter. Always. Like that idiot preacher Dad talked about who pulled out his Bible and chose his passages at random until he found the one that told him what he wanted to hear. I come back to the Letter, and it's as though my finger whirls, around and around and down, to a paragraph that says those things I want to say with a power I don't possess, with a surety I don't know, with a scope and depth that comes with the timeless voice of a King. I circle, and I point, and it works at least as well as the Bible.

I have traveled the length and breadth of Alabama, Mississippi and all the other southern states. On sweltering summer days and crisp autumn mornings I have looked at the South's beautiful churches with their lofty spires pointing heavenward. I have beheld the impressive outlines of her massive religious education buildings. Over and over I have found myself asking: "What kind of people worship here? Who is their God?" . . .

In deep disappointment I have wept over the laxity of the church. But be assured that my tears have been tears of love. There can be no deep disappointment where there is not deep love. Yes, I love the church. How could I do otherwise? I am in the rather unique position of being the son, the grandson and the great grandson of preachers. Yes, I see the church as the body of Christ. But, oh! How we have blemished and scarred that body through social neglect and through fear of being nonconformists.

Yes, Dr. King. I weep as well. Oh, I know by now I cannot take your letter and apply it as I like, for all the wrongs and ills and injustices I see in the world. I cannot take it, as a white man, and use it like *Civil Disobedience for Dummies* or as only a work of literature with meaning greater than its original focus. It is not appropriate to appropriate. I get it. But I do want to learn from it, for we really are, now, as then, as always, "caught in an inescapable network of mutuality, tied in a single garment of destiny."

My church again looks to exclude, and makes and cites laws to justify drawing lines between us. And though I have faith in my father and pride in his evolution, his words will always ring more hollow because the right ones were hardest for him to say from his pulpit in times when they were needed the most.

It is disappointment so deep it must be love. For family. For the church. For beliefs I held and expectations built over a lifetime. But for broader disappointments, too. For echoes of George Wallace that ring in the words of Donald Trump, in the condemnation of immigrants and Muslims and the poor and more. For mobs not

Murray and Steve receive the State of Delaware's Order of the First State commendation, as Delaware governor Jack Markell put it in 2013, "to bear witness to their outstanding Efforts, Knowledge, Integrity, Prudence and Ability."

just in the American South, but across the nation and the world that cheer politicians and preachers whose lips drip with hatred, who build walls to divide, who point out distinctions between people for political or financial or cultural gain.

I spoke to Governor Wallace before he died, and he claimed he regretted some of the words he used, some of the lines he drew. Now I hear the worst of him parroted across the world. Not just in the South, but in Wisconsin and Idaho and California and Europe and Australia and New Zealand and the Middle East and Africa. The Wallace strategies are employed anywhere that fear of people who don't look or talk or love or worship like the locals can be tapped to build an audience or a political base. It is anywhere the cries of anger and fear and defiance overwhelm those who hear the voices of our better angels, but are too afraid, or uncertain, or unsteady, or outnumbered to speak them to the world.

I have a friend and colleague, Kyle Whitmire, who claims all of that is evidence of the "Alabamification of America," where a common enemy is more important than the common good. I believe he thinks too small. It is the Alabamification of the earth. The politics of fear. The religion of judgment. The strategy of *Us v. Them.* Give the people someone to hate, and they will love you for it.

My father was a good man. I love him. Always. But being good is not all it takes. We are remembered, rightly or wrongly, by what we say *and* do. But we are defined just as much by what we don't say, what we lack the courage or will to speak out loud.

I wish Dad had been more vocal about race in the 1960s. I wish he had been more specific about prejudice and judgment throughout his life in the pulpit, more specific—to be more specific—about the things he clearly believed. Sometimes a parable is enough. Sometimes the world requires a rhetorical baseball bat.

I am forgiving of my father. At least he saw all as his neighbors, and helped them as he could. I am less forgiving of the church—the lax, hesitant, halting church, which damns the sinner and damns itself with its own fear and social neglect.

Then, as now, the church plays it safe, and counts its coins, and builds a tax-exempt dynasty on the body of Christ and the judgment of a mob. The Methodist Church—my church—disappoints me most, because my love for it is deepest. And because it claimed to be better, and more open in its hearts and minds and doors.

The United Methodist Church in 2019, with global influence and support from the heartland, emphasized that open minds and hearts didn't really apply at all to gay people, who were tolerated in the denomination's flowery language of acceptance, but shunned where it mattered, in its official position that continued to proclaim "the practice of homosexuality is incompatible with Christian teaching."

It was part of the steady tightening of church discipline since 1972, since that first General Conference after the merger that was supposed to show just how open the Methodists were. Delegates in February 2019 voted not only to keep the condemning language in the Book of Discipline—the book that sets out the church laws—but that United Methodist churches would have to certify adherence to it, and would be punished if they went astray. Under those changes, churches, like those reconciling congregations my brother belongs to, could be stripped of the United Methodist brand if they failed to comply. They could be barred from using the cross-and-flame logo, or the resources of the church, including money and property and all those things that really seem to matter most to religion. Any preachers who dared to conduct a same-sex ceremony could be punished, with a yearlong, unpaid suspension. Do it again and they could be expelled from the ministry. A church judicial council later declared part of the punitive policies unconstitutional in a legalistic document better fit for a court of law than a declaration of spiritual faith, but the message was again sent.

Oh, the church is quick to say gay people have worth, and encourages members not to reject gay friends or family, but demands no church money be spent on any gay group, or for the purpose of promoting the acceptance of homosexuality.

The decision, though, brought the issue to a head, revealing the disunity within the global United Methodist Church. Delegates are set to vote on a split that could break my father's beloved denomination in half, allowing the "traditionalists" to secede. But the language of those traditionalists echoes the words of another era. It sounds an awful lot like the fifties and sixties, when well-heeled and influential Methodists in Birmingham gathered to form the Methodist Layman's Union to fight the incompatible notion of desegregation.

"We are not here to attack anyone," Circuit Judge Whit Windham said in 1959 as he pushed for a church that would be all white and free to resist any integration efforts. "We wish only that the integrationists would leave us alone so we could keep our mouth shut. . . . If there is anyone here who hates Negroes he had better not join this organization because there is no place here for him."

He and others harnessed the power of fear.

Some 1,800 people gathered for that meeting, but only one person really spoke out. It was Thomas Reeves, that Birmingham-Southern student who had dared participate in the sit-ins, who would be mentioned in that Harrison Salisbury story about hatred and courage in Birmingham. Reeves stood to call bullshit. He pointed to the group's booklet of principles, which, among other things, warned against the "mongrelizing" of the races.

"We must not allow this document to become the basic idea that the Methodist Church is strictly Anglo-Saxon," Reeves said.

One young man with a voice. Reeves was dragged away from the podium after a chant of "Take him out."

Open hearts, open minds, open doors to throw somebody out, even then.

Thomas Reeves spoke. With his tiny pulpit in the place he lived, in the time he was there. In that moment it didn't seem to do a lick of good. The MLU was formed, and passed resolutions that, among other things, demanded that no church money be spent on any group that pushed for integration, or for the purpose of promoting the acceptance of integration. Sound familiar?

Reeves thought he was a voice crying in the wilderness. He was the troublemaker, the loudmouth, the thorn in the side of reputable, important people. And yet his words meant everything. Everything. Of 1,800 people gathered at that Birmingham church, his words were the only ones worth remembering. The MLU went on to fight ineffectively against integration that was, of course, inevitable.

The group was on the wrong side of history, and Reeves was right all along, no matter the consequences or what happened around him. Because to do nothing, to say nothing, is to condone what happens around you, which ensures that nothing changes. As King wrote in 1963:

> Human progress never rolls in on wheels of inevitability; it comes through the tireless efforts of men willing to be co-workers with God, and without this hard work, time itself becomes an ally of the forces of social stagnation. We must use time creatively, in the knowledge that the time is always ripe to do right.

Not just about race, but right. Whatever that right may be.

We use the voices we have, in the ways we have, to all the souls we meet, in every place we stand, as long as ever we find the strength.

In the days after the United Methodist vote to strengthen bans on same-sex marriage and gay clergy in 2019, I wrote a column under the headline METHODISTS: DON'T LET THE DOOR HIT YOU ON MY WAY OUT.

I was done. Over it. The church had closed its heart and its mind, I wrote. So I wasn't going to stick around for the rest of the show.

"I won't wait for it to shut its doors," I finished. "Thank you, I'll let myself out."

Murray, on the other hand, wrote in the CAMP Rehoboth newspaper—*Letters from CAMP Rehoboth*—that he did not plan such an exit from his church. He would stay, because that is his way. But he acknowledged his disappointment.

"Grief hit me all over again," he wrote. "Epworth has been my spiritual home for more years than I can count, and both Steve and I found friends who welcomed us, a community that shared our values, and like-minded spirits with similar beliefs. How could it not be clear to any rational person that we all deserve the right to join in worship, no matter our sexual orientation?"

Or color or nationality or income level or professional status or gender or anything else. How could it not be clear, we ask now. Thomas Reeves wondered the same thing in 1959.

Dad preached a sermon late in his career called "Like the Face of an Angel." In it he wrote of an encounter he had in Decatur in 1972, when I was in third grade, in Cub Scouts, getting ready to start my paper route and my life in the news business. I had never heard the story. It was one of the last sermons I read in his files.

Alabama was still smoldering over issues of race in 1972. Wallace was on the presidential campaign trail for the third straight election, until he was shot by Arthur Bremer in Maryland and left to spend the rest of his life in a wheelchair. School desegregation, despite all the court battles, was just coming to some Alabama cities, and was still new in Decatur. Income inequality was outrageous, and still is, and the Klan still marched occasionally in north Alabama. The 1960s were gone in the rest of the world, but everything comes five years late—at least—to the great state of Alabama.

So tensions were high as Dad sat in his office at First United Methodist Church on Canal Street, preparing a sermon that had nothing at all to do with any of that tension, except in parable. The phone rang in the office, and Dad picked it up to hear a member of the church named Paul, who was anxious and upset, who said he needed to see Dad right away.

"Of course," Dad said. "Of course." Come on over right away.

The guy was there in a matter of minutes—Decatur is not a big town. He was a tall man, usually ramrod straight, as Dad put it, but he stooped in the doorframe, worried and fidgeting. Dad didn't know if he was ill, or if someone in his family might have received bad news. He invited him in and showed him to a chair by the desk, and there Paul sagged, looking broken.

"What is it?" Dad asked, worried now.

Paul just shook his head.

"I know there is nothing you can do," he said. "But I need somebody I can talk to."

And then it all came out, in a rush. Paul was a businessman. He owned a store in Decatur and tried to do right by his customers and his workers, too, he said. He tried to know what was right in the world, and used his conscience to guide him when it seemed like he needed a guide.

It was nothing, he thought, when he hired a Black person at his store for the first time. It wasn't exactly progressive. It was 1972, after all.

But his employees didn't see it that way. They were so upset, he told Dad, that all but one of his white workers quit the store on the spot, just because he hired a Black person. They used their feet and their voices to protest, too, I guess. They used them to walk away.

Paul felt betrayed. He had to shut the store down, at least until he could hire and train more workers. He was frustrated, disappointed with people he thought he knew, fed up with the irrationality of a divisive world. But the more he talked about it, the straighter he sat, Dad said. The more he heard himself, the better he felt:

As Paul unfolded his story, the desperation gradually drained from his voice and a smile returned to his face and he said, "But, Bob, I did what is right. I can live with myself."

And I thought, "What a way to live."

What a way to live.

Epilogue

As I look at this world, there are so many things that break my heart. There is war, crime against people, poverty of spirit and poverty of body, racism, petty jealousies, hatred, strife, backbiting, and we could go on and on. Our world is divided, fractured, sick. We need to bring to this world a meaningful relationship with our fellow man.

—REV. ROBERT L. ARCHIBALD JR., October 18, 1970

There is nothing permanent. Nothing endures but change.

Grandfather Holland built our cabin on his little patch of paradise on the best ground Camp Glisson had to offer in the north Georgia mountains, where Cane Creek sings a lullaby and the air is a perfume of honeysuckle and all those generations. In the 1950s, he deeded "The Holland Hut" and the land right back to the church, in exchange for a lease that would last as long as his children.

It expired, essentially, with my mother. The most lasting place in our lives would return, as Granddaddy wanted, to the Methodists.

Nothing is permanent. Not even history. Not even memory. It shifts and changes and plays tricks. It disappears. And we hold tight to what we hope to keep in our hearts, and grieve for what's lost.

We thought the camp was ours, that all those years and the

placard on the Holland Building made it so. It was not. So some months after Mother died, we gathered to clean out five generations of memories from that cabin, with its bare wood and bowed floors and a foundation built more solidly on family than firm ground beneath.

All the siblings came: Murray, Mary Beth, Mark and me. So did two of the Holland cousins—Bill and George. We missed their sister, Sarah, who was too far away.

Of course we all mourned for that cabin, as we did for Mother, and for Uncle Harvey and all the rest. There is grief in losing a beloved place, as there is with losing a loved one. But like so many deaths after old age and long illness, the end is softened by circumstance, by pain and suffering that lets us know it is foolish to cling too long. I felt of the cabin the same thing I'd felt when we said a final goodbye to Mom and Dad. It was time.

For nothing is permanent, and the delusion that Camp Glisson was ours had expired long before any lease, long before Mother's passing. The grief had begun years ago, when the camp started to discourage fishing in the little lake, and built a castle in the middle of it, with zip lines and water slides. It came when the rustic dining hall was abandoned in favor of a retreat center with air-conditioning, of all things. It came when the charming chapel in the quiet woods was razed to build a multimillion-dollar church.

Cane Creek still sings its song, for those who listen, but it is background music now to the comforts of a generation addicted to distraction.

Nothing stands in the way of change. The Holland Building will eventually disappear to make way for a new gym, named for some generous donor. The cabin will vanish. It will become green space or a parking lot, God forbid. And no one will know we were there. Which is okay.

It was time.

The four Archibald siblings sat in that cabin in the spring after Mother's death, exhausted and quiet, after it had been all but cleared out and the Hollands had returned to their homes. We said our goodbyes, with laughter and tears and the kind of understanding that comes only after a gauntlet of too much grief. We did it exactly as I would have predicted. Together. And differently.

Murray started with ritual. Of course. He told us how places become holy because they are filled with love, and this place was holy to us simply because it was filled with as much love that day as it had been our entire lives. He asked us to tell stories about it, about our memories, and asked us to respond—church-style—with a refrain of "In this holy place there is love."

I spoke of my memories, of how I felt all those generations as if they were alive in the wood of the cabin and the woods around it, in the dark dirt and the glittering stone. I told how the image of my children running down a path toward the waterfall is etched in my mind, and when I see Drew and Ramsey and Mamie in my head I see all of the others, too, brothers and sister and parents and ancestors, as children, running alongside.

In this holy place there is love.

Mary Beth spoke of conversations with our mother about her own childhood, how Grandfather Holland built windows up high in a back bedroom so she would be able to see the creek outside from atop a bunk bed. She spoke of paper dolls and magazines and the kind of laughter that gives her strength still.

In this holy place there is love.

Mark remembered Dad showing him the little wildflower called pipsissewa, and teaching him how to tell the difference between mountain laurel and wild rhododendron, and how little moments such as those are a part of us all. He spoke of cousins and children and parents and toy boats that broke away from their moorings and sailed off down the creek, to adventure, perhaps, in parts unknown.

In this holy place there is love.

Murray recalled spitting watermelon seeds, and of how much noise we made as children, covered in sand and running with a sense of total freedom up and down the narrow path to the falls. And, of course, of love.

In this holy place there is love.

In the end we were as true to ourselves as this place had been to us. It was camp. It was us. Murray prepared a ritual, and Mark prepared a poem—"Symphony in Five Movements"—which he recited aloud, precisely, like the engineering professor he is. Mary Beth salvaged an old card from an ancient board game in a cabinet that had survived fourteen presidents. She read it aloud:

Q: What requires more patience than taking things as they come?
A: Parting with things as they go.

I prepared nothing. Like me. I laughed at old magazines in the cabin filled with recipes featuring canned meat and Jell-O, and at the ancient nutrition guide on the wall—put out by the American

Dairy Association—that recommended at least four glasses of milk and two tablespoons of butter a day. At least.

I cried at mundane memories of playing Monopoly with my children, of playing the card game Rook with Grandmother Holland—careful, or she would cheat—in those days when a deck of playing cards was the devil but Rook was just a game.

Nothing stays the same.

I am the youngest of all my cousins, the last of my generation. I made it a point to be the last one out of the cabin, even though I had to hold the door for Mary Beth to make it so. *In this holy place there really was love,* I thought to myself.

I thought later of what that place had been, and what it had seen, and heard, and how we had known it only for a fraction of time. The land had been home to Native Americans for centuries, and was preserved through much of the twentieth century with a reverence that seemed fitting. It was an escape from the world, from the events that marked those decades as seminal for mankind—from the Great Depression to World War II to the civil rights movement to the Information Age. I thought of how the escape, sometimes, was just a way to look away, to pretend songs and scriptures and summer nights in the wild made up for a world that too often bristled against its differences.

I thought of a sermon Dad gave in 1970, when he spoke of Dr. King's "Dream of justice and freedom and brotherhood."

He told of bringing us, his family, to Camp Glisson in the summer of 1969. It was a weekend, and the only people on the grounds were cabin owners and staff getting ready for the camp that would begin the following week.

Those days, at the crack of dawn, morning was broken with a song on the PA system to tell campers and staff to get out of bed.

On this day, though, the PA blared not with the music of the sixties, but with King's "I Have a Dream" speech.

Dad called it a sermon. I never really thought about that, but I guess it was. It would have been a beautiful wake-up, Dad said. Until an old cabin owner became incensed:

> He didn't like the sermon. He didn't like the young people. He didn't like to be awakened at daylight on a Saturday morning by the youth playing the sermon. He marched over to the camp office and demanded that the record be turned off. The Dream was cut off.

The Dream was cut off. On church property.

I needed to read that story, because it was important for me to see

A 2001 Easter sunset at East Lake United Methodist Church in Birmingham, where my father, the Reverend R. L. Archibald Jr., served as pastor in the 1970s, and his father, the Reverend R. L. Archibald Sr., served as pastor in the 1950s. They offered comfort to the people inside in the ways they knew how, but the congregations needed discomfort, given what was taking place beyond the stained-glass windows.

that no place is immune to those who would cut short the dreams of justice and fairness. Places are holy not because of where they are, but because they help us to remember love. Or the absence of it, which is just as important.

I was reminded that a respite is just a temporary break, an escape that requires a return to the world. It is just a reason to look inward, to gain the strength required to look outward. It doesn't depend on a place. It doesn't depend on our place in the world.

Nothing is permanent. Nothing endures but change.

Acknowledgments

I am grateful to my family. To Alecia, my wife and First Editor. To Drew, firstborn and Second Editor. To Ramsey and Mamie. I've always written about them, and they've always advised me on how it should be done. Better.

To siblings Murray, Mary Beth, and Mark. We made memories together, even when we couldn't agree on whose version was closest to truth. I think they all were. To Sally and Bob, and of course Steve, who should be here with us. For the memory of Mom and Dad, whom we will ever love. For family far and wide, past and future. Pink clouds.

To everyone this book doesn't apply to, and there are many. To all those who spoke up even when the words came hard, who stood even when legs wobbled, who marched when they saw a need, and met violence, who used their pulpits, big ones or small, to speak for goodness.

To Methodists everywhere who always welcomed the world with open doors. To Nina Reeves and Reggie Holder and Frederick Outlaw. To Sally Allocca and Kevin Higgs and so many more.

To Victoria Wilson, my editor at Knopf. We laughed, Vicky, in surprise. Thanks for bearing with me. To Marc Jaffee at Knopf, who always made things happen when they were supposed to, and to Nora Reichard for great care in making sure the words I wrote were the words I really meant.

To Steve Ross, such a special agent I think of him as 007. He encouraged me and talked me through this venture and went above and beyond. To Amy King, who gave sound and much-needed advice. To the Olivers and Pavels, who did the same.

To Lee Bains III, who was the soundtrack to this book, along with his band, the Glory Fires. To John Hammontree, who is always there to read, or to write a good letter. To Wayne Flynt and Diane McWhorter. You are friends and heroes.

To my colleagues at Alabama Media Group and Advance Local. I am proud of you. To my editors there, and at *The Birmingham News*—Glenn Stephens, Tom Arenberg, and the late great Randy Henderson—thank you for teaching me, and eventually trusting me, even when it wasn't comfortable. To the fellows. To the ballers of Old Man Hoops, you keep me sane.

To readers everywhere. I love you.

Index

Page numbers in *italics* refer to illustrations.

ILLUSTRATION CREDITS

PAGE 7 Anthony Falletta, *The Birmingham News*

PAGE 8 Alabama Media Group

PAGE 23 Ed Jones, *The Birmingham News*

PAGE 38 Ed Bruchac, *The Birmingham News*

PAGE 40 *The Birmingham News* / Alabama Department of Archives and History

PAGE 53 Special

PAGE 61 Norman Dean, *The Birmingham News*

PAGE 69 Tom Self, *The Birmingham News*

PAGE 89 *The Birmingham News* /Alabama Department of Archives and History

PAGE 107 Tom Lankford, *The Birmingham News*

PAGE 108 Louis Arnold, *The Birmingham News*

PAGE 126 Haywood Paravicini, *The Birmingham News*

PAGE 129 top: Tom Lankford, *The Birmingham News*

PAGE 129 bottom: Tom Self, *The Birmingham News*

PAGE 130 Barry Schwartz, *Staten Island Advance*

PAGE 169 Carol McPhail, Alabama Media Group

PAGE 199 © *Washington Blade* by Michael Key

PAGE 218 Beth Ann Higgs

PAGE 259 Greg Garrison/AL.com

PAGE 277 © *Washington Blade* by Michael Key

PAGE 289 Charles Nesbitt, *The Birmingham News*

All other images are from the Archibald family collection.

A NOTE ON THE TYPE

This book was set in Adobe Garamond. Designed for the Adobe Corporation by Robert Slimbach, the fonts are based on types first cut by Claude Garamond (c. 1480–1561).

Composed by North Market Street Graphics, Lancaster, Pennsylvania
Printed and bound by Berryville Graphics, Berryville, Virginia
Designed by Anna B. Knighton

A NOTE ABOUT THE AUTHOR

JOHN ARCHIBALD is a journalist for *The Birmingham News,*
where he has been a regular columnist since 2004. In 2018,
Archibald was awarded the Pulitzer Prize for Commentary. He
lives in Birmingham, Alabama.